Saul Bellow

Revised Edition

Twayne's United States Authors Series

Warren French, Editor
Indiana University

TUSAS 181

SAUL BELLOW

photograph © by Thomas Victor, courtesy of Harper & Row

Saul Bellow

Revised Edition

By Robert R. Dutton

Twayne Publishers • Boston

Saul Bellow, Revised Edition

Robert R. Dutton

Copyright © 1982 by G. K. Hall & Company
Published by Twayne Publishers
A Division of G. K. Hall & Company
70 Lincoln Street
Boston, Massachusetts 02111

Book Production by Marne B. Sultz

Book Design by Barbara Anderson

Printed on permanent/durable acid-free
paper and bound in the United States of
America.

**Library of Congress Cataloging in
Publication Data**

Dutton, Robert R.
  Saul Bellow.

  (Twayne's United States authors series :
  TUSAS 181)
  Bibliography: pp. 202–207
  Includes index.
  1. Bellow, Saul——Criticism and
interpretation. I. Title. II. Series.
PS3503.E4488Z66 1982 813'.52 81-6977
ISBN 0-8057-7353-3   AACR2

Contents

About the Author

Robert R. Dutton received his doctor of philosophy degree in English from the University of the Pacific in 1966. His dissertation on the novels of Saul Bellow, entitled "The Subangelic Vision of Saul Bellow," grew into the first edition of the present work. Mr. Dutton teaches English courses at San Joaquin Delta College in Stockton, California.

Preface to the Revised Edition

Through his critical essays, Saul Bellow urges his fellow writers to turn away from the past and to create fresh images of what it means to be a human being. He insists that it is no longer useful to elaborate upon the old theme of man as a victim trapped in naturalistic forces. Bellow says that for at least a century, such a picture of wretchedness has been thoroughly examined—and by such giants as Melville, Flaubert, Dostoevski, Lawrence, Hemingway, Faulkner, and Joyce. It is not Bellow's opinion that these novelists have presented inaccurate reflections of what it means to be human; it is just that there are other truths to be told: man is capable of integrity; he can live in dignity. Man has a power that is, say, subangelic: he is removed from the angels, but he is in a position on a "chain of being" that calls for more hope than despair.

Bellow's novels are so consistently in this vein that I have found it valuable to build this study around this theme of man as subangelic. Hence, one of the objectives of this work is to answer the following question: If Bellow the essayist prescribes a turning away from past definitions of experience, precisely what does Bellow the novelist substitute for those definitions? It is important to understand, however, that this book is not a philosophical treatise—nor has it to do with either sociology or psychology. It is a literary study; and, as such, it is concerned with the "how" of Bellow's novels: the emphasis is on Bellow's art. In any case, with the approach of "technique as discovery," to use Mark Schorer's term, an examination of the novels of Saul Bellow illuminates his strictures on the subangelic figure, as well as clarifying what seems to be one of the major literary achievements of our time.

The above remarks were set down as part of the preface to the first edition of this book (1971). They still stand, as to both Bellow's literary position and the nature of this study, although in order to avoid what has become the obvious I have not, in the present work, pursued the term "subangelic" in my comments on Bellow's more recent writing. In the decade that has passed since the first edition, Bellow has held to his position that writers should present the more positive aspects of man. We continue to hear that thesis in all of Bellow's work, not only in his fiction, but also in his essays and interviews, and certainly in his Nobel lecture in 1976. Yet in the last ten years Bellow has offered us new perspectives that extend his earlier visions and call upon us to see beyond those prospects, which, in this edition, is one of the central concerns of my comments on the later Bellow.

In this revised edition, with some exceptions I have let stand my earlier comments on Bellow's novels. I have cut severely my remarks on *Dangling Man,* and placed that novel and *The Victim* in one chapter rather than in two, since in retrospect these two books clearly form a unit in Bellow's development. The present text includes the following new material: a brief biography added to the introductory chapter, which will help the reader get some idea of Bellow's background and his developing reputation as a writer; some added observations on *Mr. Sammler's Planet*; a chapter on *Humboldt's Gift*; a chapter on *Mosby's Memoirs and Other Stories*, "The Silver Dish," and *To Jerusalem and Back: A Personal Account*; some additions to the last chapter "Looking Backward" in order to include Bellow's later work in the discussion of his technical and stylistic achievements, and to make some fresh suggestions as to where his writing will take us in the future; finally, some recent bibliographical references.

Robert R. Dutton

San Joaquin Delta College

Acknowledgments

For permission to quote from the following works, I am indebted to the following: Vanguard Press, Inc., for *Dangling Man* and *The Victim*; Viking Press, for *The Adventures of Augie March*, *Seize the Day*, *Henderson the Rain King*, *Herzog*, *Mr. Sammler's Planet*, *Humboldt's Gift*, *Mosby's Memoirs and Other Stories*, and *To Jerusalem and Back: A Personal Account*; Macmillan Company, for "Distractions of a Fiction Writer" in *The Living Novel: A Symposium*.

In this revised edition, I wish to reaffirm my gratitude to Professor Charles C. Clerc, University of the Pacific, who was my encouraging and helpful guide through a dissertation that ultimately saw its way into the first edition of this book. Then, once again, I had the good luck of being able to call upon my friend Donna Haight who was of great help with the first edition. In my earlier preface, I made clear my doubts that this book would have been completed without her assistance. The present work also owes much to her, both to her valuable perceptions and to her ability and willingness to pursue details. Finally, my warm thanks to Warren French, the editor of this volume. His thoughtful correspondence saw me through some troubling areas, and his painstaking editing helped to eliminate many technical errors.

Chronology

1959   *Henderson the Rain King.*

1960–1962   Coedits periodical *The Noble Savage.* Friends of Literature Fiction Award.

1962   "Scenes from Humanitis," early version of *The Last Analysis.* Honorary Doctor of Letters from Northwestern University. Joins Committee on Social Thought at the University of Chicago.

1963   Edits *Great Jewish Short Stories,* writes introduction. Honorary doctor of letters conferred by Bard College.

1964   *Herzog,* receives James L. Dow Award, the National Book Award, and the Fomentor Award. 29 September, *The Last Analysis* produced on Broadway.

1965   Awarded the International Prize for *Herzog.* Three one-act plays: "Out from Under," "Orange Soufflé," "A Wen." Honored by Union of Polish Writers.

1967   "The Old System." Reports on Six-Day War for *Newsday* magazine.

1968   "Mosby's Memoirs" (story); *Mosby's Memoirs and Other Stories.* Receives Jewish Heritage Award from B'nai B'rith; awarded the French Croix de Chevalier des Arts et Lettres.

1970   *Mr. Sammler's Planet.*

1971   National Book Award for *Mr. Sammler's Planet.*

1974   "Zetland: By a Character Witness," excerpt from untitled novel in progress, in *Modern Occasions.*

1975   *Humboldt's Gift.* Awarded Pulitzer Prize for Literature.

1976   *To Jerusalem and Back: A Personal Account.* Awarded Nobel Prize for Literature.

1978   "A Silver Dish."

1979   Reports for *Newsday* magazine on Sadat-Carter-Begin peace treaty signing in Washington, D.C.

Chapter One

Saul Bellow: His Vision and Background

The themes of Saul Bellow are hardly original: they include the old established counterclaims of the individual versus society and the individual in self-conflict. What Bellow offers is a clarity of vision concerning these issues that is, above all, honest. In all of his writing, Bellow faces squarely the timely issue of personal effacement and consequent degradation that every social trend seems to manifest. He never draws away from the frightening implications of an impersonal, mechanical society.

The distinctive achievement of Bellow, however, lies in his depiction of the individual in such a society, for it is the plight of the man, not society, that is emphasized throughout his work. In Bellow's world, society is rendered in an almost naturalistic manner—as an almost unchanging, indifferent, yet powerful background against which his protagonists in all of their sensitive awareness, their vitality, their frustrating absurdities, are seen. This juxtaposition of a static society and the organic individual informs all of Bellow's novels. That is, how does the individual in all of his individuality, with his dreams, aspirations, and idealism, along with his ever-present awareness of society as a naturalistic reality, find a place for himself, establish a personal and a unique identity, and still maintain an honest integrity of self?

Maxwell Geismar states the dilemma in an implicit correlation between Bellow and his protagonists: "part of our sympathy and concern with [Bellow's] career lies with his own struggle to break through a predominantly intellectual and moral approach to life."[1] Here is precisely the struggle of Bellow's protagonists—to break through to life and to achieve their possibilities; their human potentiality; and, most importantly, their individual potentiality. But they must do so without the loss of a moral and intellectual humanism basic to their views of themselves.

Bellow's heroes, then, find the complexities of their dilemma not only in an alienation from society; they are confronted by a kind of treason within themselves, which creates an even more insoluble problem. In what is perhaps an oversimplification, but a workable one, Marcus Klein states their paradoxical situations: "they face problems which are reducible to a single problem; to meet with a strong sense of self the sacrifice of self demanded by social circumstance."[2]

This "strong sense of self" is Bellow's greatest concern, for his heroes are forever troubled by the nature of this self. Society, for the most part, is or becomes a known to them. Perhaps society is uncomfortable for them, indifferent to them, at odds with their behavior and with their ideals, and antipathetic to their imaginations; but its mysteries are not beyond their apprehension. They can and do learn of its nature. But "self" eludes them: what is its nature? That it is capable of a godlike reason, that its faculty of imagination is boundless, each of Bellow's protagonists makes evident again and again. But that this same self is also capable of unbelievable stupidities, inane actions, and romantic nonsense is made equally clear. Bellow himself marks the duality in "Distractions of a Fiction Writer"—an essay, incidentally, which is a critical key to an understanding of his fictive intentions—when he observes: "There is a man's own greatness, and then there is the greatness of his imbecility—both are eternal."[3]

Philosophically, the heroes of Bellow are in the Sartrean position of the *en-soi* versus the *pour-soi*: the being-in-itself versus the being-for-itself. Unlike the stone whose being can never transcend itself, and which is therefore complete and whole in itself, a being-in-itself, man, blessed or cursed with an imaginative consciousness, is forever in a state of self-transcendence, or in a state of being-for-itself, as well as being-in-itself. Through his imagination, man would be something other than what he is or what he seems to be; for what he is, or seems to be, is an irritatingly unsatisfying and discomfiting mystery, a mystery to which depth and breadth are given with every stretch of his imagination. Bellow's novels are narrative dramatizations of the fact of this dilemma of existence; they are a working-out not to a resolution, but to a revelation of a human condition.

Bellow the critic has spoken on this issue. In "Distractions of a Fiction Writer" he maintains that novelists in the past have often failed to catch the positive factor in this human equation of the *en-soi* versus the *pour-soi*. He feels that they have too often depicted the consequent seeming absurdity of man. Taking a position against those who would depict man as completely impotent, or abjectly absurd owing to his nature, he states:

If man wretched by nature is represented, what we have here is only accurate reporting. But if it is man in the image of God, man a little lower than the angels who is impotent, the case is not the same. And it is the second assumption, the subangelic one, that writers generally make. For they are prone . . . to exaggerate the value of human personality. I don't know whether exaggeration is quite the word, but what it suggests we can certainly agree with. Why should wretched man need power or wish to inflate himself with imaginary glory? If this is what power signifies it can only be vanity to suffer from impotence. On the nobler assumption he should have at least sufficient power to overcome ignominy and to complete his own life. His suffering, feebleness, servitude then have a meaning. This is what writers have taken to be the justification of power. . . . And if no other power will do this, the power of the imagination will take the task upon itself.[4]

These comments were set down as late as 1957, yet they form an important contextual element even in Bellow's earlier novels, which would lead us to believe that he created his stories on intuitive principles that took years to formulate critically. Bellow's work as a whole is organic; the development is toward these principles. With the years of writing, he has learned to create his characters and themes with greater confidence in himself and in his ability to create a work of art that would stand the test of the exigencies of the times as he sees them.

What these exigencies are is difficult to define, but Bellow seems to feel that meaningful dialogue is noticeably absent from literature at a time when dialogue is especially imperative to any valid examination of existence; hence, he would build on what seems to him to be a decisive question of the first importance: Do we want to live? If the answer is "Yes," as it must be, then men should talk and, yes, even choose— despite what today seems such a multiplicity of choice that no knowledgeable choice exists. But in choosing, man expresses his humanity through his imagination. Bellow would agree that the best part of man, and the part of man that has been neglected in recent literature, is found not in what he is but in what he would be or wills to be. And what he would be or wills to be is also a task for the imagination.

This is not to say that Bellow is crying out for a new optimism, especially one founded on false postures. But neither would he accept a useless and hopeless pessimism. In an article "The Writer as Moralist," he states: "the idiocy of orthodox affirmation and transparent or point-less optimism ought not to provoke an equal and opposite reaction."[5] And by the "opposite reaction" Bellow means a fiction that depicts man as "wretched by nature." Bellow does not reject the validity of such interpretations; instead, such depictions seem to close all debate and to make all effort, all life, and the portrayal of that life completely ridiculous and meaningless. For such a view of man, suicide at worst or a desperate kind of quietism at best are the only sensible and logical reactions. Furthermore, Bellow would say that, instructive as such interpretations are, they are only that—interpretations. There are others that are equally valid.

What Bellow urges, as well as what he attempts to create in his novels, is a depiction of man as subangelic. But to define what subangelic man is, just what the term means, and, equally important, what it does not mean, is a difficult task. The difficulty lies in the fact that the term has nothing to do with the figure observed; the meaning is to be found within the observer. Hence, all definition is subjective. "Subangelical," when applied to man, is an attitude toward man, not a description of man.

Bellow speaks of the subangelic as the "nobler assumption" that is based on the concept that man at least has the power to "overcome ignominy" and to "complete his own life." We can conjecture that by "overcome ignominy" Bellow means that any depiction of man should grant him the power to rise above the indignities of complete subjection to unseen and unknown forces, to give him a nature not totally in the chains of a miserable naturalistic impotency. Furthermore, Bellow would say that this power must be granted to man, not only because the lack of it closes debate, and not only because its alternative is unthinkable, but also because there is good reason to believe that man actually has the power to complete his own life. It may be true that this power is difficult to find through a scientific dissection or through an objective, cold analysis: its validity is to be discovered more easily in active man, in man involved. In any case, no matter what a laboratory experiment indicates and no matter what a sociological study might conclude, the nature of man is finally defined by no one but himself, and that definition must include the power of the imagination.

This plea for a higher and better perspective on man does not come from an outsetting bard yet to deal with the grit of experience; for we are discussing the ideas of a writer who at their pronouncement in "Distractions of a Fiction Writer" was forty-two years old, had struggled through an early period of survivorship, and had completed a significant body of work that promised the major position he holds in literature today. Saul Bellow was born on 10 July 1915 in Montreal, Canada, a fourth child of Abraham and Liza (Gordon) Bellow. Just two years earlier his father had immigrated to Canada from St. Petersburg (now Leningrad), Russia, and settled in Lachine, an older section of Montreal. It was in this environment that Bellow learned his English, Hebrew, Yiddish, and French. In 1924 the Bellow family moved to Chicago, which remains Saul Bellow's home to this day. In 1933 he graduated from Tuley High School and enrolled in the University of Chicago where, we learn, he was quite unhappy. In these days, Bellow might well have suffered the "disease" of so many undergraduates; at least it seems so from the opening lines of his Nobel lecture many years later: "I was a very contrary undergraduate more than forty years ago. It was my habit to register for a course and then to do most of my reading in another field of study, so that when I should have been grinding away at 'Money and Banking' I was reading the novels of Joseph Conrad."[6] No doubt he took his wandering mind with him in 1935 when he transferred to Northwestern University; but here he earned a bachelor's degree in 1937, graduating with honors in anthropology and sociology, two areas of interest that find their way into all his later writing. Bellow then enrolled in the University of Wisconsin with a scholarship, but quit school, returned to Chicago, and married Anita Goshkin, a social worker. A son, Gregory, was born of this marriage.

It should be said that Bellow himself has described this period of his life in the 1930s in an essay entitled "Starting Out in Chicago," wherein we see him as a young man surviving the Depression, immersing himself in the works of such writers as Sherwood Anderson, Theodore

Dreiser, Edgar Lee Masters, and Vachel Lindsay, and all the time doing battle with his own yearnings to write: "So I sat at a bridge table in a back bedroom of the apartment while all rational, serious, dutiful people were at their jobs, or trying to find jobs, writing something." No doubt these efforts served their purpose, but looking back he admits, "I am glad to say that I can't remember what I was writing in Ravenswood. It must have been terrible."[7]

From 1938 to 1942, Bellow worked briefly for the Works Progress Administration, writing biographies of midwestern novelists and poets. He also served a short period as a member of the faculty at Pestalozzi-Froebel Teachers College in Chicago. The years from 1943 to 1946 saw him in various activities: serving briefly with the Maritime Service during World War II; working as a member of the editorial staff of the *Encyclopedia Britannica* on the "Great Books" project; teaching English at the University of Minnesota. Of course he was writing all this time; and in 1944 his first novel *Dangling Man* was published, to be followed by *The Victim* in 1947. The next year Bellow was awarded a Guggenheim Fellowship which allowed him to live and write in Paris and to see much of Europe. It was during these months that he started work on his third novel, *The Adventures of Augie March*.

In 1950, Bellow returned from Europe, and for the greater part of the next ten years, lived in New York City where he taught at several universities for brief periods (as well as at the University of Minnesota in 1954), contributed articles and book reviews to several publications, and saw into print four of the short stories later to be included in *Mosby's Memoirs and Other Stories*.[8] He also married again, this time to Alexandra Tschachasov. A son, Adam, was born.

The 1950s saw Bellow firmly established as one of America's foremost novelists. *The Adventures of Augie March* (1953) won the National Book Award, and was widely acclaimed, largely without dissent. With Augie, we had a new kind of literary hero, an intellectual Huck Finn, a picaro shuttling through the waste land of the first half of the twentieth century, feeding on experience. Then came *Seize the Day* (1956), a short tale that many have judged to be a classic because of its compressed account of Tommy Wilhelm, contemporary man. Finally, *Henderson the Rain King* (1959) made its appearance; and for this Africa of the mind, Bellow again received little but critical praise.

By the end of the 1950s, two points concerning Bellow's fiction had been established. First, that, while there is an understandable reticence on the part of critics of contemporary American literature to make definitive judgments, already there was a general consensus that Bellow's novels represented the contemporary American novel at its best. Moreover, this consensus came not only from critical journals with an exclusive and limited circulation, but from publications of wider appeal—weekly news magazines and book reviews in daily newspapers. The second point is that, by this time, Bellow, unlike many other good writers, could count on a wide reading public. Our most discerning critics and the general reader were in agreement—not an everyday development.

From 1960 into 1962, Bellow acted as coeditor with Keith Botsford and Aaron Asher, of a cultural periodical called *The Noble Savage.* Like so many events in Bellow's life, this short-lived effort found its way into *Humboldt's Gift,* in which we find Charlie Citrine engaged in a similar effort with his *The Ark,* a journal "to improve mankind." Charlie bumps his head against the apathy and economics that often sink such ventures, and that is probably what happened to *The Noble Savage.* Bellow continued to teach in the 1960s, but confined his instruction to the University of Chicago, except for a year at the University of Puerto Rico in 1961. That year he married Susan Glassman with whom he had another son, Daniel. In 1962, he joined the Committee on Social Thought at the University of Chicago, a prestigious group formed to unify recent discoveries in the arts and sciences. To this day, Bellow has worked with the Committee, serving as chairman from 1970 to 1976.

Herzog was published in 1964. It received several awards, including another National Book Award; and if there was ever any doubt about Bellow's leading role in American fiction, this novel removed it. In a *Book Week* survey of postwar fiction from 1945 to 1965, the authors, critics, and editors who submitted answers cited Bellow most frequently as the author who had "written the most distinguished fiction during the period." In the list of twenty American books chosen as best for the period, Bellow was represented by four of his then six novels: *Herzog* (fourth), *Seize the Day* (fifth), *Augie March* (sixth), and *Henderson the Rain King* (fifteenth).[9] The reading public kept *Herzog* on the best-seller lists for many weeks.

The year of 1964, however, was not all upbeat for Bellow. He tried his hand at drama with *The Last Analysis,* a full-length play that ran for but twenty-eight days on Broadway at the David Belasco Theatre (the present writer saw it in San Francisco). For the faithful reader of Bellow's novels, the play deserved better; yet one can understand the failure. *The Last Analysis* is heavy with farcical elements that simply get out of hand; the stage is quite often entirely too busy, in an uproar most of the time; there are no strong characters, certainly none to sympathize with—even the leading character Bummy, the comic who turns serious and declares his intention to bring psychology to the masses through television, loses us through his slapstick behavior. It is not a good play, not good comedy—except for those of us who delight in Bellow's mind in whatever form it is presented.[10] A year or two later, a like fate greeted three one-act plays: "Out from Under," "Orange Soufflé," and "A Wen." These were privately shown off-Broadway in 1965; then in 1966 they were staged in London, then at the Festival of Two Worlds in Spoleto, Italy, and finally back on Broadway, this time with the collective title *Under the Weather*; but they never caught on. It is little wonder that Bellow has turned away from further dramatic endeavors.

Toward the end of the decade, in 1967, Bellow reported on the Six-Day War in Israel for *Newsday* magazine, then published by Bill Moyers. The chaos and carnage that Bellow witnessed were obviously still heavily on his mind when he wrote his *To Jerusalem and Back* almost ten years later. The following year he began work on his sixth novel, *Mr. Sammler's Planet,* which was published in 1970; and for the third time, Bellow gained the National Book Award. Again a best-seller, this novel received high critical acclaim, yet not without some reservations. There was some discomfort with the long interior monologues of old Mr. Sammler, as well as some objection to dialogue that turned into wandering speeches lasting several pages. Also in this novel, Bellow introduced some metaphysical elements that were bound to draw some narrowing side-glances. It is difficult to appeal to our modern conception of a hero with a man who is in his seventies and "interested in little more than Meister Eckhardt [a thirteenth-century priest] and the Bible." Yet Bellow's technical skills and the force of his ideas will keep this work among his best, whatever else he writes.

In 1975, *Humboldt's Gift* was published, and for it Bellow received the Pulitzer Prize for Literature. More in the tradition of *Augie March* and *Herzog,* and less in that of *Mr. Sammler's Planet,* this work, too, was widely read, became another best-seller, and was generally praised by critics and reviewers. Still, it contained metaphysical elements, initiated in *Mr. Sammler's Planet,* that caused some consternation. When the protagonist Charlie Citrine makes his plea for a perspective on our existence that must be described as metaphysical, there was a good deal of confusion in the critical ranks, and certainly in the minds of many readers, about how to take it. In an age in which scientific logic rules, we are simply not prepared for ventures running counter to that logic. Once again, however, Bellow's larger-than-life figures, his comic spirit, and the astonishing depth and breadth of his mind prevailed; and for many the book takes a place alongside, or perhaps second to, *Herzog.*

The following year (1976) Bellow wrote *To Jerusalem and Back,* his first nonfiction book. An immediate success, widely attended to, it is "a personal account" of Bellow's several months' visit to Israel. Since this work is focused on the problems of the survival of Israel, the reading public and the critics were especially interested in just how this man of the imagination would explore the exasperatingly real conditions in that war-torn land. The year 1976 also brought to Bellow what most of us think to be the highest award for literature—the Nobel Prize. In view of his achievements, there would seem to be little reason for astonishment at the choice. Yet, according to Alfred Kazin, the announcement brought "a vast tremor from the Village of Columbia, forced smiles, clenched teeth, much headshaking from New York's two million authorities in literary history."[11] Kazin explains this response, and proceeds to defend Bellow's fiction—for most of us, unnecessarily. For the consistent reader of Bellow's novels and his commentaries, the Nobel lecture Bellow delivered in Sweden holds little that is new. He makes many of the same pleas to writers that he has been making over the years: to reexamine traditional attitudes or orthodoxies; and to strike through the deadening acceptance of widespread ideologies that leave us nakedly isolated and insignificant. His last sentence makes the claim that, since art is built on unification, so should art emphasize the unity of man: "What Conrad said was true: art attempts to find in the universe, in matter as well as in the facts of life, what is fundamental, enduring, essential."[12] Here is the principle that provides the underlying theme in all Bellow's work and that is especially pressed home in his last two novels, *Mr. Sammler's Planet* and *Humboldt's Gift.*

At the present time, Bellow and his fourth wife, Alexandra (Tulcea), live in Chicago, and Bellow continues to write; reportedly, another novel is in progress. As late as 1979, he reported once again for *Newsday* magazine, this time on the Sadat-Carter-Begin Middle East peace treaty signing in Washington, D.C.

Chapter Two
Dangling Man and *The Victim*

Saul Bellow's first two novels, *Dangling Man* and *The Victim,* may be considered apprenticeship work, if we do not read "apprenticeship" as stumbling first steps, or as work to be read only in adumbration of the later Bellow. While these early novels do lack the depth and breadth of his later work, and more importantly, the distinctive voice of the mature Bellow, they stand on their own, and must be taken into account in any survey of Bellow's career.

Dangling Man (1944) and the War

The title of Saul Bellow's first novel, *Dangling Man,* conjures up precisely an image of a subangelic figure caught in a scheme of being, for the adjective "dangling" describes with varying nuances the general state in which Bellow sees his heroes and, by extension, humanity. With the use of this word, he indicates a situation of helpless waiting, of ambiguous swaying, of an airy suspension between two worlds. We shall return to a further discussion of this topic, but for the moment we must consider the plight of Joseph, the protagonist in *Dangling Man.*

The novel opens during World War II with Joseph, a resident of Chicago for eighteen years, in a state of alienation and isolation. Owing to a snarl of red tape, the draft call he is expecting simply fails to come. He has given up his job, moved to a lower middle-class rooming house, and is being supported by his wife. He has severed relationships with his friends and acquaintances because "the main bolt that held us together has given way." He is patronized almost beyond restraint by his in-laws and by his brother and his brother's family. Joseph and his wife Iva no longer seem to have anything to say to each other. He has even stopped reading books, which until this time "had stood as guarantors of an extended life, far more precious and necessary than the one I was forced to lead daily."

With his "freedom" from the usual family and social obligations, Joseph also experiences a loss of self insofar as the self is directive. For, within his vacuum, there are no comparatives, none of the established values, no directions that ordinarily serve to channel effort and, thereby, to make that effort meaningful. Bellow's hero—perhaps antihero[1]—is in much the same situation as those in which the characters of Joseph Conrad often find themselves: he is in strange "territory" where all of his values break down. He is out of context, hence lost, a condition to which he freely resigns himself at the end of the story when he gives up the struggle to live with his freedom and demands that he be taken into the army without any more delay:

> And I am sorry to leave her [his wife, Iva], but I am not at all sorry to part with the rest of it. I am no longer to be held accountable for myself; I am in other hands, relieved of self-determination, freedom canceled.
> Hurray for regular hours!
> And for the supervision of the spirit!
> Long live regimentation![2]

With this hysterical praise for "the leash," Bellow's hero falls to an unheroic submission.

Inasmuch as *Dangling Man* is set during the period in which Joseph awaits induction, the title evidently refers to his dangling between civilian life and the army; and the war is directly responsible for a drastic change in his life. In a sense, then, the novel is a war story about what can happen to a man when he is caught in the exigencies of a national military struggle. But the book is about Joseph and World War II only in much the same sense that *Huckleberry Finn* is a book about Huck Finn and the antebellum South. The setting of Bellow's work is indeed World War II, but that fact serves only as background for an experience that extends far beyond the confines of any time and certainly of any war.

The Use of Time

That Joseph's private hell is not the result of the war is made conclusively evident if we look at Bellow's handling of time. *Dangling Man* is in diary form, a highly effective form when it is used to depict the struggles and tensions of a troubled mind. Bellow uses the form loosely, allowing Joseph to recreate incidents that occurred many months before the story proper. Moreover, in the recreation of these incidents, Joseph is allowed to recall at will verbatim conversations that took place at the time. At this point, it is necessary to note that the diary is begun by Joseph in December. He is writing in December when he speaks of his "seven months' delay," which means that he must have received his first draft call no sooner than the previous May. Yet several of these recalled events and conversations take place before May, and in each case, Bellow is careful to state the time when they occurred. For example, it was at the Servatius party last March when Joseph realizes that his efforts to create a "colony of the spirit" were based on romantic idealism; the affair with Kitty Daumler, who offers companionship when Joseph becomes alienated from his wife, was begun over "two years ago"; Joseph's disillusionment with the Communist party took place several years before; and his violent quarrel with his first landlord happened "last winter." These incidents constitute a substantial part of the story, indicating that Bellow feels that the part of Joseph's story before he receives his draft notice is fundamentally significant to his present plight. It would seem, then, that Bellow intends that different and more substantial "strings" than those of the war are involved in Joseph's "dangling."

One such string runs through these four incidents: an isolation that strikes ever more deeply at Joseph during his enforced idleness. We find that step by step he moves toward an alienation from those around him—alienation from the Communist party, from his wife, from his friends, and even from his own principles, as when he violently confronts his landlord. In each of these cases, the reality of the experience does not match his ideals. Through these events Bellow's protagonist is being lowered to a subangelic position that not only takes into account man's godlike imagination and his limitation, but also punishes anyone who fails to recognize those limits. Joseph's past, then, sets the stage upon which is to be played out a most painful reappraisal of his relationship to society and to himself.

Kitty

The period of time encompassed by the seven months' delay—from the time of Joseph's first draft call in May to his diary entry in December—continues the pattern of Joseph's failure to reconcile satisfactorily the ideal with the real, which leads to his ever-increasing alienation. This deterioration is nowhere more clearly illuminated than in Joseph's affair with Kitty Daumler, whom he meets at the travel bureau where he has been working. Although their relationship begins on a Platonic basis, Joseph's biological subangelic nature is increasingly attracted to her. After a span of two months, however, he explains to Kitty, "A man must accept limits and cannot give in to the wild desires to be everything and everyone and everything to everyone" (101). In this dramatic scene, rich in self-contradiction, Joseph reasonably explains his limitations, but then denies his own words by continuing to see Kitty. At a later time, Joseph is finally and sharply confronted with the *sub*angelic facts when he visits Kitty to get a book she borrowed from him: he finds her in bed with another man. Upon this discovery he feels "ambiguously resentful and insulted," a reaction that is the result of having his images smashed again, images of "ideal constructions" made possible by his angelic nature. It is important to understand that Joseph is no fool. His keenness in diagnosing the drives that led to his first and subsequent sexual unions with Kitty shows a man of awareness, of insight into natural motivations, and of a partial understanding of himself. Only an honest and an alert mind more nearly allied to the angelic than to the demonic could so accurately chart a course of such complexity. Poor Joseph's motives are laudably high and well-intentioned, while his practical knowledge of basic human needs and relationships is sadly incomplete.

In order to add depth and meaning to the experience with Kitty, Bellow shows Joseph returning home in a setting that symbolically reinforces the discovered world of reality with which he has just been confronted. After Kitty closes the door, Joseph is left standing like a little boy, "staring up at the transom" as if he would see into the life of things were he tall enough. As he walks down the stairs, he sees: "a woman in a slip, sitting before the mirror with a razor, her arm crooked backward, a cigarette on the ledge of the radio beside her, and from it two curling prongs of smoke rising. The sight of her held me momentarily; then, possibly because the sound of my steps had ceased, or sensing that she was being watched, she looked up, startled—a broad, angry face" (104).

In this embodiment of the subangelic nature of humanity, a woman, surrounded by objects of civilization, is in the act of attempting to

disguise her animalism; and she is angry at the possibility of being
discovered. The correlation between this scene and that which just took
place with Kitty a few moments before can hardly be missed. Certainly
Joseph feels it, if he does not intellectualize it. And, as Joseph proceeds
downstairs to the vestibule, his attention is drawn to a lamp: "On a
pedestal a bronze Laocoön held in his suffering hands a huge
barbarically furred headpiece of a lampshade with fringes of blackened
lace" (104).

This lamp reflects the wellsprings of the affair with Kitty—a human
condition, a subangelical station. Man is capable of illuminating
insight, of reasoning awareness, of moral humanism; yet he must bear
the modifying burden of a biological shade that dims the light of an
otherwise angelical nature. His "suffering hands" are forever entwined
in his own history, a history out of the sea that shuts out all prophecy of
reason and morality, even as the truth of Laocoön was stifled. This
history includes a "furred headpiece" and "blackened lace."

The episode concludes with Joseph's boarding a streetcar along with
a drunken soldier and young girl, an old woman, a rumpled policeman,
and a woman in a "short skirt and fur chubby" (106). This last person
draws a pitying comment from the conductor of the car about her
reasons for being out on an icy winter's night, but this pity moves to
derision as he adds, "Unless she's out on business." Joseph responds by
telling us: "I jumped off and struggled homeward against the wind,
stopping for a while under the corner awning to catch my breath. The
clouds were sheared back from a mass of stars chattering in the
hemispheric blackness—the universe, this windy midnight, out on its
eternal business" (105–6). Bellow would have us see that at times the
world is an ugly, wind-swept waste. But, if the woman is "out on
business," it is encompassed within the business of the universe, as are
Joseph and Kitty. There is, however, a kind of universal reconciliation:
there are stars "in the hemispheric blackness." Also, Joseph sees no
more of Kitty; and, when he returns home, he and Iva are reconciled.

Life's Double Reality

This artful use of setting as source for commentary on the action is
not consistent throughout the novel; more often than not, Joseph acts as
his own commentator. On a visit to the home of his brother Amos,

Amos's wife Dolly, and their daughter Etta, Joseph reacts to an
awkward and uncomfortable discussion concerning his idleness and
lack of money by retiring defensively to the attic, where, listening to
Haydn records, he confesses that he is "still an apprentice in suffering
and humiliation. . . . Surely no one could plead for exception; that was
not a human privilege." He also says he will not "catch at any
contrivance in panic. . . . No, not God, not any divinity in order to
meet suffering and humiliation with grace, without meanness" (67).
Surely this spirit is angelic, a spirit aware of reach exceeding grasp, but
still reaching. However, when Etta intrudes on his solitude, they
scream childish accusations at each other. Joseph ends the skirmish by
soundly spanking her. Again, his godlike reason is checkmated by his
own treasonous emotions.

This scene demonstrates Bellow's concern with the doubleness of
man. At every opportunity Bellow marks the distinction between the
en-soi and the *pour-soi*. We see Joseph's awareness of life's double reality
as we are coincidentally aware of his seeming incapacity to apply his
insight to his actions.

The Limits of Imagination

This incapacity of Joseph is reflected in his inability to live in his
"freedom." He finds that his own resources are not enough to sustain a
self-definition and, therefore, a meaningful life. Bellow supports this
thesis with a parallel incident in another man's life that examines the
extent to which one may rely upon his own imagination to find his place
in the world. The incident revolves around John Pearl, an artist friend
of Joseph, who has left Chicago for New York, where he has a position
with an advertising agency. While denigrating his job in a letter to
Joseph, Pearl contends that "the real world is the world of art and of
thought. There is only one worthwhile sort of work, that of the
imagination" (90–91). Joseph envies his friend and decries his own
inability to find salvation in the elevating power of the imagination.

In "Distractions of a Fiction Writer" Bellow holds that "Men are
active. Ideas are passive."[3] He also suggests that the artist who forgets
this truism becomes an abject creature, creating contemptible art. The
artist, Bellow is saying, is after all a man. As such, he must be involved
with man, not only passively through a world of ideas but actively in

concert with man. This pattern is carried out in John Pearl, who later writes about his "peeling environment" and his longing for Chicago; he has found that the imagination has its limits. Joseph, in his turn, expresses understanding of Pearl's defeat; for he is learning that man is part of his environment and that he cannot separate himself from the past. He is what he is because of what he was. Imagination, a godlike extension of man, is of value only when it is rooted in reality, when it remembers that its source is within man. To Bellow, the imagination in all its creativity must never attempt to create a world beyond man. It is bound to fail any test of art or life.

The Failure of Reason

Joseph's effort to build a foundation on which he can establish some purpose and direction is directly dramatized by Bellow through Joseph's philosophical discussions with his Spirit of Alternatives, whom he calls "Tu As Raison Aussi." This Spirit, of course acts as Joseph's other self. In one of these sessions the following exchange occurs in which Joseph speaks first:

"There's a lot of talk about alienation. It's a fool's plea."
"Is it?"
"You can divorce your wife or abandon your child, but what can you do with yourself?"
"You can't banish the world by decree if it's in you. Is that it, Joseph?"
"How can you. . . . The world comes after you. . . . Whatever you do you cannot dismiss it."
"What then?"
"The failing may be in us, in me. A weakness of vision."
"If you could see, what do you think you would see?"
"I'm not sure. Perhaps that we were the feeble-minded children of angels." (137)

All of Bellow's protagonists are nowhere better described than in this phrase "the feeble-minded children of angels." Then, somewhat later in this discussion, Joseph asks:

"But what of the gap between the ideal construction and the real world, the truth?"

"Yes. . . ."
"How are they related?"
"An interesting problem."
"Then there's this: the obsession exhausts the man. It can become his enemy. It often does."
"H'm." (141)

When this Spirit persists in his refusal to provide any answers to Joseph's dilemma, Joseph erupts explosively, flinging orange peels at the departing Spirit. As with imagination, reason has its limitations. If a man persists in not recognizing and accepting those limitations, he is thrown back on the natural resources of violence. There is always that recourse for the subangelical man.

The last encounter with the Spirit of Alternatives prepares for Joseph's surrender. He and "Tu As Raison Aussi" are discussing the proper role for Joseph: whether he is to maintain a freedom whose "value is decreasing everyday" or to insist that his draft number be called at once. While Joseph maintains that it is necessary to preserve his freedom, he recognizes that his weariness comes from the inability to be free "because it is not accompanied by comprehension." Because of this ignorance we "soon run out, we choose a master, roll over on our backs and ask for the leash." As for the war, it is but an incident; the real nature of the world will not be changed by it. He adds: "The war can destroy me physically. That it can do. But so can bacteria. I must be concerned with them, naturally. I must take account of them. They can obliterate me. But as long as I am alive, I must follow my destiny in spite of them." To which "Tu As Raison Aussi" replies:

"Then only one question remains."
"What?"
"Whether you have a separate destiny. Oh, you're a shrewd wriggler," said "Tu As Raison Aussi." "But I've been waiting for you to cross my corner. Well, what do you say?"
I think I must have grown pale.
"I'm not ready to answer. I have nothing to say to that now."
"How seriously you take this," cried "Tu As Raison Aussi." "It's only a discussion. The boy's teeth are chattering. Do you have a chill?" He ran to get a blanket from the bed.

I said faintly, "I'm all right." He tucked the blanket around me and, in great concern wiped my forehead and sat by me until nightfall. (168–69)

The possibility, or even the probability, that Joseph has no individual meaning, purpose, or existence of any consequence stuns him. If all this is true, such phrases as "individual freedom" and "personal justice," and the romanticism of ideal constructions are surely games of the ego, and of an imaginary ego at that. It is little wonder that Joseph desperately reaches for the group in order to achieve a degree of self-identification and meaning.

The Burden of Man

When Joseph gives up the battle and makes preparations to join the army, he feels a great sense of relief. Once more, he and Iva are at least in a state of peaceful coexistence. He makes peace with his fellow tenant Vannaker, an old man, hard of hearing, a drunk and a thief, who had annoyed Joseph progressively throughout the seven months' delay. These and other positive adjustments seem to indicate a kind of consolation in defeat. Joseph also returns to his reading, and it will be remembered that he refers early in the novel to his books as "guarantors of an extended life, far more precious and necessary than the one I was forced to lead." Evidently, Joseph learns finally that books, hence art, are complementary to life, certainly not more precious or more necessary.

Through Joseph, Bellow does not intend the darker views of our existence that some readers have seen. Chester Eisinger says, "Joseph cannot reconcile his two worlds, and he cannot exist as a whole man with dignity in the real world. . . . Worse than this, Joseph cannot exist in his own independent world, carved out of his own inner resources of mind and will and sensibility."[4] And Marcus Klein says: "Joseph must give himself to idiopathic freedom, and that way is madness, or submit to the community's ordinary, violent reality. . . . He surrenders."[5] These interpretations are indeed within the framework of Joseph's experience, but they do not hit squarely the central point of that experience, which is, that we do not and cannot live alone in a world of which we are a part; that we need ties and

connections for self-meaning as well as social meaning; and that freedom and independence are but ideals if they are not functioning in the
reality of a social context—even if that context is military with its
demands against individualization and freedom. This is the state of
man, dangling in a subangelic position.

The Victim (1947)

The negative implications of the title of Saul Bellow's second novel,
The Victim, are difficult to reconcile with the positive concepts of the
subangelic attitude; for, by definition, the term "victim" seems to
preclude the dignity, the integrity, and the hopefulness usually assumed within that attitude. Yet we must accept the author's title as a
clear indication of intention: he does mean to cast Asa Leventhal, the
protagonist, as victim. Furthermore, the text bears out the intention:
Asa is trapped by forces that are surely not of his own making.

In this work, however, there are explicit and implicit affirmations
which show an unbroken line of development in the work and thought
of Bellow: the subangelic spirit is neither forgotten nor laid aside in *The
Victim*; instead, it is evidenced through a kind of indirection. Just how
Bellow manages this complexity, how he contrives to place in conjunction the demonic and the subangelic, is of primary interest.

In order to understand the more specific intentions of the author, we
may begin by examining the general nature of the novel and the
personality of its hero. This examination might best be done through
comparisons with his first novel, *Dangling Man,* inasmuch as both
works are founded on the victim theme. *The Victim* is set in contemporary New York City. The primary action develops out of the relationship of Asa Leventhal and Kirby Allbee,[6] "one of those guys," says Asa,
"who want you to think they can see to the bottom of your soul."[7] A
few years prior to the action of the story, Asa, a Jew, through the help of
Allbee, a Gentile, had secured an interview from Allbee's superior,
Rudiger, in an attempt to obtain a much-needed job. Rudiger was rude
beyond Asa's self-restraint, and there ensued between them a loud,
chaotic scene filled with general and specific recriminations. Within a
few days, Allbee himself was dismissed by Rudiger.

Shortly after the novel opens, Allbee, who presents himself to Asa,
whose wife Mary is away for the summer, insists that Asa had malici-

ously contrived the scene with Rudiger in order to avenge an anti-Semitic remark made earlier by Allbee during a party which Asa had attended. Allbee contends that the sole responsibility for his dismissal and subsequent decline (Allbee is a derelict: his wife had left him and is now dead; he is without money, without work; and he is a heavy drinker) rests solely on the conscience of Asa. At first, the charge seems so ridiculous to Asa that he refers to Allbee as "some kind of nut." But, as his accuser continues to plague him, both with his presence and with his complaints, Asa, although convinced that he is dealing with a lunatic, seeks reassurance from his friends.

Through Harkavy and Williston, Asa had got an editing job for a trade paper. Since they had helped him once, he now turns to them. Harkavy gives him some words of encouragement; but somehow his comments, "outrageous . . . how annoying . . . how disagreeable," fail to bring Asa any peace. Williston seems to agree with his indignant reactions; but he is so reserved that Asa demands a concrete and immediate vindication. Williston not only does not insist on Asa's innocence but also states that Asa is probably not without responsibility. Now even Asa doubts his own innocence.

But Allbee, with his unpredictable behavior and slovenly habits, is not an easy one to help; and the working-out of the Asa-Allbee relationship is made up of scene after scene of intense and at times violent confrontations of accuser and accused. Soon it is difficult to tell which is which. After one particular vicious encounter in the apartment, Allbee, who tries to commit suicide, almost kills Asa in the process and he then disappears. The two meet several years later at a theater; during the intermission Allbee, now at least superficially successful, confesses a debt to Asa and explains that he is "the type that comes to terms with whoever runs things" and that he now realizes "the world wasn't made exactly for me." This primary plot ends with Asa's call to Allbee to "wait a minute, what's your idea of who runs things?" (294). But the curtain is going up, and Asa receives no reply.

The second plot in *The Victim* serves as support and counterpoint to the primary action. Asa's brother Max, who is working in Texas, has left his wife Elena and their two children in New York. When one of the children becomes ill, Asa assumes the responsibility of watching over the family. During this caretaking Asa is forced into another examination of his responsibility, perhaps guilt, through his efforts to help and advise. This subplot ends with the death of the child and with the return of Max and his family to Texas.

The Victimization of Asa

A comparison of *The Victim* and *The Dangling Man* reveals general likenesses between the created worlds; Bellow depicts in both works existences that are torn between a frustratingly partial recognition of implacable naturalistic forces and a humanly stubborn insistence upon an active self-determination. Certainly both novels reach their intensities through an examination of this theme of deterministic limits. Then, there are general similarities between the two protagonists: Asa and Joseph are, in a sense, antiheroes; both are isolated and alienated; both find that exigencies of the moment are usually beyond their anticipation and restraint; and, finally, both are left with an unquiet apprehension of an existence that seems to be beyond their control. In a very real sense, Asa and Joseph are both "dangling" and both "victims."

There are, however, sharp and informative distinctions between Bellow's two works that are useful in extending the author's concept of man as subangelic. *Dangling Man* has for its center an examination of the meanings of freedom, and the implications of them to the individual. In *The Victim,* the author moves to a consideration of another human condition, the burden of guilt and responsibility; and the issues become more complex in that they are more immediate, more tangible, less abstract in the sense that their resolutions are called for many times over. In *Dangling Man,* Joseph at least has an alternative: he can continue his struggle toward a personal and individual integrity or he can give up his freedom, as he does, and "collectivize." For Asa Leventhal, such a choice does not and cannot exist; he simply must make the best of an existing situation which is largely beyond his control. His situation calls for decisions and conclusions that are impossible of intelligent and reasonable resolutions, not only because of his confused and limited personality, but also because of the intricacies of the problem itself: those of determining guilt and responsibility regardless of modifying circumstances.

Certainly there is less drama in the experiences of Asa Leventhal than in those of Joseph, simply because Asa has no clear-cut alternative. The question of whether or not Leventhal will win his fight is somehow not germane. Asa, who has no choice, seems to live on Matthew Arnold's "darkling plain, swept with confused alarms . . . where ignorant armies clash by night." In such chaos, friend and foe are unrecognizable; victory and defeat, meaningless. In such conflicts, survival itself is the only end to be devoutly wished.

Moreover, Joseph is a highly sympathetic figure. The reader identifies with him and participates in his battle for freedom. In spite of his behavioral "brinksmanship," he has a keen intelligence that is actively aware, though usually too late, of its own weaknesses. He is defeated, but his defeat comes about only after a conflict in which there is to be seen a kind of clear-eyed nobility and a searching integrity. The reader trusts Joseph, and he trusts Joseph's diary with its confessional approach and candid directness. In his near proximity, then, the reader feels that Joseph, in Bellow's words, "has the power to complete his own life," and to "overcome the ignominy" of the blows of a seemingly mechanical universe. The most important point is that, while Joseph has difficulty in determining his relationship with society, he does have a complete understanding of self—not, perhaps, an angelic understanding, but one not too far removed.

Such is not the case with Asa Leventhal, or at least serious modification of statement is called for. In fact, ignorance of self is largely responsible for Asa's victimization. Bellow indicates this confusion early in the novel when Asa is first described: "burly, his head large; his nose, too, was large . . . his eyes under their intergrown brows were intensely black and of a size unusual in adult faces. But though childishly large they were not childlike in expression. They seemed to disclose an intelligence not greatly interested in its own powers, as if preferring not to be bothered by them, indifferent; and this indifference appeared to be extended to others. He did not look sullen but rather unaccommodating, impassive" (13).

The hints of childish innocence and the clear indications of anthropoidal characteristics make it impossible for us to reach the closeness, the fine degree of identification, that we immediately attain with Joseph. Moreover, this description of Asa is just the stuff of which victims are made: a basic inability coupled with an innocence that seem to defy experience.

Asa is also set at a distance from the reader by a "sickness" that is largely owing to a sense of guilt arising from a mind limited by a long history of anti-Semitism. A victim of a persecution complex, he defines his entire relationship to the world in terms of persecution. Early in the story, Bellow presents his protagonist's problem when Harkavy urges Asa to forget about his encounter with Rudiger and the consequent possibility of his being blacklisted: "There isn't a thing he can do to you. Whatever you do, don't get ideas like that into your head. He can't persecute you. Now be careful. You have that tendency, boy, do you know that?" (46). This "tendency" accounts for the suspicion and defensiveness that are a part of Asa's personality. All of his reflections and conclusions are founded upon "that tendency."

Asa's excited and apprehensive Jewishness, for example, makes possible his reactions to Elena's mother, who is a devout Catholic: "And the grandmother? If anything happened to the boy she would consider it in the nature of a judgment on the marriage. The marriage was impure to her. Yes, he understood how she felt about it. A Jew, a man of wrong blood, of bad blood, had given her daughter two children, and that was why this was happening. No one could have persuaded Leventhal that he was wrong" (62).

This accentuated Jewishness also confuses Asa to the point of inaction when he is confronted by the anti-Semitic Allbee, "a Gentile . . . from an old New England family." In what is one of the most illuminating scenes of the novel, a scene discussed in more detail later, Asa fully reveals the pattern of behavior that comes from his persecution complex. In a discussion of Disraeli's role in the political life of England, Asa gives his views of the motives behind the prime minister's success: "I don't have it in for him. But he wanted to lead England. In spite of the fact that he was a Jew, not because he cared about empires so much. People laughed at his nose, so he took up boxing; they laughed at his poetic silk clothes, so he put on black; and they laughed at his books, so he showed them. He got into politics and became the prime minister. He did it all on nerve" (130).

Through this interpretation of Disraeli's motives, Asa unconsciously reveals the sources of his own actions, or of his reactions. He is the victim of tunnel vision: all of his thinking is channeled along the lines of defensive Semitism. Furthermore, the reader soon discovers that, as a result of this singular sight, Asa has a distorted picture of his environment: Rudiger does not really interfere with his efforts to seek employment; the hidden anti-Semitic vengeance of Elena's mother is probably imaginary; and, as will be shown, Allbee's constant negative references to his Jewishness are merely reflected self-impressions. The point is that, as soon as we feel or see the distortion in Asa's thinking, we immediately step back and view Bellow's protagonist as a victim. And, if we recall for a moment Joseph in *Dangling Man,* the contrast is evident. Joseph's view of the world is trusted; therefore, it is easy to make a friendly and sympathetic identification with him.

It should be added that Bellow also sets some distance between Asa and the reader through the practice of referring to his protagonist as merely "Leventhal," rather than by the more familiar "Asa," as if Asa Leventhal were the subject of a study, a case report. In *The Victim* Bellow achieves a distance between reader and protagonist because the point of view is quite important to the attitude that the author would have us take toward his theme, in which there are issues of guilt, morality, justice, and responsibility.

In such a framework, judgment is necessary; and that judgment, which must come from the reader, calls for a measure of distance and objectivity. But, more directly to the purpose, the distance from Asa, which is accomplished through point of view, accounts in large part for the view of Asa as victim. Through the detachment of reader and protagonist there is a certain loss of sympathetic participation. Of course this whole matter of distance is not a matter of black and white, and there is some truth in what Jonothan Baumbach states in his *Landscape of Nightmare:* "Much of the impact of *The Victim* resides in Bellow's ability to keep the reader's point of view limited to Leventhal's, making the reader a sympathetic participant in his nightmare experience."[8] Yet Leventhal's point of view is distorted. And, when the reader discovers this lack of clear vision, as he does early in the novel, he may remain sympathetic; but his will to participate is subject to the extent of the distortion.

Asa's Dilemma

It is difficult at this point to regard Bellow's protagonist as sub-angelic because there seems little if anything he can do to "overcome ignominy" and to "complete his own life." He simply has a built-in "suffering, feebleness, and servitude" that seem to be totally without help or meaning. He labors the stone of Sisyphus up the hill, but he walks down for his next effort with a mind that is largely unable to grasp even a piece of the nobility and the dignity of his humanness.

Unlike many other contemporary novelists, Saul Bellow never creates his worlds in terms of a complete victimization, nor are his characters absolute grotesques. The subangelic attitude does not permit such a frozen outline; Asa is depicted as victim; but this condition is shown to be but one, the nature of which is, to an extent, dependent upon the victim himself. And here part of what Bellow intends in his use of the term "subangelic" is made clear in the depiction of Asa's state as a complex rather than as a singular one. It has been pointed out that Asa's problems are largely the result of a sickness, specifically, his insecurity owing to Semitic feelings of guilt; but it is important to see that this guilt is only an unnatural condition, one in which there are possibilities of development and change. Those possibilities are evident if Bellow's protagonist is considered in another light.

Asa has an honest mind: he wants to do what is right. He is even capable of a kind of idealism. When he reflects upon the implications of human responsibility, he does so with strength: "he liked to think [that] 'human' meant accountable in spite of many weaknesses—at the last moment, tough enough to hold" (154). And, more often than not, at least within the limits of his ability, he abides by his ideals: he is humanly accountable in the best sense of the term. His own effort and his own time, often valuable time, are given to help his brother's family. Furthermore, his visits are not perfunctorily passive. When Elena fearfully refuses to allow her sick child to be sent to the hospital, Asa is actively concerned: "With unconscious grimness, Leventhal prepared himself to struggle with her. . . . The prospect of interfering, rushing in to rescue the boy, was repugnant to him; it made him feel, more than ever, that he was an outsider" (52). Yet Asa sees the unpleasantness through.

And he does so with Allbee. In spite of the seeming unreasonableness of his accuser's complaints and demands, Asa cannot completely sever the relationship because, regardless of his certainty that he intended no evil toward Allbee, he is not convinced of his own innocence. He understands abstract accountability, and he suffers from this understanding in spite of his attempts to rationalize the subject into nonexistence. When he reflects on Williston's reluctance to support his case against Allbee, and on "the whole affair," he concludes: "It was, after all, something he could either take seriously or dismiss as an annoyance. It was up to him. He had only to insist that he wasn't responsible and it disappeared altogether. It was his conviction against an accusation nobody could expect him to take at face value. And what more was there for him to say than that his part in it was accidental? At worst, an accident, unintentional" (96).

Asa's rationale is quite logical, and it is well within the framework of social dictates. Its only weakness, however, is its lack of humanity. It does not take into consideration Asa's deep feeling of accountability; hence, it is little wonder that such a cold analysis of his responsibility gives him no comfort whatever. After all, as he says, "it is up to him"; and laboratory logic cannot remove him from that felt and very human position.

"It was up to him," hardly the statement of a victim, is another brick in the subangelic foundation. When Bellow says that the reality of this responsibility "may be an exaggeration of the value of the human personality," the fact of Asa's feeling that it is not an exaggeration is also a reality, a truth that must be reckoned with in the depiction of the human personality. Certainly there is a dilemma, and it often leads to helplessness, to a loss of the name of action; but the very recognition of the problem points to a potentiality. Again and again, Bellow shows that Asa is working in this field of recognition, perhaps blindly, but working. When he is pondering his "meddling" into Elena's family difficulties, he pauses to examine the deeper and more meaningful extensions:

judging from what he had seen . . . well, her fear of the hospital was an indication of her fitness to bring up children. Some people would say that she loved them and that her love made up for her shortcomings. . . . Love, by all means. But because the mother and the child were tied together in that way, if the child died through her ignorance, was she still a good mother? Should someone else—he thought of it seriously—have the right to take the child away? Or should the fate of the two of them be considered one and the same, and the child's death said to be the mother's affair only because she would suffer most by its death? In that case, the child was not regarded as a person, and was that fair? Well, that was the meaning of helplessness; that was what they meant when they said it. Now with that in mind you could understand why little children sometimes cried the way they did. It was as if it were in them to know. Unfair, thought Leventhal, not to say tragic. (52)

Such extensions of meaning as those found in this passage help to inform *The Victim* above and beyond the immediate issue of anti-Semitism. Bellow is concerned with Asa as a victim of a religious inheritance, but he is also interested in him as an issue of a human condition that exists with the vague and indecisive, the gray and shadowed, area of accountability. As Frederick Hoffman concludes, "the ultimate issue is one of general morality specifically grounded."[9]

In any case, Asa is aware of the wider implications of his particular dilemma; he sees beyond his immediate confusion. While such an awareness does not necessarily admit of concrete resolutions, it does point to the possible positive in its pursuit of revelations. It affirms man's potentiality. And so it is with Asa, who, while a victim, embodies what Ihab Hassan refers to as "the basic morality of the *eiron*" in that Asa's nature allows for an "evoking of possibilities where none but limitations exist."[10]

With these modifying affirmatives introduced into Asa's character, Bellow is saying that, while Asa's limitations tend to victimize him, his deep and honest feelings of responsibility and accountability, his sense of the real and the ideal, and his empathy for his fellowman, whether founded on logic or not, give him the dignity of development and the possibility of change. Bellow urges that, while man's limitations might be inherent, so are man's potentialities. Moreover, this positive side of Asa gives to the reader another point of view—this time, a closer view, one with which he can identify and sympathize more easily. But this new position neither negates nor lessens Asa as victim; it merely shows an extenuation, a complexity that denies any view of man that is singular in nature.

The Theater of Man

In a pivotal chapter 10, in the middle of *The Victim,* Bellow deepens his meanings. This chapter acts as a wheel upon which the issue of guilt and responsibility in Asa turns to a consideration of that issue in modern man. Moreover, Asa's dilemma, or that of contemporary man, is clarified through an examination that sets the conflict in historical perspective. The scene takes place in a cafeteria where Asa and his friend Harkavy join Goldstone, Shifcart, and Schlossberg. Each of this group, with the exception of Asa, is or has been closely connected with the world of the theater. Their conversation centers generally on acting and specifically on the merits of particular actresses.

Bellow often uses images of the theatrical world as metaphors to assert the distinctions between what man is and what he pretends to be. For Bellow, these are images of escape through which he depicts man's attempts to escape the facts of his existence.[11] With this metaphor in mind, Bellow turns the cafeteria into a setting whose sights and sounds evoke reminiscences of the theater. Asa is described as he steps inside: "He had come in as much to escape the hot winds as to eat. The glass door shut on the dirty rush behind him, and he advanced a few steps over the green tile floor and paused. . . . The trays were on a stand nearby, and he picked one up and started toward the counter. The cashier called him back. He had forgotten to pull a check from the machine" (122). We can almost see the omnipresent theater signs that read "20° cooler inside." The glass doors, the fading of street noises, the machine from which the patron pulls his ticket—all might be seen as theatrical setting, as well as might the description of the change of menus which recalls the setting up of new programs on a theater marquee: "Behind the steam tables, one set of white-lettered menu boards was hauled down and another sent up in the steel frame with a clash" (130). Bellow even puts the scene in motion: "It was a slow hour in the restaurant. On all sides there were long perspectives of black-topped tables turned on an angle to appear diamond-shaped, each with its symmetrical cluster of sugar, salt, pepper, and napkin box. From end to end their symmetry put a kind of motion into the almost empty place. At the rear, under the scene of groves painted on the wall, some of the employees sat smoking, looking toward the sunlight and the street" (131).

Here are the stagehands standing in front of some scenery, looking out and over what appears to be the setting of and action for a harlequinade. Then, when Asa and his companions leave, Harkavy calls to them in the manner of a hat-check girl at the theater:

"Don't forget your hats, gentlemen."
The musical crash of the check machine filled their ears as they waited their turn at the cashier's dazzling cage. (135)

The last three lines give to the reader the sights and sounds of a ticket line in front of a theater.

Bellow creates the image of the theater primarily for Mr. Schlossberg, whose function is to dramatize an attitude of the past that Asa, as modern man, finds no longer tenable. As a symbol of the past, Schlossberg is provided with Victorian trappings, including a family that might have been drawn from a Victorian novel. His son, who is thirty-five years old, still lives with him—"hasn't made up his mind about a vocation," Harkavy explains to Asa before they join the group; and "there are daughters, too. Worse yet" (123). He is somewhat jaded but still active:

> He was a large old man with a sturdy gray head, hulking shoulders, and a wide, worn face; his eyes were blue and disproportionately small, and even their gaze was rather worn. But he was vigorous and he must once have been (some of his remarks evoked him for Leventhal as a younger man) sensual, powerful, flashy, a dandy—as his double-breasted vest and pointed shoes attested. He wore a knitted tie which had lost its shape with pulling and was made up with a bold, broad knot. Leventhal felt himself strongly drawn to him. (123–24)

Schlossberg is the Victorian "dandy" whose tie, vest, and shoes are fashionable for the era. When he derides the actresses who have attempted the role of Victoria, he says, "I could play a better Victoria myself," with which Asa agrees "with more respect than amusement" (132).

Schlossberg is extremely critical of every contemporary actress whose name comes into the discussion, for none of these can match the performances of the past. He is especially distressed to hear Goldstone praise one actress, Livia Hall. When Goldstone says, "I don't know what your standards are. A perfect piece of casting. Who else could have done it?" Schlossberg replies:

> "Wood, so help me. She poisons her husband and she watches him die. She wants the insurance money. He loses his voice and he tries to appeal to her she should help him. You don't hear any words. What is she supposed to show in her face? Fear, hate, a hard heart, cruelness, fascination." He shut his eyes tightly and proudly for a moment, and they saw the veins in his lids. Then he slowly raised them, turning his face away, and a tremor went through his cheeks as he posed.

"Oh, say, that's fine!" Harkavy cried, smiling.

"That's the old Russian style," said Shifcart. "That doesn't go anymore."

"No? Where's the improvement? What does she do? She sucks in her cheeks and stares. A man is dying at her feet and all she can do is pop out her eyes. . . . She is not an actress because she is not a woman, and she is not a woman because a man doesn't mean anything to her. I don't know what she is. Don't ask me. I saw once Nazimova in *The Three Sisters*. She's the one whose soldier gets killed in a duel over nothing, foolishness. They tell her about it. She looks away from the audience and just with her head and neck—what a force! But this girl. . . !" (125–26)

At the end of the chapter, Schlossberg gives his final soliloquy:

"It's bad to be less than human and it's bad to be more than human. . . . Good acting is what is exactly human. And if you say I am a tough critic, you mean I have a high opinion of what is human. This is my whole idea. More than human, can you have any use for life? Less than human, you don't either."

He made a pause—it was not one that invited interruption—and went on.

"This girl Livia in *The Tigress*. What's the matter with her? She commits a murder. What are her feelings? No love, no hate, no fear, no lungs, no heart. I'm ashamed to mention what else is missing. . . . You see right away she has no idea what is human because her husband's death doesn't mean to her a thing. . . . Now maybe somebody will answer me 'This sounds very interesting. You say less than human, more than human. Tell me, please, what is human?' And really we study people so much now that after we look and look at human nature . . . after you look at it and weigh it and turn it over and put it under a microscope, you might say, 'What is all the shouting about? A man is nothing, his life is nothing. Or it is even lousy and cheap. But this your royal highness doesn't like, so he hokes it up. With what? With greatness and beauty. Beauty and greatness? Black and white I know; I didn't make it up. But greatness and beauty?' But I say, 'What do you know? No, tell me, what do you know? You shut one eye and look at a thing, and it is one way to you. You shut the other one and it is different. I am as sure about greatness and beauty as you are about black and white." (133–34)

Bellow's intentions are clear in these passages only if the reader understands, first, that Schlossberg's strictures on acting are to be equated with an attitude toward the nature of man, and, second, that Schlossberg, as an actor himself—"He shut his eyes tightly and proudly for a moment"—represents an attempt to escape from the facts of that nature. In more detail now, Bellow intends Schlossberg as an ironic figure who does not realize the significance of what he says, or better yet, of what he does not say. His entire criticism of the actress is based on her not responding properly to the death of her husband. He claims that her inappropriate reactions show her to be less than human. And when he says in the final passage, "She commits a murder. What are her feelings?" the irony is especially evident in his blindness to the central issue—she *did* kill her husband. But about this deed there is no comment; the important issue to him is how she responded.

This blindness is again emphasized when Schlossberg, speaking of her response, says, "it should be so awful the whole audience should be afraid positively to look in her face" (134). Again the fact of a nature that allows murder, and in cold blood as the use of the poison indicates, *that* animal fact is overlooked. There is an irony, too, in Schlossberg's statement that "good acting is what is exactly human. And if you say I am a tough critic, you mean I have a high opinion of what is human." Schlossberg, the Victorian, is deeply anxious about the forms, but he misses the substance, or closes his eyes to it. Act correctly—that is the key to the Victorian definition of man. The poisoning of a husband can be overlooked if the wife shows her humanity by clearly suffering the death of the husband. Schlossberg's "high opinion of what is human" is founded only on the appearance of things rather than on the nature of them.

In the last few lines of the final soliloquy Bellow points directly to Schlossberg as representative of the past. Through self-deception this old Victorian idealist insists upon viewing man as "greatness and beauty" in contrast to what seems to him to be the modern attitude that man is "lousy and cheap." He takes the polar extreme, the Victorian attitude; and he is extremely disturbed at the idea that man is less than that attitude dictates. To him, the actress (mankind) is a goddess. Of significance to this study, she is angelic; he will not subscribe to a lesser vision.

Asa's response to this encounter is intensely meaningful because of its revelation of his dilemma as well as for its statement of it in terms of modern man. Asa is drawn to Schlossberg; he admires his opinions on the "greatness and beauty" of man. Some twenty pages after the scene in the cafeteria, Asa is thinking about his brother's responsibility to his wife and children:

On Max's side an acknowledgement would be made. After all, you married and had children and there was a chain of consequences. It was impossible to tell, in starting out, what was going to happen. And it was unfair, perhaps, to have to account at forty for what was done at twenty. But unless one was more than human or less than human, as Mr. Schlossberg put it, the payments had to be met. Leventhal disagreed about "less than human." "More than human" was for a much smaller number. But most people had fear in them—fear of life, fear of death, of life more than of death, perhaps. But it was a fact that they were afraid, and when the fear was uppermost they didn't want any more burdens. At twenty they had vigor and so were careless, and later they felt too weak to be accountable. . . . But either they found the strength to meet the costs or they refused and gave way to dizziness—dizziness altogether, the dizziness of pleasures before catastrophe. Maybe you could call it "less than human" to refuse; he liked to think "human" meant accountable in spite of many weaknesses—at the last moment, tough enough to hold. But to go by what happened in the majority of cases, it was the last dizziness that was most typical and had the best claim to the name. (154)

In what Asa likes to think—to be human means to be accountable—Bellow shows Asa's yearning, or that of contemporary man, for the past—or for what he judges to be a less complex interpretation of life and hence, a more solid guide by which to judge the meaning of man. But Asa cannot agree with Schlossberg's singular definition of what is less than human. Asa knows that his dilemma, his guilt or innocence in the case of Allbee, is much more complicated than Schlossberg's view allows. And the nature of man has greater complexity than the Victorian attitude admits.

Bellow intends no resolution, only the revelation of a human condition. Yet it can be said that through chapter 10 the author shows an attitude toward the present that is positive in its implications. Asa, at least, is looking at the nature of man and the facts of his existence much more honestly than does Schlossberg—with an honesty, Bellow seems to imply, that allows for learning. That learning is to be gained through experience. At the end of Schlossberg's final speech, Harkavy and Shifcart applaud his theatrics with comic condescension:

"Amen and amen!" Shifcart laughed. He drew a card out of his wallet and threw it toward him. "Come and see me; I'll fix you up with a test."

The card fell near Leventhal, who seemed to be the only one to disapprove of the joke. Even Schlossberg himself smiled. . . . It seemed to Leventhal that Shifcart, though he was laughing, looked at him with peculiar disfavor. Still he did not join in. *He picked up the card* [italics mine]. The others were rising. (135)

It is not to the smiling Victorian that the card falls; it falls to Asa, the modern. He accepts the test—a test that adds to the examination of what it means to be human.

Alter Ego

Up to this point, we have been concerned with Bellow's technique in presenting the duality of his protagonist, a duality that is functional in that it supports the major conflict in *The Victim*—man's struggle with himself. This struggle is seen primarily in the strange and mystifying relationship that exists between the two major figures, Asa Leventhal and Kirby Allbee. Most important for the purposes of this chapter, it is the working out of this relationship that makes clear the nature of Asa as victim and as subangel.

On one level, Kirby Allbee is a character who represents an outer force working on Asa; on a deeper and more significant level, he is an inner adversary, an alter ego,[12] born of Asa's desire of punishment for his assumed and felt Semitic guilt and of his personal confusion and indirection regarding his place in relation to society. While Bellow depicts Allbee as a believable character in his own right, he gives ample evidence that he wishes the reader to see the close mental and physical identification between Asa and Allbee. At their first meeting, Asa asks Allbee if they are related. Allbee laughs, "By blood? No, no . . . heavens!" (29).

The implication, of course, is that there is another kind of relationship. When, in spite of Asa's antagonism, Allbee prevails upon him to sit down, Asa thinks desperately, "Damn him, he's got me, he's got hold of me" (30), as if he were dealing with a sort of mysterious force from which he cannot escape. Staring at Allbee, "Leventhal suddenly felt that he had been singled out to be the object of some freakish, insane process . . ." (31). And so he has, for this meeting with his alter ego is the beginning of a tortuous, painful journey to the depths of himself.

In Allbee, all of Asa's fears, weaknesses, insecurities, and contradictions are seen in their logical extensions. Although the reader sees these extensions, Asa does not. It is the reader who realizes that Allbee is source and goad behind the self-exploration of Asa. For example, Asa's fears of poverty hover over his every thought and action. When Asa honestly and sympathetically appraises the broken condition of Allbee, the reader is told, "It was something like this that Leventhal was thinking of when he occasionally said that he had gotten away with it" (38). Allbee's very presence, along with his lamentations, gives rise to and sustains these fears of economic insecurity; for in his double, Asa sees, indeed, feels, the threat of his own fears. When Allbee insists that Asa knows nothing of poverty, Asa snappishly replies:

"What do you mean? I've been down and out." . . .There rose immediately to Leventhal's mind the most horrible images of men wearily sitting on mission benches waiting for their coffee in a smeared and bleary winter sun; of flophouse sheets and filthy pillows; hideous cardboard cubicles. . . . And if it were *his* flesh on those sheets, *his* lips drinking that coffee, *his* back and thighs in that winter sun? . . . Allbee was right to smile at him; he had never been in such a plight. "So I'm mistaken," he reflected. (69–70)

Again and again, Allbee forces Asa to look deeply into himself, into his confused and frightened frustrations. He recalls the interview with Rudiger: "He was ready to accept the blame for losing his head. . . . But why had he lost it? Only because of Rudiger's abuse? No, he, he himself had begun to fear that the lowest price he put on himself was too high and he could scarcely understand why anyone should want to pay for his services. . . . 'He made me believe what I was afraid of,' Leventhal thought" (120).

But such insights as these come to Asa only as a result of Allbee's badgering and baiting him. In effect, what is happening is that Asa is being forced to face his fears; in so doing, he is discovering them. More precisely, rather than "being forced," Asa makes a choice of his own volition. Early in the story, when he hears Allbee approaching his apartment, "It occurred to him that he could escape Allbee by going to the roof. If he went out stealthily he could still get away. . . . He could go even now. Even *now*. Yet he stood firm and strangely enough he felt that he had proved something by doing so. 'I won't give ground,' he thought" (67). Now whether Asa is being forced or whether he chooses leads to a discussion of determinism and free will, and we will have something to say of these extensions later. For now, suffice it to say, Asa is learning about Asa.

Allbee's words and actions are deeply confusing to Asa. It is impossible to tell when he is lying, when he is just acting, how he really feels, what he wants, and what he expects. He constantly keeps Asa off balance with his intermittent outrages (as when he brings a woman to spend the night in Asa's apartment), and with his pleas for pity and help. This confusion of Asa's, of course, traces the confusion of his journey into himself. At the end of a particularly violent encounter with Allbee, Mrs. Nunez, who is the wife of Asa's landlord and "who lay on the bed near the window in a white slip," whispered "'Que Pasa?' Leventhal looked at her in bewilderment" (78). Asa, too, would like to know what is happening.

Asa plunges even deeper into his own being when he returns to his apartment one evening to discover Allbee and "a woman who was dressing in great haste" (269). Asa's horror at his first thought that the woman is Mrs. Nunez arises from a vague but incisive revelation that he has occasionally had sexual inclinations toward her. When he finds that it is not she, "He felt enormously lightened, but at the same time it gave him a pang to think of his suspicion" (269–70). One can only conclude that the pang arises from an instant's awareness of his own lust.

In any case, Allbee is ultimately living in Asa's apartment, wearing his clothes, eating his food, reading his mail (even the letters from Asa's wife), and sleeping in his bed; for Bellow would make it clear not only that Allbee is Asa's mental counterpart but that he is also a parner in a kind of negative-positive symbiotic attachment. At the zoo with Phillip, Elena's eldest son, Asa is sure that Allbee is following them: "Leventhal . . . was so conscious of Allbee, so certain that he was being scrutinized, that he was able to see himself as if through a strange pair of eyes: the side of his face, the palpitation in his throat, the seams of his skin, the shape of his body and of his feet in their white shoes" (107). This physical duality, which is depicted by Bellow intermittently throughout the novel, is indicative of the intention that the reader see these two as a Dostoevskian double (cf. 160, 224).

Allbee, then, symbolically embodies Asa's victimizing characteristics, which are born and extended, given breadth and depth, through Asa's imagination. It is supremely ironic to hear this creature of the imagination exclaim, when Asa demands that he leave his apartment after the bedroom scene, "You don't care about the woman. You're just using her to make an issue and break your promise to me. Well, and I thought I had seen everything in the way of cynicism. . . . I guess there's an example in the world of everything a man can imagine, no matter how great or how gruesome" (272). Here is Asa listening to his alter ego, a product of his imagination, using him as an example of what a human being can imagine. Bellow always uses such turns and twists as this exchange in order to show the intricate and complex binding of these two together.

But Allbee leaves under threats and violence, and it seems that this time we may have seen the last of him. Even Asa feels so. As he surveys the disarray of his apartment, he is "angry, but exultant also: he felt dimly that this disorder and upheaval was part of the price he was obliged to pay for his release" (274). His final release, however, is not to come until later that night when Allbee returns to the apartment and attempts to commit suicide by gas. Asa awakens in time to prevent his accuser's death and to save his own life. After this last outrage, Asa thinks desperately, "I have to kill him now"; and the clear implication is that the struggle between him and Allbee has reached the point of immediate self-preservation:

> He caught the cloth of his coat in his teeth while he swiftly changed his grip, clutching at Allbee's face. He tore away convulsively, but Leventhal crushed him with his weight in the corner. Allbee's fist came down heavily on his neck, beside the shoulder. "You want to murder me? Murder?" Leventhal gasped. The sibilance of the pouring gas was almost deafening.
> "Me, myself!" Allbee whispered despairingly, as if with his last breath. "Me. . . !" (282–83)

Some of the implications of this scene become clear only as the story progresses; at the moment, it is evident that Bellow suggests that the fate of Asa is closely dependent upon that of Allbee. If Asa had not taken command of the situation, he would have died with Allbee. And with

Allbee as alter ego in mind, it would seem that Asa is brought to the realization that he must destroy this inner force for his own survival.

With this savage scene, Asa successfully casts out his alter ego; and it is years before he sees him again. The narrator says: "Things went well for him [Asa] in the next few years. . . . His health was better. . . . Something recalcitrant seemed to have left him . . . he looked years younger. . . . He lost the feeling that he had, as he used to say, 'got away with it,' his guilty relief, and the accompanying sense of infringement" (285). Then, when we are told that Mary is pregnant, Bellow clearly points to a regained or new power for Asa and a kind of rebirth.

One night at a theater Asa sees Allbee again, but it is not the old Allbee. As we have noted, he is no longer whining, self-pitying, accusing, and troublesome. Under his gaiety and superficial well-being, he appears old and decayed. He explains to Asa with a "short and faint" laugh: "I'm not the type that runs things. I never could be. I realized that long ago, I'm the type that comes to terms with whoever runs things. What do I care? The world wasn't exactly made for me. What am I going to do about it?" (294). Asa's last desperate question to Allbee, who moves off in the crowd, is, "Wait a minute, what's your idea of who runs things?" (294). Allbee has gone, but the question remains. Its answer will be seen to pierce the heart of Bellow's intentions.

A Victim with Possibilities

The Victim is the story of man's struggle to free himself from a state of victimization—an ironic struggle of self-encounter.[13] Moreover, it is within this conflict that the reader once again is made aware of the subangelic in action. At the outset of this chapter, we discussed Bellow's title and its intent to indicate that the nature of Bellow's victim was in need of clarification. The contention here is that in Asa Leventhal we do see a victim, a man whose limitations are indeed severe. Perhaps the most serious of these limitations is his inability to know himself and his place in the scheme of things, an ignorance that might seem to make his apprehension of dignity and integrity impossible.

But we also maintain that the subangelic spirit is manifested in Asa Leventhal, not, perhaps, through a conscious awareness of his potentialities and thence of his nobility, but through Bellow's depiction of him, in the last analysis, as a human being with the "power to complete his own life." It might well seem that with Asa's last question, blindly flung at Allbee, "Wait a minute, what's your idea of who runs things?" Bellow intends his protagonist to remain a victim, to embody the title of the work. From time to time, however, we see that Bellow is depicting what to some may be a paradox: a victim with possibilities.

First of all, we must remember that Asa, early in the novel, stands up to his fears, in spite of a strong inclination to run away. He does not run away, and, consequently, he does "prove something." That "something" Bellow could only intend to be an element of the subangelic—a measure of free will. Again, Bellow points to the power of Asa when, at their first meeting, Allbee says "I don't want to wrestle. I'm probably no match for you" (29). Taken by itself, this statement might be insignificant; yet throughout the novel it is always Allbee who backs down in the face of Asa's wrath. Moreover, in what turns out to be one of the most illuminating encounters in the work—not only for its philosophical implications but also for its function of foreshadowing—Bellow has Allbee set guide lines for Asa that, in hindsight, clearly anticipate final intentions. Allbee states:

> Don't you worry. . . . I know what really goes on inside me. I'll let you in on something. There isn't a man living who doesn't. All this business, "Know thyself!" Everybody knows but nobody wants to admit. . . . Now let me explain something to you. It's a Christian idea but I don't see why you shouldn't be able to understand it. "Repent!" That's John the Baptist coming out of the desert. Change yourself, that's what he's saying, and be another man. You must be and the reason for that is that you can be, and when your time comes here you will be. There's another thing behind that "repent"; it's that we know what to repent. How? . . . *I* know. Everybody knows. But you've got to take away the fear of admitting by a still greater fear. I understand that doctors are beginning to give their patients electric shocks. They tear all hell out of them, and then they won't trifle. You see, you have to get yourself so that you can't stand to keep on in the old way. . . . It takes a long time before you're ready to quit dodging. Meanwhile, the pain is horrible. . . . We're mulish; that's why we have to take

such a beating. When we can't stand another lick without dying of it, then
we change. And some people never do. They stand there until the last lick
falls and die like animals. Others have the strength to change long before.
(226–27)

This passage is highly important to an understanding of what Bellow
means when he urges the subangelic attitude. Bellow would make it
clear that his thesis rests upon an assumption of free will, that man can
make choices. As Asa concludes much earlier in the story, it is up to
him. Even though we must remember that Allbee is speaking at this
point, it is also to be remembered that the working out of *The Victim*
follows the lines of his argument; for, when Asa (and Albee, too, for
that matter) "can't stand another lick without dying of it," Asa makes
his decision to act. Now it is true that the experience of Asa—the fact
that it is he who determines his limits of endurance—seems not to have
made much of an impression on him; for at the end he is still asking,
"Who runs things?"

What Asa does not seem to grasp is the lesson of his experience: that
he is running things, that *his* decision has brought about a change of
direction. And surely to the extent that he remains blind to the
meaning of his experience, just to that extent are the possibilities of his
victimization. More important, however, is that as surely as he can face
himself and say, paradoxically, perhaps, that it is up to him, he will
remain within the sphere of the subangelic. His "suffering, feebleness,
and servitude" will then have meaning; and he will have "at least
sufficient power to overcome ignominy and to complete his own life."
And this position is precisely descriptive of how Bellow leaves Asa at
the end of his novel.

Bellow Looks Back

In a 1967 Paris interview, Bellow said that he would prefer not to
discuss *Dangling Man* and *The Victim* because with their completion he
had moved away from certain attitudes and standards that went into
their making. Looking back, he says, "I had to touch a great many
bases, demonstrate my abilities, pay my respects to formal requirements" (182);[14] "I was doing nothing very original by writing another

realistic novel and calling it *The Victim*" (187). Particularly revealing is his statement that after their writing he simply became a different person, "very tired of solemnity of complaint" (187). There is indeed a messianic tone in these two early novels, almost as if the young Bellow wanted to "set us straight," to preach, to insist dramatically that new and more positive definitions of man are called for. Finally, when he says, "These books, though useful, did not give me a form in which I felt comfortable," (183) we can look ahead to his third novel, *The Adventures of Augie March,* a wide, loose, sprawling tale that Bellow moves through freely, unhampered by "formal requirements" or the need to persuade.

Chapter Three
The Adventures of Augie March

The Adventures of Augie March (1953) must be read as a multilevel work if the reader is to comprehend fully its significance. First, the novel is to be seen as a story in which a picaresquelike hero, who is also the narrator, advances through a series of adventures which, in varying degree and nature, are relevant to a general life experience. Second, the work is to be regarded as Bellow's strictures on an existing relationship between literature and society. More specifically, on this second level, *Augie March* is a fictional history of American literature; it serves as an evaluation of a literary attitude, whose existence is reflected in the experiences of the protagonist and his reactions to those experiences. Third, the character and experiences of Bellow's hero may be seen as encompassing a contemporary human condition as well as dramatizing a wider and deeper comment on literature and society.

As a character in his own right on the first level, Augie plays the role of the philosophic picaro. A man of no commitments,[1] he wanders from incident to incident and from place to place, never getting so deeply involved in any experience that he cannot continue in search of what he insists is his "better fate." Since his experiences are endless in number and infinite in variety, the following examples are only the highlights: he works as a stock boy in a department store, sells trivia in a railway station, steals and sells textbooks, begins a university education, becomes a coal salesman, enters the fringes of the underworld, helps to manage a professional fighter, takes care of dogs for the socially elite, falls in love twice, becomes a union organizer, trains an eagle to catch giant lizards in Mexico, skirts the edges of joining Trotsky's cause, joins the Merchant Marine; and he finally marries and settles in Paris, where he is last seen participating in some form of shady international business. Augie is, as he says, "varietistic." Early in the novel he confides, "Saying, 'various jobs,' I give out the Rosetta stone, so to speak, to my entire life."[2]

The reader is likely to feel some confusion when he finishes the story of Augie March, for Bellow's protagonist ends with the same attitude with which he set forth: he still lacks commitment. Still without purpose or direction, he continues his uninvolved existence. The main source of this confusion lies in the reader's inability to penetrate Augie's attractive personality, through his keen awareness and obvious intelligence, and through his independent objectivity down to the blunt facts of his total experience: Augie is one of life's failures. It is a difficult conclusion to reach, for the reader sees in Bellow's hero many of the traits that have long been assumed to be heroic—heroic in terms of what may be called a modern mythology of heroic behavior. This heroism is founded on a rebellion from and on an opposition to, even a separatism from, established institutions. This mythology tends to blind the reader to the facts of the text inasmuch as—given this opposition and rebellion, and other qualities to be pointed out later—there seems to be a predisposition on the part of the reader to judge Bellow's protagonist, both as to character and function, on the basis of issues apart from his actual experience.

Augie's Appeal

For the reader, Augie is certainly a sympathetic character; he has abilities and qualities often thought to be necessary for integrity, nobility, and intellect. One of the most obvious and most immediately apparent of these abilities is his clear vision. A keen observer, he has all the insight of Huck Finn, with whom he has been compared as many times as the novel has critics. A case in point is evinced in Augie's reactions to one of the major characters of the novel, Einhorn, the shrewd, rapacious, cantankerous, lecherous, old man who employs Augie to run his errands and to carry around his crippled body. Of him, Augie says:

And Einhorn? Jesus, he could be winsome—the world's charm-boy. And that was distracting. You can grumble at it; you can say it's a ruse or feint of gifted people to sidetrack you from the viper's tangle and ugly knottedness of their desires, but if the art of it is deep enough and carried far enough into great play, it gets above its origin. . . . I every time had high regard for him.

For one thing, there was always the fight he had made on his sickness to consider. . . . weighing it all up, the field he was put into and the weapons he was handed, he had made an imposing showing and, through mind, he connected with the spur gear. . . . So why be down on poor Einhorn, afflicted with mummy legs and his cripple-irritated longing. (99–100)

Such keen descriptive insight, along with the objective ability to see all sides of a person, helps to convince us of Augie's reliability. Then his sympathetic fairness—his ability to see the good in people—comes to light. Finally, if it is true that the ability to generalize is a mark of intelligence, Augie must be seen in this passage as a figure of intellect.

Augie is also trusted and admired for his knowledge of the limits of his understanding and for his measurable honesty to self. When he is reflecting upon Einhorn's fear of death, he states, "Often I thought that in his heart Einhorn had completely surrendered to this fear," but he quickly adds: "But when you believed you had tracked Einhorn through his acts and doings and were about to capture him, you found yourself not in the center of a labyrinth but on a wide boulevard; and here he came from a new direction . . ." (83).

And then Augie says of the simple and natural Willa, who is one of his many romances: "I think I could have been perfectly happy with Willa and lived all my life in a country town if the chance had ever presented itself. Or, anyhow, I sometimes tell myself that" (204). We cannot help being impressed with such candor, such an open willingness on Augie's part to suspend judgment even when his own ideas and conclusions are the subjects of consideration. Understood also is his yearning for simplicity.

Moreover, there is an admiration for Augie in his generous acceptance of people for what they are. "However, I had a high regard for him," he says of Einhorn. And, when he sees Joe Gorman, a thief with whom he has been involved over a stolen car, sitting dazed and beaten in the back seat of a police car, Augie laments, much in the fashion of Huck to the tar-and-feather fate of the King and the Duke, "I felt powerfully heartsick to see him" (165). Augie is an unconditional humanitarian, for he knows that Gorman had lied to him, that he was carrying a gun and would have used it, which would have implicated Augie far more than was anticipated. But Joe Gorman is a human being; therefore, Augie accepts him as such and feels for him.

And so it is with Grandma Lausch; his mother; his brother Simon; the frank and rebellious Mimi; the Renlings who wish to adopt him; Thea, his sweetheart; Bateshaw, the ship's carpenter; and all the rest. Augie sees them clearly, sympathetically; he knows what they are and what they want; he accepts them; and, without malice, he removes himself from their spheres of influence: "He has a better fate."

Augie makes one of his strongest appeals for the reader's sympathies when he philosophizes about his personal destiny of high ideal—a destiny peculiarly American in its virtuous optimism, and immediately recognizable. Early in the story he recalls his reactions as a young boy to the plans of his Aunt Anna that he will someday marry her daughter, Freidl: "Even at that time I couldn't imagine that I would marry into the Coblin family. . . . My mind was already dwelling on a better fate" (28). These words, "a better fate," or their equivalents, are asserted by Augie again and again—each time, in fact, that some person or institution attempts to convert him. Whether marriage, a career, or money, nothing stands in the way to his future. Bellow's protagonist certainly seems a figure of strength, courage, and foresight.

His view of life, his *weltbild,* reinforces this favorable image. He simply refuses to see the world as a Valley of Despair, in spite of the obvious painful wounds and the scars of thunder sitting entrenched around him: age and deterioration are catching Grandma Lausch; his mother is growing blind; his younger brother Georgie is born an idiot; Simon's early ideals have been replaced by his mad and dismal search for money and power. Augie is surrounded by the greedy, the cynical, the shameful, the ignorant, the hopelessness of the poor, the arrogance of the rich, and by other elements that would undermine the most reasonable of stoics. Yet Augie does not despair. When he explains why he will not stop reading, even though he knows nothing will come of it, he states:

> Why, I knew there were things that would never, because they could never, come of my reading. But this knowledge was not so different from the remote but ever-present death that sits in the corner of the loving bedroom; though it doesn't budge from the corner, you wouldn't stop your loving. Then neither would I stop my reading. I sat and read. I had no eye, ear, or interest for anything else. . . . Why everybody knows this triumphant life can only be periodic. So there's a schism about it, some saying only this

triumphant life is real and others that only the daily facts are. For me there was no debate, and I made speed into the former. (194)

So Augie's reality lies in a vision of life as triumphant, a goal that he is ever speeding toward. He is the soul of cultural optimism and great self-destiny—to him, all is possible, even in a world not the best possible. This generous, high-minded spirit is seen when Mimi urges Augie to agree or disagree with her negative opinion of Einhorn, to speak up, and to say what he thinks: " 'No,' I said, 'I don't know. But I don't like low opinions, and when you speak them out it commits you and you become a slave of them. Talk will lead people on until they convince their minds of things they can't feel true' " (209).

While there may be other truths to consider in what Augie says, he is right. Low opinions are uncomfortable companions, and not those of nobility. Of course, Mimi does not accept his "speak no evil" attitude, which he seems to have retained from Grandma Lausch's strictures on the three idols that sat in their house (9); but Mimi has a heatedly cynical view of life and society and of man's goodness. As for Augie, even if Mimi's cynicism is well founded, he "couldn't think all was so poured in concrete" (225) that change is impossible. He quite under-standably observes with pleasure Thea's snakes as they shed: "Toughest of all was the casting of the skins. . . . But then they would gleam out, one day, and their freshness and jewelry would give even me pleasure, their enemy, and I would like to look at the cast skin from which they were regenerated in green or dots of red like pomegranate seeds or varnished gold crust" (369). Augie refuses to see a world of deterministic ugliness and low opinions. Such a world is not compatible with his "spur-gear" of enthusiasm nor with his anticipation of a better fate.

Part of the mythology of our cultural hero is his opposition to whatever would cause him to lose his individuality, and it is a proud and exciting moment for Augie when Einhorn discovers that such a distinction is an element of Augie's personality. When Einhorn is lecturing him to stay away from the likes of Joe Gorman and "those thieves," Einhorn suddenly exclaims: "But wait. All of a sudden I catch on to something about you. You've got opposition in you. You don't slide through everything. You just make it look so" (117). Augie is delighted to hear this, and so is the reader; for the reader, also an admirer of opposition, would be an individual, indifferent, unique, not on the market of malleable commodities as is the world around him.

Another source of pride in Augie is his refusal to become really involved in any action or cause that does not arouse his enthusiasm. He will go along, for a time, but with only a passive acceptance; all depends on how he *feels* about the particular issue. It is a part of the convention of the hero that he remain detached and coolly observant until he feels a strong emotional call to involvement.

Bellow's drawing on the voices of America's literary past and assigning them to his protagonist also increases Augie's prestige with the reader. Through these faint echoes, especially to the literary minded, Augie acquires an added depth, wisdom, authority, and, equally important, a certain nostalgic and romantic aura of courage and integrity. The presence of Twain's Huck has already been noted, and he is omnipresent throughout the story. When the fear of one of Einhorn's lectures is upon Augie, he describes his fright: "the candles were now as genial to me as though they had been the ones stuck into loaves of bread by night and sailed on a black Indian lake to find the drowned body sunk to the bottom" (180).

When Mimi becomes sarcastic over Augie's letting Simon lead him to the practice of having his nails polished, Augie merely thinks, "I let it be done. I didn't consider my fingers much" (223). Then reminiscences are sung of Whitman when Augie is forced to remember his "parentage, and other history, things I had never much thought of as difficulties, being democratic in temperament, available to everybody and assuming about others what I assumed about myself" (147). Echoes of Emerson (and perhaps of Thoreau) are heard when Augie looks out over the landscape: "Meanwhile the clouds, birds, cattle in the water, things, stayed at their distance, and there was no need to herd, account for, hold them in the head, but it was enough to be among them, released on the ground as they were in their brook or in their air. I meant something like this when I said occasionally I could look out like a creature." Then, immediately thereafter, Augie asks in Emersonian terms, with the style of Huck Finn, "How is it that human beings will submit to the gyps of previous history while mere creatures look with their original eyes?" (330).

There are other voices of the past, as is later shown. For now, the point is that the reader tends to identify Augie with the free-wheeling style and with the independent spirit of these eminent figures. Their honesty, integrity, and courage are judged to be part of Augie's character. Their heroic stance becomes his.

The Failure of an Ideal

Bellow gives to Augie other "advantages of the American folk hero": he comes from a poor family; he does not know the identity of his father; he refuses to be trapped by fine clothing, social position, or wealth; he admits that he "gives his affections too easily" and that "he has no grudge-bearing power." Bellow has endowed his narrator with the entire list of requisites to a folk hero of our time and culture; consequently, it is difficult for us to imagine Augie as one of life's failures.

But Augie does fail. In spite of his objective insights, his intelligence, his self-knowledge, his generous and humane spirit, his personal ideals and sought-for destiny; in spite of the nobility of his opposition and his discriminating enthusiasm; and, finally, in spite of the powerful and impressive voices of the past, through which he often states his case, he fails. In fact, as is seen in more detail later, there are implications at the end of the novel of a general deterioration not only of Augie's purpose but of his character.

And any confusion over Bellow's final intentions, at least one of them, is centered in this irony of the failure of greatness; for it is all too easy, once again, to see Bellow's protagonist in the light of what we have called "the mythology of heroic behavior," and to close our eyes to the obvious deficiencies of that mythology, as—strangely enough in view of the textual facts that leave Augie in a position of ignominy—Irving Malin seems to have done when he states that "He [Bellow] favors Augie's ideal, without completely noting its inadequacies."[3] Malin is misled by what Augie says, not noting carefully enough what he does.

But Bellow knows that, for every action, there is an equal and opposite reaction; for every strength, the possibility of a weakness or a disability. Or, as he has Augie say on the opening page of the book, "Everybody knows there is no fineness nor accuracy of suppression; if you hold down one thing you hold down the adjoining" (3). As a result, Augie's keen ability to observe accurately seems to carry with it the curse of estrangement: his clear insight into the characters and motivations of others has as its companion an emotional and, therefore, a functional immaturity of purpose. Consequently, as he drifts from incident to incident, he uses his "better fate" as his rationale.

Augie's generous and humane acceptance of others is, therefore, questionable. At one point, when Mintouchian, the shady and cold lawyer, asserts, "You think I'm a bandit, only you wouldn't say it on a bet. You fight your malice too much," Augie replies, somewhat proudly it seems, "Everybody says so. It's as if you were supposed to have low opinions. I'd never say I was angelic, but I respect as much as I can" (479). Perhaps Augie respects too much, or at least too widely; for his nondiscrimination—his life without malice—permits him to dissipate his ideals through his objective passivity toward every one of his confrontations with people or with institutions. From the very beginning he passively and acceptingly joins, first, Grandma Lausch and her deceptions; second, with Simon's misplaced ambitions; third, with his aunt's plans for his marriage to Freidl; and so on through the novel— with the plans and teachings of Joe Gorman, Einhorn, the Magnuses, the Renlings, Thea, and Mintouchian. In each case he refuses to take a stand, to assert his ideals in the form of action and positive commitment. When someone calls him to join a parade, he does so; and he stays—until someone calls him to join another.

The enthusiasm that Augie calls his "spur-gear," as he terms Einhorn's wellsprings to resolute commitment, is also double-edged. There is little doubt as to its worthwhile function in great and little enterprises; but Bellow seems to say that, as a key to the action, it may open the wrong doors. Augie manages a deep enthusiasm just twice in the novel: he falls in love twice—first, with Thea (his infatuation with her sister Esther is only temporary); second, with Stella. The first experience fails completely; and the second, as the novels ends, is failing. Evidently Bellow is saying that, with or without enthusiasm, some work is to be done, some direction and function assumed.

We have noted that Augie is proud of what he likes to think of as his "opposition," or his refusal to be drawn into the plans of others, unless they are temporary plans, of course, or unless they have the sanctions of his enthusiasm. Here again Bellow depicts the hero of rebellion, one who will not be deprived of his individuality. But also, again, he depicts the consequences: one can alienate himself to the point of uselessness and absurdity, even grotesqueness, by pushing this rebellion to its furthest extensions.

Bellow makes this consequent alienation quite clear. At the end of the novel, one of Augie's missions for the cynical Mintouchian can only be described as grotesque: "And what have I been doing? Well, perhaps

I had a meeting with a person who used to be in Dachau and did some business with him in dental supplies from Germany. That took an hour or two." And then he adds, "After which I may have gone to the cold halls of the Louvre and visited in the Dutch School . . ." (522). Bellow could only intend a comment on the dismal and useless existence of Augie. What kind of life casually profits from the dentistry that took place in Dachau? And surely the sensuous painting of the Flemish Rubens and the Dutch Vermeer's depiction of the isolated, comfortable burgher, removed from the world of involvement and interested only in his pipe and lucrative shipping trade, are reflections of Augie's life.

In any case, we wonder about Augie's "better fate" and about his enthusiasm, about his high-spoken ideals concerning man's potentialities, about his generous acceptance of all living things, and certainly about his pride of opposition. We think about his language and words, noble and courageous; and we wonder if they are not mere tools to a self-betrayal.

But this view is an overly bleak and slightly distorted picture of the way in which Bellow wants us to see Augie. He is not a figure of fatalistic determinism; for, through Augie, Bellow is not saying, "Look at man with all of his endowments, to these depths he comes." Instead he is saying that man comes to these depths only through his mistaken goals and wasted abilities. For Bellow endows Augie with all of the weapons needed to achieve a better fate, "to overcome ignominy," if he will only see the contradictions between his ideals and reality. And at times, Augie does see. When Thea and he come to the end of their romance, Augie makes an attempt at self-examination:

> Now I had started, and this terrible investigation had to go on. If this was how I was, it was certainly not how I appeared but must be my secret. So if I wanted to please, it was in order to mislead or show everyone, wasn't it, now? And this must be because I had an idea everyone was my better and had something I didn't have. But what did people seem to me anyhow, something fantastic? I didn't want to be what they made me but wanted to please them. Kindly explain! An independent fate, and love too—what confusion! (401)

So Augie *is* willing to examine his own life honestly. And in this particular passage it is evident that he at least has a temporary insight into the center of his problem. Augie, for the most part, sees himself clearly; and he sees others with a fine facility. His whole difficulty is in seeing himself *in relation to* those others: he does not take the rest of the world into consideration when he is asserting his better fate, his ideals, and his "spur-gear" of enthusiasm. When thinking of the causes behind his break with Thea, he concludes, "My real fault was that I couldn't stay with my purest feelings" (402). Exactly! The real as opposed to the ideal is not an uncommon problem. The only way that one can stay with his purest feelings is by living in a cave. "An independent fate and love too" is as impossible as a marriage of purest feelings and a functional existence. Something must give, or one ends in a cave, useless and isolated, as Augie does.

But Augie can and does learn, even though such self-insights are partial in self-revelation. Intermittently throughout the novel he summarizes a reflection by adding that he did not know "that" at the time, as when he says, "You do all you can to humanize and familiarize the world, and suddenly it becomes more strange than ever. . . . I see this now, at that time not" (285). And then, describing his feeling for Thea, he says: "Not even the eagle falconry distressed me as much as that what happened to her had to happen to me too, necessarily. This was scary. This trouble of course wasn't clear to me then . . ." (323). This ability, the capacity to grasp even a piece of the significance of experience, is a structural cornerstone of Bellow's subangelic ideology.

Augie still does not see that the thing everybody has that he does not have is direction and purpose, involvement with life, even though these involvements might be criticized. The full meaning of his experience is lost to him, as his rather pathetic assertion, while not one of hopelessness, at the end of his story indicates: "It must be clear, however, that I am a person of hope, and now my hopes have settled themselves upon children and a settled life. I haven't been able to convince Stella as yet. Therefore while I knock around . . . it's unborn children I pore over far oftener than business deals" (529).

Augie will probably go his picaresque way with hope and with children still unborn; for hope alone creates nothing but despair or an "animal ridens," as Augie describes himself at the end of the book (536). Yet perhaps Augie will come to know, even as does Joseph in *Dangling Man,* that there is no identity, no integrity, no better fate, no creation, of children or anything else, without a social commitment, without an understanding of one's relationship to others. It is only hoped that he comes to this knowledge with less hysteria and less despair than did Joseph. Bellow leaves Augie, for the time being, in a position that seems to be a comment on those who rest on the claim that the game is not to their liking, not to their enthusiasms, and that they are waiting for a higher, freer reality. But Bellow also leaves them Augie's abilities and his hope, pathetic or otherwise.

Bellow makes his position clear when Augie closes the story: "I may well be a flop at this line of endeavor. Columbus too thought he was a flop, probably, when they sent him back in chains. Which didn't prove there was no America" (536). All of which is to say that Augie knows his ideals are right, in spite of his less-than-high fortune. In Augie's view of himself as Columbus, Bellow intends an illumination for his protagonist—a discovery of likenesses between himself and another explorer. While both seem to have failed, their hope, vision, judgment, and courage are realities of their natures which give to them powers and potentialities that allow them the possibilities of a "better fate." Bellow leaves it to the reader to understand that Augie's failure lies not in his high ideals but in his refusal to live them through positive action and personal involvement—and in his seeming willingness to be used by those who are actively involved but who do not possess his vision of existence as subangelic.

Literature and Society

In his introduction to *Literature in America*, Phillip Rahv states: "Art has always fed on the contradiction between the reality of the world and the image of glory and orgastic happiness and harmony and goodness and fulfillment which the self cherishes as it aspires to live even while daily dying."[4]

The statement expresses the theme of the second level of *The Adventures of Augie March*, a theme seemingly of primary importance in Bellow's conception of the novel. For, although *Augie March* is a meaningful work in its depiction of a human condition, much of its significance is to be found in the ideas of its protagonist, in his reflections, and not in his confrontations with life. To be sure, reflection follows confrontation; but we sense that something is out of balance, that perhaps reflection outweighs confrontation, giving philosophy a major role and literature a minor one.

Somehow incident fails to support the weight of narrative, as Robert Penn Warren concludes: "if Augie plunges into the aimless ruck of experience, in the end we see that Saul Bellow has led him through experience toward philosophy. That is, the aimless ruck had a shape, after all, and the shape is not that of Augie's life but of Saul Bellow's mind. Without that shape and the shaping mind, we would have only the limited interest in the random incidents."[5]

Although Warren is rather vague, inasmuch as he does not trace the "shape" of Bellow's mind, the statement has a general validity—if the novel is confined in meaning to its first level: the depiction of a human condition. In that case, there is an "aimless ruck of experience"; therefore, the incidents in Augie's life would indeed be "random" and of "limited interest." Once again, Bellow's philosophy seems to hold the work together. Furthermore, if the novel is read with Augie as a fictional creation, it is difficult to place much value, in spite of National Book Awards, on either the theme or its dramatization. It is the old theme of nonconformity, the refusal to be trapped in social quagmires, the commitment to self and the exploration of that self. In American letters, such breast-beating goes back at least to Melville, Emerson, and Thoreau; it grew to tribal orgies in the 1920s; it still has an army of adherents.

Moreover, the ignominious state in which the protagonist ends, owing to the age-old conflict of the individual against society, is hardly a revelation to the reader schooled in Frank Norris, Stephen Crane, Theodore Dreiser, Sherwood Anderson, Ernest Hemingway, John Dos Passos, James Farrell, and their many disciples. As Frederick Hoffman says of the novel, "In the end there is something wrong with the picture: there is too much to know, and the knowing and living have too little to do with each other."[6] Once again, we do not say that Bellow's novel on a first level is not meaningful; at the very least it is an intellectual picaresque that cannot be ignored no matter how thin the total structure and development, no matter how tired the theme, and no matter if the philosophy exceeds the rendered life.

In any case, we must examine the work as something other than a philosophical travelogue, as something more than an "aimless ruck of experience" and "random incidents." We must consider *Augie March* as presenting not so much the "shape of Bellow's mind" but as showing the relationship between literature and society in general and the condition of American literature in particular. As for the novel's concern with American literature, Maxwell Geismar's comment and question are to the point: "Thus the novel which opens in the Chicago slums ends with the exotics and expatriates of Mexico and Europe: which is also a curious parable of the course of American literary realism during the last half-century. But what can we really make of all this?"[7]

Geismar's question deserves an answer, for Bellow has included within the story of Augie some materials that can best be accounted for only in metaphoric terms. As we stated earlier, *Augie March* may be read as a study of the relationship between the artist, or literature, and society. What Bellow does is to show that relationship as it exists universally, through a dramatized depiction of American realism. Bellow has made his position clear on this subject of the artist and society in works other than fiction. In his acceptance speech for the National Book Award (1964) for his novel *Herzog,* he said:

> The fact that there are so many weak, poor, and boring stories and novels written and published in America has been ascribed by our rebels to the horrible squareness of our institutions, the idiocy of power, the debasement of sexual instincts, and the failure of writers to be alienated enough. The poems and novels of these same rebellious spirits, and their theoretical statements, are grimy and gritty and very boring too, besides being nonsensical, and it is evident now that polymorphous sexuality and vehement declarations of alienation are not going to produce great works of art either.
>
> There is nothing left for us novelists to do but think. For unless we think, unless we make a clearer estimate of our condition, we will continue to write kid stuff, to fail in our function; we will lack serious interests and become truly irrelevant. Here the critics must share the blame. They too have failed to describe the situation. Literature has for generations been its own source, its own province, has lived upon its own tradition, and accepted a romantic separation or estrangement from the common world. This estrangement, though it produced some masterpieces, has by now enfeebled literature.
>
> The separatism of writers is accompanied by the more or less conscious acceptance of a theory of modern civilization. This theory says in effect that modern mass society is frightful, brutal, hostile to whatever is pure in the human spirit, a waste land and a horror. To its ugliness, its bureaucratic regiments, its thefts, its lies, its wars, and its cruelties, the artist can never be reconciled.

This is one of the traditions on which literature has lived uncritically. But it is the task of artists and critics in every generation to look with their own eyes. Perhaps they will see even worse evils, but they will at least be seeing for themselves. They will not, they cannot permit themselves, generation after generation, to hold views they have not examined for themselves. By such willful blindness we lose the right to call ourselves artists; we have accepted what we ourselves condemn—narrow specialization, professionalism, and snobbery, and the formation of a caste.

And, unfortunately, the postures of this caste, postures of liberation and independence and creativity, are attractive to poor souls dreaming everywhere of a fuller, freer life. The writer is admired, the writer is envied. But what has he to say for himself? Why, he says, just as writers have said for more than a century, that he is cut off from the life of his own society, despised by its overlords who are cynical and have nothing but contempt for the artist, without a true public, estranged. He dreams of ages when the poet or the painter expressed a perfect unity of time and place, had real acceptance, and enjoyed a vital harmony with his surroundings—he dreams of a golden age. In fact, without the golden age, there is no Waste Land.

Well, this is no age of gold. It is only what it is. Can we do no more than complain about it? We writers have better choices. We can either shut up because the times are too bad, or continue because we have an instinct to make books, a talent to enjoy, which even these disfigured times cannot obliterate. Isolated professionalism is death. Without the common world the novelist is nothing but a curiosity and will find himself in a glass case along some dull museum corridor of the future.

We live in a technological age which seems insurmountably hostile to the artist. He must fight for his life, for his freedom, along with everyone else—for justice and equality, threatened by mechanization and bureaucracy. This is not to advise the novelist to rush immediately into the political sphere. But in the first stage he must begin to exert his intelligence, long unused. If he is to reject politics, he must understand what he is rejecting. He must begin to think and to think not merely of his own narrower interests and needs.[8]

Augie March is a dramatic rendering of a good part of these same strictures. Bellow sets his protagonist-narrator in motion in order for these ideas to come alive: Augie, too, practices "separatism"; he, too, is one of the "poor souls dreaming . . . of a better life"; he dreams of "a perfect unity of time and place."[9] And there is good reason to doubt that he will create children (or works of art) through "declarations of alienation." Moreover, Augie has "failed to make a clear estimate of [his] condition"; he "has failed in . . . function"; he "lacks serious interests"; and he has "become truly irrelevant." Other parallels between Bellow's speech and the characterizations of Augie will be discussed later; for now, these serve to point out that, through his protagonist, Bellow is making the same observations concerning the state of contemporary literature in its relation to society that he made in his speech.

Literary Influences

If we accept Augie as a paradigm for artist, as that artist reflects the state of contemporary literature, then part of his role is that of the contemporary American writer who is a product of the roots of his own national literature. In order to cast his protagonist in this role, Bellow gives Augie what might be thought of as heredity and environment: past and present literary influences. Augie's heredity manifests itself in a mind and tongue highly reminiscent of nineteenth-century American authors, all of whom are representative of the kind of artistic integrity that would define them as rebels of one sort or another.

Such names as Emerson, Thoreau, Whitman, and Twain have already been mentioned earlier in this chapter; but there are others. When Augie is stranded after his abortive career in crime with Joe Gorman, he reports: "I took the excursion to Niagara Falls where nobody seemed to have any business that day, only a few strays beside the crush of water, like early sparrows in the cathedral square before Notre Dame has opened its doors; and then in the brute sad fog you know that at one time this sulphur coldness didn't paralyze everything, and there's the cathedral to prove it" (165). Augie finds proof in the cathedral of the existence of an active, warming force that sets itself against the numbing coldness of the fog, just as Henry Adams found proof in cathedrals of Europe of the driving force of the Virgin as against the cold, detached, godlike power of the steam engine or dynamo.

And, in Mexico while training the eagle Caligula, Augie philosophizes: "When Caligula soared under this sky I sometimes wondered what connection he made with this element of nearly too great strength that was dammed back of the old spouts of craters" (338). Melville's Ishmael, in the chapter in *Moby Dick* entitled "The Symphony," ponders the relationship of the sun, "aloft like a royal czar and king," with the sea and the sky; and Augie wonders at the soaring Caligula, this king of birds, and his connection with the earth and sky around him.

Of particular interest is the fact that all of the writers Bellow calls up from the past created works that speak for the same philosophic and idealistic alienation or rebellion that Augie brings into the world. From the beginning he sets a course of idealistic noninvolvement in the interests of a "better fate." And Bellow points directly to Augie's environment when he has his protagonist state early in the novel: "All the influences were lined up waiting for me. I was born and there they were to form me which is why I tell you more of them than of myself" (43). For the most part, Bellow sets these influences in motion through the people with whom Augie associates. That is, these people, in a complex and at times confusing way, are symbols of literary movements, trends, ideas, fictive characters, and authors that have in one way or another made lesser or greater marks on American literature.

A few examples illustrate Bellow's technique in the treatment of symbolic function of character. Augie is born in Chicago, where he lives with his brother Simon, his mother, his idiot brother Georgie, and Grandma Lausch, who is the first influence to be reckoned with. This old woman is really no relation to the Marches: sometime earlier she had rented a room in their house and has stayed to exercise a dominant authority over the entire family. As Simon says to Augie, "She's really nothing to us, you know that, don't you, Aug?" (33). Her roots are in Europe, and Augie as a young boy is fearfully impressed: "That isn't to say that I stopped connecting her with the highest and the best— taking her at her own word—with the courts of Europe, the Congress of Vienna, the splendor of family, and all kinds of profound and cultured things as hinted in her conduct and advertised in her speech . . . " (30).

Grandma Lausch often sends Augie to the library after books: "Once a year she read *Anna Karenina* and *Eugene Onegin* [also *Manon Lescaut,* we learn later, p. 14]. Occasionally I got into hot water by bringing a book

she didn't want. 'How many times do I have to tell you if it doesn't say
roman I don't want it?' " (11). Grandma Lausch is symbolic of the
Victorian mores to which American literature was largely bound during
the nineteenth and early twentieth centuries. With the references to
"the courts of Europe," "the Congress of Vienna," "the splendor of
family"—along with Grandma Lausch's stage appearance and her interest in Russian and French romances—Bellow intends this figure to
represent a literary authority based on reaction and tradition. It is a
fading authority, one that must find its comfort through the romantic
past and by steadfastly denying the ugly present, or at least by not
speaking of it. Augie recalls:

> Monkey was the basis of much thought with us. On the sideboard, on the
> Turkestan runner, with their eyes, ears, and mouth covered, we had see-no-
> evil, speak-no-evil, hear-no-evil, a lower trinity of the house. . . . the
> monkeys could be potent, and awesome besides, and deep social critics when
> the old woman . . . would point . . . [and] say, "Nobody asks you to love
> the whole world, only to be honest, *ehrlich*. Don't have a loud mouth. The
> more you love people the more they'll mix you up. A child loves, a person
> respects. Respect is better than love. And that's respect, the middle
> monkey." It never occurred to us that she sinned mischievously herself
> against that convulsed speak-no-evil. (9)

In the last line Augie notes the duplicity and hypocrisy of his tyrannical
Victorian grandmother. And, of course, Grandma Lausch's "speak-no-
evil" monkey is the cultural primate that the artist had to battle during
the nineteenth and early twentieth centuries.

When Augie comments on Grandma Lausch's failing authority, he
explains, "I never repudiated her that much [as much as Simon did] or
tried to strike the old influence, such as it had become, out of her
hands" (58). Here Augie might be seen as a paradigm of American
literature; and it is particularly suitable to his passive character that he,
like literature in general, accepts, for a while, all influences. He makes
no direct attempt to hold aloof from them nor to diminish their
influences on him: when Grandma Lausch simply grows old, she is sent
to an old-folks home; and her loss of power is noted by Bellow through
Augie: "The house was changed also for us; dinkier, smaller, darker;
once shiny and venerated things losing their attraction and richness and

importance. Tin showed, cracks, black spots where enamel was hit off, threadbarer, design scuffed out of the center of the rug, all the glamour, lacquer, massiveness, florescence, wiped out" (58–59).

This passage depicting a house of the realistic is at the close of chapter 4: the next chapter begins with Augie's statement that "Einhorn was the first superior man I knew" for whom Augie "went to work awhile . . . a high school junior, not long before the great crash" (60). While it is difficult to state the precise significance of Bellow's use of time, the publication dates of the following works are provocative: Faulkner's *The Sound and the Fury* and *Sartoris* (1929); Wolfe's *Look Homeward Angel* (1929); Hemingway's *The Sun Also Rises* (1926) and *A Farewell to Arms* (1929); Fitzgerald's *The Great Gatsby* (1925); Dreiser's *An American Tragedy* (1925). In any case, the time was one for dispossessing the old and looking to the new; for with these novels—and, on the chronological fringes, the work of Anderson, Lewis, Dos Passos, O'Neill, and Mencken—the full tide of a new wave of literature was to flood the land: a realistic literature, something on the order of the personality and character of Einhorn, who becomes the second major influence on Augie.

Einhorn is a complete figure of the 1920s, or perhaps of the myth of the 1920s because of his pursuit of money, power, and sex; and, in spite of his crippled legs, he has absolute confidence in his own strength and abilities.[10] His cynical view of life overrides all opposition. He is demanding, knavish, petty, and knowing, but he is confused and driven by a sexual greed that is without limits, "singlemindedly and grimly fixed on the one thing, ultimately *the* thing, for which men and women came together" (78). Einhorn, utterly devoid of illusions, knows the wellsprings of man and draws on them with staggering jerks and sly pulls. Above all social dictates, he tells Augie: "Besides, there's law, and then there's Nature. There's opinion, and then there's Nature. Somebody has to get outside of law and opinion and speak for Nature. It's even a public duty, so customs won't have us all by the windpipe" (67). In such a voice naturalism and realism announce their presence. When we think of Einhorn, we think of a powerful determinism, as does Augie when his "superior man" falls victim to the Depression: "I'm thinking of the old tale of Croesus, with Einhorn in the unhappy part" (106). And the story of Croesus is about the reversal of simple fate, the god of determinism.

Einhorn's activities are instructive. Primarily in real estate, his
interests are without end, as Augie relates:

> The stuff had to be where he could lay his hands on it at once, his clippings
> and pieces of paper, in folders labeled Commerce, Invention, Major Local
> Transactions, Crime and Gang, Democrats, Republicans, Archaeology, Lit-
> erature, League of Nations. . . . Everything was going to be properly done,
> with Einhorn, and was thoroughly organized on his desk and around
> it—Shakespeare, Bible, Plutarch, dictionary and Thesaurus. *Commercial
> Law for Laymen,* real-estate and insurance guides, almanacs and directories;
> then typewriter in black hood, dictaphone, telephones on bracket arms and a
> little screwdriver to hand for touching off the part of the telephone
> mechanism that registered the drop of the nickel . . . wire trays labeled
> Incoming and Outgoing, molten Aetna Weights, notary's seal on chain,
> staplers, flap-moistening sponges, keys to money, confidential papers,
> notes, condoms, personal correspondence and poems and essays. . . . (66)

And the end of his interests is nowhere in sight; for, as Augie concludes, "He had to be in touch with everything" (70). Through such a
comprehensive and minute cataloging, Bellow's creation is to be seen as
an embodiment of the naturalistic or the realistic, the distinctions
between which are somewhat too fine for precise delineation. But
Einhorn's drives are certainly reminiscent of the "chemisms" of Dreiser
and the style in which Bellow indicates the activities of the old man is
blatantly realistic in its enumeration of every last detail.

While Einhorn may be read as a generalized depiction of the new art
and emerging culture of the 1920s, there is some evidence that Bellow
means to be more precise—that he intends this figure to be representative of Hemingway, or, in part, to be seen as a Hemingway creation.
Admittedly conjectural, the likenesses are interesting: Augie carries
Einhorn on his back, even as Hemingway during this period was the
master, guide, and controlling force of American literature. Einhorn's
useless legs recall the wounds suffered by several Hemingway characters; his deep concern, perhaps even fear, of death is an everlasting
omnipotent subject of Hemingway's; his stocking cap is in the
Hemingway mode; Hemingway's almost fanatical emphasis on physical endurance and well-being is seen as Augie describes Einhorn at the
table: "Then Einhorn took a white spoonful of Bisodol and a glass of

Waukesha water for his gas. He made a joke of it, but he never forgot to take them and heeded all his processes with much seriousness, careful that his tongue was not too coated and his machinery smooth. . . . he was zealous about taking care of himself; and with this zeal he had a brat's self-mockery about the object of his cares . . ." (74).

But there is more at issue than Hemingway's stamina, and the further significance lies in the references to the "tongue" and "machinery," as well as to the "self-mockery about the object of his cares." While Hemingway's manner was to behave with a bravado in spite of his bodily fears, of more importance in this instance was his inclination to speak disparagingly of literary technique but to take an almost obsessive care with his own. Bellow shows this high degree of fidelity to art through Einhorn's son, Arthur, who attends the university and in whom Einhorn puts all his hope and trust, counting on him to carry on the Einhorn name. Augie is made ever aware of his position in relation to that of Arthur: "I wasn't ever to get it into my head that I was part of the family. There was small chance that I would, the way Arthur, the only son, figured in their references. . . . I don't think I would have considered myself even remotely as a legatee of the Commissioner [Einhorn's father] if they hadn't, for one thing, underlined my remoteness from inheritance, and, for another, discussed inheritances all the time" (72). And later, "Arthur's brainy authority made his dad occasionally sound off . . ." (293).

The threads of Bellow's intent are closely woven and of complex design; but the passages must be read as a specific comment on Einhorn as Hemingway or as a general comment on the writers of the 1920s, and perhaps as on both. In any case, Bellow indicates the weakness of these writers: they refused to admit into their thinking the uses and values of American literature (symbolized by Augie) as it had been handed down to them, inasmuch as their single-visioned emphasis on artistic technique (represented by Arthur) made them somewhat blind to their function as artist, a function that Bellow unfolds in his speech previously quoted.

At this point, it is necessary to say a word about the Commissioner who, again conjecturally, acts the role of Mark Twain. Hemingway's repeatedly acknowledged debt to Twain is a possible parallel to Einhorn's realization of his debt to his father. Augie states the case: "He

[Einhorn] had his father to keep up with, whose business ideas were
perhaps less imaginative but broader. . . . The old commissioner had
made the Einhorn money" (66). Then, when Augie describes the
Commissioner, the personality of Mark Twain is clearly evident:

> The Commissioner, in a kindly, sleepy, warm-aired, fascinated way,
> petted and admired all women and put his hands wherever he liked. . . .
> You couldn't say it was a common letch he had; it was a sort of a Solomonic
> regard of an old chief or aged sea lion. . . . You could feel from the net
> pleasantness he carried what there had been between him and women now
> old or dead, whom he recognized, probably, and greeted in this nose or that
> bosom. . . . His sons didn't share this quality. Of course you don't expect
> younger men to have this kind of evening—Mississippi serenity, but there
> wasn't much disinterestedness or contemplation in either of them. . . .
> Einhorn . . . took the joking liberties his father did, but his jokes didn't
> have the same ring; which isn't to say that they weren't funny but that he cast
> himself forward on them toward a goal—seduction. (76–77)

Evident in this passage is the literary relationship between the sen-
sibilities of Twain and Hemingway. Furthermore, with Twain's re-
nowned lack of business sense in Bellow's mind, the Commissioner, it is
discovered upon his death, "had made loans to these men and had no
notes, only these memoranda of debts amounting to several thousand
dollars" (105). Then, in what may be Bellow's opinion of the relative
merits of Twain and Hemingway, Augie says: "Kreindl, who did a job
for him once in a while, thought he was as wise as a god. 'The son is
smart,' he said, 'but the Commissioner—that's really a man you have to
give way to on earth.' I disagreed then and do still, though when the
Commissioner was up to something he stole the show" (61). Through
Grandma Lausch, the Commissioner, Einhorn, and Arthur, then with
Augie, Bellow shows the drift of literary influences; and those influences play directly upon his protagonist, the artist or symbol of
American literature.

Even as naturalism or realism remains a force in literature, so
Einhorn remains a figure throughout the book, but in a somewhat
weakened condition, or changed position, from his earlier one of power.
Augie reports the change: "His spirit was piercing, but there had to be
mentioned his poor color, age-impoverished and gray; plus the new

flat's ugliness; dullness of certain hours, dryness of days, dreariness and shabbiness—mentioned that the street was bare, dim and low in life, bad; and that there were business thoughts and malformed growths of purpose, terrible, menacing, salt-patched with noises and news, and pimpled and dotted around with lies, both practical and gratuitous" (155).

And Einhorn has grown bitter. When Simon, who is distracted by love, fails to send money to Augie so he can get back home, Einhorn contends that Augie should "take advantage" of the situation, should "have satisfaction" and not let Simon off easy. Augie guesses at the reasons for Einhorn's vindictive manner: "He intended that, as there were no more effective prescriptions in old ways, as we were in dreamed-out or finished visions, that therefore, in the naked form of the human jelly, one should choose or seize with force; one should make strength from disadvantages and make progress by having enemies, being wrathful or terrible; should hammer on the state of being a brother . . ." (183).

Finally, Bellow makes additionally clear what the realistic movement has become, how it has, in the words of his speech, "enfeebled literature," through Einhorn's reaction to Augie's becoming a union organizer. When Augie asks him, "Then you think it's a waste of time, what I'm doing?," Einhorn replies: "Oh, it seems to me on both sides the ideas are the same. What's the use of the same old ideas? . . . To take some from one side and give it to the other, the same old economics. . . . You think that with a closed shop you're going to make men out of slobs. . . . Look here, because they were born you think they have to turn out to be men? That's just an old fashioned idea" (293). The possibility of man bettering himself is an old idea, held by such romantic dreamers as Grandma Lausch. Einhorn is clearly preaching ideas of isolation here, a noninvolvement, the uselessness of effort—the same behavior that Bellow condemns in his speech and, ultimately, in his depiction of Augie's existence. Yet Einhorn has seen better days. Augie recalls that "you could always get part of the truth from Einhorn" (386). Much earlier he tells Augie: "But I'm not a lowlife when I think, and *really* think. . . . In the end you can't save your soul and life by thought. But if you *think,* the least of the consolation prizes is the world" (117). This is the voice of Bellow, it will be recalled, speaking to his fellow novelists and saying, "there is nothing left for us novelists to do but think."

Through *The Great Gatsby*, Fitzgerald left his mark not only on the literature but on the culture of this country; for Jay Gatsby embodies the sad estrangement, the disappointment, and the disillusion of those who feel that the 1920s witnessed the death of the American dream. In *Augie March*, Bellow gives this role to Augie's brother Simon. Like Gatsby, who in his childhood was faithful to Benjamin Franklin ideals and to dreams of self-improvement, Simon begins his adolescence. When Augie describes Simon's not participating in the deception of the Charities, he explains that his brother "was too blunt for this kind of maneuver and, anyway, from books, had gotten hold of some English schoolboy notions of honor" (4). Simon, unlike Augie, never has trouble with the neighborhood gangs; he has other interests: "School absorbed him more, and he had his sentiments anyway, a mixed extract from Natty Bumppo, Quentin Durward, Tom Brown, Clark at Kaskaskia, the messenger who brought the good news from Ratisbon, and so on, that kept him more to himself. I was a slow understudy to this, just as he never got me to put in hours on his Sandow muscle builder" (12).

Simon even gets odd jobs and works diligently. But one summer, and in this case, much in the manner of Dreiser's Clyde Griffith of *An American Tragedy*, Simon leaves home to work in a resort hotel. When he returns, Augie recognizes that something has happened: "he went through a change the summer he waited on tables . . . and came back with some different aims from his original ones and new ideas about conduct" (31). And Simon, like Fitzgerald's Gatsby or Dreiser's Griffith, begins his long road in search of power and wealth. Simon even talks like Gatsby; for, when he anounces his engagement, he says to Augie, "Well, sport, we may be married in the next few months. You envy me? I bet you do" (150).

Augie also gets his chance to play the role of a Fitzgeraldian figure. When he takes up with the Renlings, we cannot miss the tone and flavor of indolent glamor. With chapter 8, Augie announces his new life: "From here a new course was set—by us, for us: I'm not going to try to unravel all the causes . . . I don't know how it all at once came to me to talk a lot, tell jokes, kick up, and suddenly have views. When it was time to have them, there was no telling how I picked them from the air" (125).

And Augie describes himself during this period: "There was a spell in which I mainly wished to own dinner clothes and be invited to formal parties and thought considerably about how to get into the Junior Chamber of Commerce. Not that I had any business ideas. . . . It was social enthusiasm that moved in me, smartness, clothes-horseyness. The way a pair of tight Argyle socks showed in the crossing of legs, a match to the bow tie settled on a Princeton collar, took me in the heart with enormous power and hunger. I was given over to it" (134).

Bellow's attempt to define Augie as a cultural and literary wind is obvious in the choice of words. "I picked them from the air" and "I was given over to it" appropriately describe Augie not only as character but also as a symbol of the way an institution such as literature adopts and is ultimately dominated by a particular inclination or influence.

Bellow depicts the Fitzgeraldian world in which Augie lives:

> It was sundown, near dinnertime, with brilliant darkening water, napkins and broad menus standing up in the dining room, and roses and ferns in long-necked vases, the orchestra tuning back of its curtain. I was alone in the corridor, troubled and rocky, and trod on slowly to the music room, where the phonograph was playing Caruso, stifled and then clear cries of operatic mother-longing, that ornate, at heart somber, son's appeal of the Italian taste. Resting her elbows on the closed cabinet, in a white suit and round white hat, next thing to a bishop's biretta, bead-embroidered, was Esther Fenchel; she stood with one foot set on its point. (142)

Making the portrayal complete, Esther turns out to be something of Gatsby's Daisy, a "deadhead," as her sister Thea describes her, one incapable of accepting or fulfilling Augie's dreams.

But Augie leaves the Renlings for good reason: "Just when Mrs. Renling's construction around me was nearly complete I shoved off. The leading and precipitating reason was that she proposed to adopt me . . . Why should I turn into one of these people who didn't know who they themselves were? And the unvarnished truth is that it wasn't a fate good enough for me . . ." (151). So Augie is ready to leave the 1920s and its influences and to move into the 1930s and new pressures, new longings, new ideas, and new adoptive-minded people.

Separatism and Self-appraisal

The entire track that Bellow lays down cannot be traced here. But Augie's association with the Magnuses, the unions, his trip to Mexico, the near association with the dreams of Trotsky, Bateshaw, service in the merchant marine, Mintouchian, and all the rest are reflections of different literary and cultural interests at various times. Augie's function within this framework is highly complex; for he is both a part of it and outside it. He is outside it insofar as he fails to get enduringly involved with any particular force or influence. Pursuing "a better fate," he moves on. In this role of wanderer, Augie is intended by Bellow to be what we may call the backbone of American literature, or, as he has been referred to here, the spirit of that literature. At the end of the novel, as will be seen, Bellow shows the present state of literature through his protagonist; when all of the literary influences finally come to rest on him, they make of Bellow's hero a symbolic figure of contemporary writing.

But, for now, the interest is in Augie as the participant who is inside the framework, and is responding to these influences. And there is added complexity to Bellow's protagonist in this role: for, on the one hand, he represents a specific trend in the particular literature of the period, as when he assumes a Fitzgeraldian guise; and, on the other hand, he represents what may best be described as the artist responding to these various pressures. Augie as artist may be seen, for example, when he is in that period of self-examination which was referred to in the first part of this chapter. It will be recalled that Augie is searching for his own character right after Thea has left him. For convenient reference, we cite the passage again: "Now I had started, and this terrible investigation had to go on. If this was how I was, it was certainly not how I appeared but must be my secret. So if I wanted to please, it was in order to mislead or show everyone, wasn't it, now? And this must be because I had an idea everyone was my better and had something I didn't have. But what did people seem to me anyhow, something fantastic? I didn't want to be what they made me but wanted to please them. Kindly explain! An independent fate, and love too— what confusion!" (401).

On the surface, Augie's self-appraisal arises from his realization that he seems to be unable to commit himself, to become really involved with life. It is more important, however, to see Augie as an artist of whom Bellow is asking the same questions he poses in his National Book Award speech. When Augie asks, "But what did people seem to me, something fantastic," Bellow is commenting on the theory of literature that seems to demand a theme of alienation, or, as he states, "This theory [that] says in effect that modern mass society is frightful, brutal, hostile to whatever is pure in the human spirit, a waste land and a horror." Bellow questions the vision that sees only a society uninhabitable and grotesque, not only as to its validity, although "it produced some masterpieces,"[11] but for its consequence—"the separatism of writers." Then Augie says, "I didn't want to be what they made of me but wanted to please them."

Of course, Augie is posing the often contradictory position of the artist: he refuses to become actively and positively involved, either in his art or in his personal life, with the very group from which he seeks approval. As Bellow says more directly, "This is not to advise the novelist to rush into the political sphere. But in the first stage he must begin to exert his intelligence, long unused." And Augie has every right to be confused in his impossible demands for "an independent fate and love too," for here is the confusion manifested by the artist who, as Bellow says, exhibits "postures of liberation and independence and creativity." Because love and independence are mutually exclusive, modification of one position or the other is an absolute necessity. So it is with independence and creativity: for, as Bellow makes clear, "vehement declarations of alienation are not going to produce great works of art either."

Augie's adventures in love are extremely germane to his role as artist. To Bellow, love is a symbol of creation; as such, he often equates love with the creative abilities of the artist. In his essay, "Distractions of a Fiction Writer," he says:

"To believe in the existence of human beings as such is love," says Simone Weil. This is what makes the difference. It is possible—all too possible—to say when we have read one more modern novel: "So what? What do I care?

You yourself, the writer, didn't really care." It is all too often like that. But this caring or believing or love alone matters. All the rest, obsolescence, historical views, manners, agreed views of the universe, is simply nonsense and trash. If we don't care, don't immediately care, then perish books both old and new, and novelists, and governments, too! If we do care, if we believe in the existence of others, then what we write is necessary. . . . A book, any book, may easily be superfluous. But to manifest love—can that be superfluous? Is there so much of it about us? Not so much. It is still rare, still wonderful. It is still effective against distraction.[12]

Ihab Hassan, while he does not pursue the significance of his observation, draws a useful distinction: "For Thea love is a preparation to a more exalted state; for him [Augie] it is a worthy end."[13] Love as an end in itself—all very romantic. But all for love or the world well lost is precisely the issue. Augie loves in a vacuum; he loves his ideas and ideals; but he does not "believe in the existence of human beings *as such* [italics mine]." His Emersonianisms and Whitmanisms are kept apart from the actual human condition. As Thea says to him, "But perhaps love would be strange and foreign to you no matter which way it happened, and maybe you just don't want it" (396). Real love would seem foreign to Augie because he would not be able to reconcile his ideals with reality.

And so it is, Bellow says, with the artist. He must care—and care, immediately and now—within the framework of the human condition, and not only in some abstract way. Caring in the abstract is worse than useless; it has a deteriorating effect. Bellow makes this effect clear in his essay: "But it is not only ideas of evil that become destructive. Ideas of good, held in earnest, may be equally damaging to the passive thinker. His passivity puts him in self-contempt. This same contempt may estrange him from ideas of good. He lives below them and feels dwarfed. On certain occasions a hero in thought, he has become abject in fact, and he cannot be blamed for feeling that he is not doing a man's work. . . . Men are active. Ideas are passive."[14]

Although Bellow is talking to the novelist, he is describing Augie's condition. Because he lives below his ideas of good, he has become, at the end of the novel, abject in fact. His idea of love, high and noble, is barren and uncreative; indeed it is self-damaging because it is not based on the real condition of its object—the human condition. How ironic the statement of David Galloway: "Augie's point of view—the maintainance of an intention which is opposed at almost every turn by reality—begins gradually to define him as an absurd man."[15] So Bellow would define the artist who insists on a "separatism" until a "fuller, freer life" arrives, and who spends his time in "dreams of a golden age."

This paradigm of Augie as artist, once understood, is evident throughout the novel. Indeed, in almost every word that Augie speaks we can see Bellow's dual intent: first, to develop Augie as a character in his own right; second, to use him as a symbol of literary issues.

Augie and Western Literature

Up to this point, *Augie March* has been regarded as a comment on American literature, but Bellow has set his novel on a wider stage: he would have his work read as a depiction of the relationship throughout the Western world between literature and society. In his "Distractions" essay, he says:

But I should like to point out that impotence has received more attention from modern writers than any other subject. . . . Here is a brief list:

Oblomov: he spends his life in bed.

Moreau in Flaubert's *The Sentimental Education:* a life spent on trifles, utterly spoiled.

Captain Ahab: "I have lost the low enjoying power." He means that he is distracted. Natural beauty is recognized by his mind but it doesn't move him.

Clym Yeobright in *The Return of the Native:* empty of the feeling which Eustacia desires.

The hero of Henry James's "The Beast in the Jungle": empty of feeling.

Dostoevski's hero or anti-hero in *Notes from Underground:* his spite, his coldness, his venom, combined with the greatness of his mind, give him an exceptional stature.

Leopold Bloom: the distracted and impotent man.

I could add hundreds more to this list, from Lawrence or Proust or Hemingway and their innumerable imitators. They all tell the same story. The dread is great, the soul is small; man might be godlike but he is wretched. The heart should be open but it is sealed by fear.[16]

Bellow is not only concerned with American literature; he sees the stain on a larger canvas. For this wider picture, he turns to mythology.

Augie's travels and relationships have their counterparts in mythology; there are, for example, some striking similarities in Augie as archetype of both Aeneas and Apollo. It will be remembered that Augie, in his own words, is born the result of "the by-blow of a traveling man" (125) and that he has no father, at least none living with him. His mother is an object lesson "in her love-originated servitude" (10). Moreover, Augie says of his mother: "[She] occupied a place, I suppose, among women conquered by a superior force of love, like those women whom Zeus got the better of in animal form and who next had to take cover from his furious wife" (10). As far as the punishment which was administered to "those women" by the "furious wife. . . . Grandma Lausch was there to administer the penalties under the standards of legitimacy, representing the main body of married woman-kind"[17] (10). This background parallels the birth of Apollo to Zeus and Leto, and Leto's subsequent difficulties. Inasmuch as Apollo is the god of poetry, it seems that Bellow means in this relationship to reinforce the view of Augie as a spirit of literature.

Augie is also Aeneas. First, both are travelers. Then, as Aeneas carries his father on his back from Troy, so does Augie carry Einhorn (literary father to Augie) on his. In fact, Augie speaks of this ancient event in connection with Einhorn (122). More than in any other way, however, it is the travels of Aeneas and his destiny that are of significance. Several times before reaching Carthage and Dido, Aeneas, whose fate is to found Rome, starts to build a city; but each time he, with his followers, is driven off by various omens and misfortunes. So it is with Augie as he tries his constructions on crime, education, social position with the Renlings, wealth with the Magnuses, on a career as a union organizer, and so on through his travels. Each time, he, too, moves on to his "better fate."

There is also a close parallel between the stay of Aeneas with Dido in Carthage and the short time together of Augie and Thea in Mexico. Both Dido and Thea are beautiful widows, and both dress their men in lavish fashion (314). Of particular interest is the plan of Venus, mother to Aeneas, to contrive a plan which will make it certain that Aeneas' feeling for Dido is of no great depth so that he, at the proper time, has the strength of purpose to continue his fated journey to Rome. This situation precisely applies to Augie; he seems to exist with Thea not as a person but as a kind of extension, on her terms, as a passive but highly willing and obedient follower. He, like Aeneas again, has "a better fate." Both Dido and Thea plan hunting trips for their men. Then, both Aeneas and Augie leave their women crying in anguish and despair: Aeneas, to build the foundations of Rome; Augie, appropriately enough, to reach for Stella (or "star").

Another archetypal pattern springs from Aeneas' search for the Sibyl in order that she may guide him through the underworld where he is to seek his father for advice and guidance. The Sibyl tells Aeneas he must find in the forest a golden bough, break it off the tree, and carry it in his hand as a passport throughout Hades. When these actions are accomplished as fated, Aeneas, through the aid of the Sibyl and his father, is set on the right track to his destiny. Bellow, however, is not so generous to his protagonist. When Augie is in Florence toward the end of the novel, he gives one of his hours to visit the gold doors of the Baptistery on which one may see depicted the history of mankind. There, he is accosted by an elderly woman, "this aged face of a great lady covered by mange spots and with tarry blemishes on her lips" (517), who is carrying a stick with a purse on it. She wants to act as guide to Augie, to explain the story on the doors, but he doubts her knowledge. Besides, he does not want to be bothered. When he refuses her services, she begs: "Give me five hundred [lire] and I'll show you the cathedral and I'll take you to Santa Maria Novella. It's not far, and you won't know anything if someone doesn't tell you" (519).

But Augie dismisses her: "As a matter of fact, I have to meet a man right away on business. Thanks just the same" (519). So, unlike Aeneas, Augie turns away from his "better fate," perhaps because he is drawn away by a very immediate personal fate. We may conjecture that Bellow intends a comparison here, not only in that Aeneas heeds the Sibyl and Augie does not heed his prophetess, but in the nature of their two goals: Aeneas is engaged in the creation of Rome, an act that extends beyond himself; Augie's goal has deteriorated to personal, even perhaps illicit, trivia. And Bellow's final words of his speech are to be heard again: "He [the novelist] must begin to think, and to think not merely of his own narrower interests and needs."

Both Aeneas and Augie have the same destiny—to create. But the latter has lost his way. At the end, Augie, it will be remembered, spends his time in "the cold halls of the Louvre" (522). Bellow describes his fallen state, even as he speaks to his fellow novelists: "For unless we think, unless we make a clearer estimate of our condition [but Augie doesn't listen to the Sibyl] . . . we will lack serious interest and become truly irrelevant [surely Augie's job with Mintouchian fits] . . . he dreams of a golden age [as does Augie]. . . . Without the common world the novelist is nothing but a curiosity and will find himself in a glass case along some dull museum corridor of the future [and Bellow seems to have left Augie looking for a likely spot for his case]."

Retreat from Reality

The failure of Augie to estimate his condition is central to Bellow's meaning of Augie, as a depiction both of a human condition and of contemporary literature and the artist. Augie is still a man of hope despite the reality of sordid and irrelevant affairs. But his deterioration is almost complete. When he and his maid Jacqueline are walking across the fields in the freezing cold, she urges him to sing in order to prevent his stomach from freezing: "And because I didn't want to argue with her about medical superstitions and be so right or superior wising her up about modern science I decided, finally, what the hell! I might as well sing too. The only thing I could think to sing was 'La Cucaracha.' I kept up La Cucaracha for a mile or two and felt more chilled than helped" (535).

This passage reflects what Augie as modern man has become, and here, Bellows intends, is too often what modern literature has become—the victim of microscopic vision. Life is only what may be seen in the laboratory. Augie tries to sing, but all he can manage is a song reminiscent of Kafka's "Metamorphosis" in which the protagonist slips to a lower form of life because he has not recognized his condition, because he has refused to face reality and suffer his freedom. It is little wonder Augie feels more chilled than helped.

Bellow points to this alienation from reality when Augie and Jacqueline are approaching the farmhouse where her uncle lives, after their car stops and leaves them stranded: "Then she pointed. 'Vous voyez les chiens?' The dogs of the farm had leaped a brook and were dashing for us on the brown coat of the turf, yelling and yapping. 'Don't you worry about them,' she said, picking up a branch. 'They know me well.' Sure enough they did. They bounded into the air and licked her face" (536).

Jacqueline and nature are friends. They know each other. One does not fear nor frighten the other. But immediately after, in the last paragraph of the novel, Augie says:

I cut out for Dunkerque and Ostend. Where the British were so punished the town is ruined. Quonset huts stand there on the ruins. The back of the ancient water was like wolf gray. Then on the long sand the waves crashed white; they spit themselves to pieces. I saw this specter of white anger coming from the savage gray and meanwhile shot northward, in a great hurry to get to Bruges and out of this line of white which was like eternity opening up right beside destructions of the modern world, hoary and grumbling. I thought if I could beat the dark to Bruges I'd see the green canals and ancient places. (536)

Through a careful choice of words, Bellow equates the dogs running to greet Jacqueline with the landscape and its threat to Augie. Augie, still retreating from reality, is like fragmented modern man: he is frightened by his vision of a destructive nature. He yearns for what Wallace Stevens calls the "old complacencies" in his poem "Sunday Morning." Augie would escape to the artificiality of Bruges, a city born of Hanseatic man; he feels comfortable with its canals and palaces of the past as he does with his coveted and protected philosophies. And he cannot help laughing at the image of poor, unattractive, middle-aged Jacqueline, "yet still hopefully and obstinately seductive": "What's so laughable, that a Jacqueline, for instance, . . . will still refuse to lead a disappointed life? Or is the laugh at nature—including eternity—that it thinks it can win over us and the power of hope" (536). Augie, still fighting nature, still does not believe in the reality of the human condition; and he establishes his battle lines between the real and his ideal—*ils ne passeront pas.* Again, he is very noble but self-defeating.

Augie's state, Bellow would say, is too often the state of the contemporary novel and of too many novelists: they, like Augie, practice separatism from the world. Frightened by it, as if it would contaminate them, they hurry to their laboratories to gain evidence of the world's

worldliness, and profess great single truths. Once again, they see only
Sisyphus struggling up the hill with his task; they are blind to his trip
back down. But Jacqueline lives on the hill and senses if she does not
see; unlike Ahab, she has not lost the "low enjoying power."

In the last few lines, Augie assumes the role of literature, as Bellow
contemplates its present and future: "Why, I am sort of a Columbus of
those near-at-hand and believe you can come to them in this immediate
terra incognita that spreads out in every gaze. I may well be a flop at this
line of endeavor. Columbus too thought he was a flop, probably, when
they sent him back in chains. Which didn't prove there was no
America" (536). Augie's statement is, first, an interpretation of the
function of literature—to establish lines of discovery and communication. At the present time, though, literature is in chains of denial, "in
the bondage of strangeness for a time still" (523), as Augie describes
himself, which does not prove that literature (or the novel) is dead.
Everybody knows that August—March is a dormant period; and if
winter comes. . . .

To return to Phillip Rahv's statement concerning the natural contradiction between art and reality, it is important to understand that
Bellow is not asking for a dissolution of that relationship. Once again,
the distinction between Augie's ideals and reality is not the problem: it
is the failure on the part of the artist to "estimate his condition," to see
himself within the framework of the ideal-real nature of this world.
Augie says that he does not claim to be angelic, but he turns out to be a
fallen angel, what with his wasted ideals, because he removes his
abilities from the human condition in the name of "a better fate" that
has its roots only in his imagination. So it is with the artist of
alienation. It is the subangelic attitude for which Bellow calls—an
attitude that will create within the existing state, and not above or
below it.

Chapter Four
Seize the Day

Seize the Day (1957) is a clear example of what Bellow means when he urges the novelist to depict man as subangelic, or as having the power to overcome ignominy. For in this novel, or novelette, the protagonist Tommy Wilhelm has such an ability. *De profundis* he arises to some positive apprehension of what it means to be a human being. More specifically, he achieves a reconciliation, first, with an unsympathetic society that neither knows nor cares to know of his existence; second, with a world that offers no helpful spiritual guidance; and, third, with a self that seems to be a piece of flotsam driven by dark forces of malevolent intent. Tightly interwoven and often overlapping, these are the three levels of meaning in *Seize the Day*. But we need to note how Bellow develops these themes and to understand the significance of their resolutions.

Bellow is concerned with the well-worn dilemma of the individual desperately isolated and profoundly alone, intermittently shunned and used, in a society whose only God is Mammon. As the story opens, Tommy is in just such a state of ignominy. Forty-three years old, huge, bearlike, overemotional, and heavily dependent, he is caught in a world devoid of heart, one in which there is no caring and no real communication among men. In this lower-middle-class, densely populated section of New York City, where Tommy lives in the less than swank Hotel Gloriana, people talk to each other, do business, pass the time of day, but somehow do so only superficially; the human heart is never reached; masks and deceptions are the rule; there is no compassion, no understanding, and no love but that it is frustrated. Tommy is nakedly and miserably alone.

This theme of ignominious isolation is established in the first several pages of the novel when Tommy stops to get his morning newspaper from Rubin, the newspaper vendor. They talk only about the weather,

Tommy's clothes, last night's gin game; for, even though both men know many intimate details of each other's personal lives, "None of these could be mentioned, and the great weight of the unspoken left them little to talk about."[1] And a few lines later, during the same meeting, Tommy thinks: "He [Rubin] meant to be conversationally playful, but his voice had no tone and his eyes, slack and lid-blinded, turned elsewhere. He didn't want to hear. It was all the same to him" (8).

Even Tommy's father, Dr. Adler, refuses to become involved in his son's desperate loneliness. Tommy needs money which his father could easily supply; but Dr. Adler is greatly pained, even shies away, when the subject is mentioned. More than money, however, Tommy needs communication with an understanding heart; again and again, he appeals to his father for compassion; and, at the same time, he hates himself for being so weak as to do so. The appeal is always futile, for his father's response is ever a cold, detached, yet bitter and angry, analytical denunciation of Tommy's past failures and present ignominy: "It made Tommy profoundly bitter that his father should speak to him with such detachment about his welfare. Dr. Adler liked to appear affable. Affable! His own son, his one and only son, could not speak his mind or ease his heart to him . . . couldn't he see—couldn't he feel? Had he lost his family sense?" (10–11).

And, in a different way, the circumstances are the same with the rather mysterious Dr. Tamkin, a sort of a second father to Tommy. Tommy feels that he can talk to and be understood by him; but here, too, a barrier of communication exists. In the words of Dr. Tamkin, it is impossible to separate truth from fiction, intellect from idiocy. At times, there is no doubt in Tommy's mind that there is truth, even profound truth, in his philosophical and psychological teachings; at other times, Tommy knows he is being victimized by this combination psychologist, psychiatrist, broker, poet, gambler, counselor, father, and world-traveling philosopher. Hence, no consolation comes from this quarter. Only toward the end of the novel does Tommy finally decide that he has merely been used, that Dr. Tamkin does not truly care about him or his problems: "I was the man beneath; Tamkin was on my back, and I thought I was on his. He made me carry him, too, besides Margaret [Tommy's estranged wife]. Like this they ride on me with hoofs and claws. Tear me to pieces, stamp on me and break my bones" (105).

There are other characters with whom Tommy finds no comforting solace: his wife Margaret,[2] who has left him but will not agree to a divorce; his children; Maurice Venice, the talent scout, another agent of disillusion; Mr. Perls, a German refugee from a concentration camp; and Mr. Rappaport, an elderly, clutching player of stock markets. The role of each of these figures only reinforces Tommy's aloneness.

One of the major themes of *Seize the Day*, then, is the isolation of the human spirit in modern society. The appeal is for caring, for a sincere feeling of involvement with mankind. Bellow is urging that a loving recognition of the natural bond between hearts is the only answer to a society which seems to have lost or seems to be denying all social kinship. At the end of the novel, Tommy recognizes this kinship when he finds himself at a funeral, while searching for Dr. Tamkin. As he looks down on the corpse of a stranger, he understands or at least feels the basic relationship between himself and all men—a relationship established, in spite of superficial and man-made barriers, by the bond of mortality. Tommy, no longer isolated, absorbs into his being the full meaning of the line of poetry that had earlier slipped from his mind: "Love that well which thou must leave ere long" (12). This understanding, Bellow implies, allows Tommy the dignity of position in a social order. There is no triumphant promise here, but neither is there cause for miserable and hopeless lamentation—that is, no reasonable cause—for Bellow is stating a case beyond dispute. All shall die—live with joy and live in harmony. It is the only answer to the ultimate design. Tommy sees it, even if the other "mourners" do not when he looks down into the casket on his own fate:

The great knot of ill and grief in his throat swelled upward and he gave in utterly and held his face and wept. He cried with all his heart.

He, alone of all the people in the chapel, was sobbing. No one knew who he was. . . .

"Oh my, oh my! To be mourned like that," said one man and looked at Wilhelm's heavy shaken shoulders, his clutched face and whitened fair hair, with wide, glinting, jealous eyes.

"The man's brother, maybe?"

"Oh, I doubt that very much," said another bystander. "They're not alike at all. Night and day" (118).

But they are alike. The reality of brotherhood is not to be diminished by illusory trivia that constructs fortresses of sand among the living.

Source, Setting, Structure

There is no doubt that *Seize the Day* may be read with accuracy as the state of the individual trapped in the chaos of an egoistic and driving society, a society detached and cold, refusing the pleas of the individual for a meaningful and enduring relationship, as in the blunt rejections of Dr. Adler and in the disillusioning promises and confusion of Dr. Tamkin. Yet Bellow has in mind a wider scope of universal intent. He is depicting a world wherein spiritual guidance, grown old and useless, seemingly offers no answer to the exigencies of man. Moreover, man finds nothing but disillusionment as he sets up his own gods of materialism. These are the second and third states of ignominy in which Tommy progressively finds himself.

To examine Bellow's methods of expression at these deeper levels, there must be a consideration in some depth of source, structure, and setting and of techniques of characterization and imagery; for in these materials we may see Bellow's intentions more clearly. The source of *Seize the Day* may be traced to a single paragraph in Dostoevski's *The Brothers Karamazov*: to the incident in which the Grand Inquisitor confronts Christ with angry accusations. In this passage Christ visits Seville, "during the most ghastly period of the Inquisition when, to the greater glory of God, bonfires blazed day in and day out all over the land. . . ."[3] Christ is promptly arrested by the Grand Inquisitor, who feels that the Son of God blundered when He left a burden too difficult for man to carry; for He left him, regardless of intent, his freedom. The Inquisitor points to Christ's refusal to turn rocks into bread, and to jump off the pinnacle—in short, to give man miracles. Christ's reasoning that man should not turn to miracle but to God is unrealistic, says the irate Inquisitor: it is even meaningless, in view of man's limitations. He says to Christ:

But thou didst not know that no sooner would man reject miracle than he would on the instant reject God as well, for it is not so much God as miracles that man seeks. And since it is beyond man's strength to remain without miracles, he is bound to create for himself a mess of new miracles, this time all his own, and will bend his knee this time to the miracle of the witch-doctor, to the black magic of the witch-woman, though he may be a rebel, a heretic and an atheist a hundred times over.[4]

What Bellow in *Seize the Day* shows is his protagonist in the position of man described by the Inquisitor—as rejected by divinity and disillusioned by his own contrivances.

For the working-out of Tommy's rejection and disillusionment, Bellow creates a kind of morality play, a drama whose structure falls into a pattern of function. Allowing for flashbacks, the action takes place in five acts. The first serves as a introduction to the characters and presents Tommy's relationship to these in a manner that describes the nature of his isolation. The second act is set during breakfast in the hotel cafeteria at which time the confrontation between Tommy and his father further clarifies their deteriorated relationship. In the third act, Tommy and Dr. Tamkin visit the stock market where their mutuality is made evident. The fourth act shows Tommy eating lunch with Dr. Tamkin and Tommy's subsequent disillusionment. In the final act, there is the dramatic gathering of loose ends, a recapitulation of former actions, and a resolution of conflicts. Of course, much has been omitted from this outline; but the major actions take place within this framework.

The function of this structure is evident, especially when Dostoevski's passage is kept in mind: Dr. Adler fails Tommy, just as Christ may be said to have failed man; then Tommy turns to Dr. Tamkin, just as the Inquisitor says that man will "create for himself a mess of new miracles, this time all his own, and will bend his knee this time to the miracle of the witch-doctor. . . ." As a matter of fact, Tommy himself describes the plot early in the work when he reflects upon his father's unsympathetic attitude: "I wouldn't turn to Tamkin. . . . If I could turn to him."

The technique, therefore, is clearly allegorical. Bellow intends Tommy's story to be seen as a general condition of man beset by rejection from both divine and materialistic sources. And, in a sense, there are shades of the old morality dramas here—body versus soul. Even as the body and soul fight over their respective influences on man, so there is a struggle between Dr. Tamkin and Dr. Adler as to whose constructions, whose teachings, shall prevail with Tommy. Dr. Adler makes his animosity toward the influence of Tamkin on his son quite clear in his warnings against trusting him (40). Tamkin's opposition to Adler is less open, but it exists in his promises of a get-rich-quick formula as opposed to the work-hard advice of Adler.

Because of Bellow's extended purposes, he expands the setting of *Seize the Day* in order for his allegory to have a universal state. He manages this additional breadth and depth by paralleling Spenser's *The Fairie Queen* and by drawing on the allegorical figure of Gloriana. The reader learns almost immediately that, even as the quest of the Red Cross Knight begins with his setting forth from the court of Gloriana, so Tommy starts his day of fate when he steps out of the Hotel Gloriana. While there are few likenesses between these two protagonists, they do have common situations: both figures are involved in quests; there are confrontations to be suffered; their fields of action are filled with a confusion of guile, love, innocence, truth, envy, lust, and other projections of humanity (Dr. Tamkin is a forest of confusing ambiguities in himself). Finally, both are victorious, although in the case of Tommy we must call again upon Sisyphus to understand the nature of his victory. Or better yet, perhaps, we must learn to count the dubious blessings of being a man. However, through the use of Spenser's materials, Bellow serves notice that his work is to be an allegory. It is through Tommy's experiences that the allegory is carried out, a universal action dealing with no lesser subjects than man's relationship to society, self, and God.

Father and Son

Through structure and setting Bellow creates a field of action in which his characters may function in their symbolic roles as guiding forces on Tommy. Such forces as Dr. Adler and Dr. Tamkin assume a far greater meaning than that of father and counselor.[5] Bellow creates their further meanings largely through a linguistic ambivalence that, in the case of Dr. Adler, appears within the first few pages of the story. His role as divinity, probably God, is evident when his person is described:

The handsome old doctor *stood well above* the other old people in the hotel. He was idolized by everyone. This was what people said: "That's old Professor Adler who *used to teach internal medicine.* He *was a diagnostician,* one of the best in New York, and *had a tremendous practice.* Isn't he a *wonderful-looking* old guy? It's a pleasure to see such a fine old scientist, clean and *immaculate.* He stands straight and *understands every single thing you say.* He still has all his buttons. *You can discuss any subject with him."* The clerks, the elevator operators, the management flattered and pampered him. *That was what he wanted. He had always been a vain man.* To see how his father loved himself sometimes made Wilhelm madly indignant. . . . *The doctor had created his own praise* [italics mine]. (11–12)

The symbolic implications are clear: Dr. Adler's role as divinity is especially evident when he is described as "idolized," as a teacher of "internal medicine," as "immaculate," and as creating "his own praise." This last phrase—"created his own praise"—is typical of many of Bellow's ambivalencies. It is, in a sense, but not in a very clear one, appropriate to Dr. Adler as a character in his own right. Yet, if the phrase is so read, it seems somewhat useless, at least gratuitous. If its function is symbolic, however, Bellow's intent is immediately evident: Dr. Adler, in addition to being Tommy's father, is God.

This lengthy description of Dr. Adler takes place in Tommy's mind before Dr. Adler actually makes his appearance. With his appearance, Bellow supports his role as God with at least four direct references to the Deity. Within the dialogue there are interspersed such introductory expletives as "God knows!" and "Lord knows why . . ." (33); "God, they have some queer elements in this hotel" (34); "God alone can tell why" (35). Before these pages and after, there are no other such references. Seemingly, Bellow deliberately announces the allegorical arrival of Dr. Adler:

If Dr. Adler's function of God can be accepted, Tommy, his son, must be seen as Christ. And there are some such vague indications. When Dr. Adler is hiding Tommy's financial failures by praising him to Mr. Perls, Tommy thinks, "It's Dad . . . who is the salesman. He's selling me. *He* should have gone on the road"—again, a highly gratuitous remark, in view of Dr. Adler's background and profession, unless one interprets the comment in the light of Tommy as Christ "on the road," selling Christianity. Again, when Tommy is explaining his complaint against his former employers, he says:

"I have to do something to protect myself. I was promised executive standing. . . . I was the one who opened the territory for them. I could go back for one of their competitors and take away their customers. *My* customers."

"Would you offer a different line to the same people?" Mr. Perls wondered. (37)

In business jargon, Christ might be thought of as the one who "opened the territory." And, in the same sense, all Western cultures are "customers" of Christ. Then Mr. Perls's question, while appropriate enough to the conversation, could refer to the same point that Dostoevski makes, that Christ's first "line" has no value, not even a negative one, especially when Tommy answers Mr. Perls: "Why not? I know what's wrong with the Rojax product" (Rojax is the name of the company for which Tommy worked). Other suggestions support Tommy in this role, but none are more telling than those cited. A point that should be kept in mind, however, is that Bellow's symbolic patterns are often quite complex and overlapping; they are not restricted to one-to-one relationships. Hence, it is possible that Bellow intends Tommy as Christ only in the sense of his suffering and his possible disillusionment with his historical and theological roles.

In any case, a more substantial argument can be made for Tommy as Adam, or as mankind in general: for example, in the passage just cited, Adam was promised "executive standing," or perhaps immortality; and Adam certainly "opened up the territory." Then, at another point, Tommy reflects upon his decision to change his name: "The changed name was a mistake, and he would admit it as freely as you liked. But this mistake couldn't be undone now, so why must his father continually remind him of how he had sinned? It was too late. He would have to go back to the pathetic day when the sin was committed. And where was that day? Past and dead. Whose humiliating memories were these? His and not his father's" (25). In one sense, these words fit Tommy as Dr. Adler's son, for Tommy has made mistakes that his father never ceases to recall. Yet here, too, are dramatized implications of Adam and his fall, of the tortured questionings to which man is ever subjecting himself and God.

The complexity of Bellow's symbolism is also evident in the references to Tommy's mother. There are strong hints that she may be identified as Eve, which would be appropriate to Tommy as mankind, but hardly in keeping with him as Adam or Christ, nor with Dr. Adler as God, inasmuch as she was his wife. In any case, Tommy's thoughts about his inheritances are interesting:

> In middle age you no longer thought such thoughts about free choice. Then it came over you that from grandfather you had inherited such and such a head of hair which looked like honey when it whitens or sugars in the jar; from another, broad thick shoulders; an oddity of speech from one uncle, and small teeth from another, and the gray eyes with darkness diffused even into the whites, and a wide-lipped mouth like a statue from Peru. Wandering races have such looks, the bones of one tribe, the skin of another. From his mother he had gotten sensitive feelings, a soft heart, a brooding nature, a tendency to be confused under pressure. (25)

Here, through a juxtaposition of anthropology and the specific inherited characteristics of Tommy, Bellow attempts to place the mother deep in history, even in prehistory. Then the shift from the anthropological physicalities to the emotional qualities of Tommy and his mother are interesting. We might assume that, since Tommy is the protagonist and therefore the primary focus, Bellow is more interested in just these qualities than he is in the other, that he merely uses the facts of anthropology in order to show the universal and timeless intent of his subject. Aside from technique, however, the description in the last line could well be applied to Eve, especially in the last phrase. Although Tommy, too, has a "tendency to be confused under pressure," if his mother is meant to be allegorical, and if she is to be placed in the far distant past, Eve's fatal decision may be regarded as a result of the same tendency.

Whatever the identity of Tommy's mother, if we can accept Dr. Adler as divinity and Tommy as mankind, the relationship that exists between the two is precisely that described by Dostoevski. With God's inability or refusal to alleviate man's anxieties or to sympathize actively with his weakness and limitations, there is a loss of mutual trust, respect, and communication between Him and man. This complete lack of understanding shows itself, for example, when Tommy and his father are discussing the death of Tommy's mother:

> Then Wilhelm had asked, "Yes, that was the beginning of the end, wasn't it, Father?"
> Wilhelm often astonished Dr. Adler. Beginning of the end? What could he mean—what was he fishing for? Whose end? The end of family life? The old man was puzzled but he would not give Wilhelm an opening to introduce his complaints. He had learned that it was better not to take up Wilhelm's strange challenges. So he agreed merely pleasantly, for he was a master of social behavior, and said, "It was an awful misfortune for us all."
> He thought, what business has he to complain to *me* of his mother's death? (28)

Interpreted allegorically, this whole passage has echoes of the enduring problem of free will. On the one hand, Tommy as mankind and as a child of Eve, is vaguely blaming Dr. Adler as God for the death of his mother. Yet Dr. Adler as God never questions but that free will was operative when Eve made her mortal choice; therefore, he is surprised and puzzled by Tommy's insinuations. It never for a moment occurs to him that he (He) might have been involved in the event. Communication and understanding between these two have so deteriorated that hints as to responsibility are merely regarded as "strange challenges," which Dr. Adler as father, and, most appropriately here, as God, refuses to dignify with answers. And, as for Tommy as man, he is equally puzzled as he timidly, obliquely, searches for those answers.

In the last few pages of the novel, in the final act, Tommy makes one more attempt to seek help from his father. Here, Bellow turns again to Aeneas, to the mythological tales in which the hero seeks wisdom and advice in Hell. Tommy finds his father deep in the basement of the hotel taking a steam bath. Under the guidance of Dr. Tamkin, Tommy has just suffered a ruinous loss on the stock market:

> "You took some gamble? You lost it? Was it Tamkin?"
> "Yes, Dad, I'm afraid I trusted him." . . .
> "Well, I won't remind you how often I warned you." . . .
> "Nobody likes bad luck, eh Dad?"

"So! It's bad luck now. A minute ago it was stupidity."

"It is stupidity—it's some of both. It's true that I can't learn. But I—".

"I don't want to listen to the details," said his father. "And I want you to understand that I'm too old to take on new burdens. I'm just too old to do it. And people who will just wait for help—must *wait* for help. They have got to stop waiting."

"It isn't all a question of money—there are other things a father can give his son." He lifted up his gray eyes and his nostrils grew wide with a look of suffering appeal that stirred his father even more deeply against him.

He warningly said to him, "Look out, Wilky, you're tiring my patience very much."

"I try not to. But one word from you, just a word, would go a long way. I've never asked you for very much."

He recognized that his father was now furiously angry. Dr. Adler started to say something, and then raised himself, and gathered the sheet over him as he did so. His mouth opened, wide, dark, twisted, and he said to Wilhelm, "You want to make yourself into my cross. But I am not going to pick up a cross. I'll see you dead, Wilky, by Christ, before I let you do that to me." (108–10)

In this passage, Bellow shows the end of man's hope for divine providence. Man must turn elsewhere for help.

Dr. Tamkin: Contemporary Witch Doctor

It is quite clear that Dr. Tamkin, to whom Tommy turns in the face of his father's rejections, is Dostoevski's "witch doctor." Bellow certainly describes him in this light. He is "shrewd and wizard-like . . . secret, potent" (64); "There was a hypnotic power in his eyes (62); he smiles "like a benevolent magician" (81); and even his bathrobe is patterned with "lightning streaks of red and white" (106). And the fraudulent deceit is evident in his physical appearance, which, if not intended to be that of the devil, is surely devilish:

What a creature Tamkin was when he took off his hat! The indirect light showed the many complexities of his bald skull, his gull's nose, his rather handsome eyebrows, his vain mustache, his deceiver's brown eyes. . . . His bones were peculiarly formed, as though twisted twice where the ordinary human bone was turned only once, and his shoulders rose in two pagoda-like points. At mid-body he was thick. He stood pigeon-toed, a sign perhaps that he was devious or had much to hide. The skin of his hands was aging, and his nails were moonless, concave, clawlike, and they appeared loose. His eyes were as brown as beaver fur and full of strange lines. (62)

From such a creature Tommy hopes for a "mess of new miracles." In order to show the stretch of man's octopuslike reach for "new miracles," in the absence of a helpful divinity, Bellow adds many distinctive touches to his figure, Dr. Tamkin. Tamkin, as noted earlier, is a little bit of everything—psychologist, psychiatrist, poet, broker, gambler, counselor, traveler, philosopher; but he is more—ex-husband, doctor, lover, benefactor, teacher of Greek, scientist and inventor, with hints, from himself of course, of even wider knowledge and abilities. He generously and confidently offers the benefits of his never-ending capacities to Tommy. He assures him: "I read the best of literature, science and philosophy. . . . Korzybski, Aristotle, Freud, W. H. Sheldon, and all the great poets" (72).

Of course, Bellow intends in these references a catalog of grails which man everlastingly seeks in his pursuit of happiness and well-being, quite hopelessly because they offer no satisfactory answer to "the heart's ultimate need" by which Bellow means a feeling of place, of value, with the integrity of identity. They are only toys that amuse, dry grails, empty of any real and lasting nourishment. Tamkin is a combination of all the elixirs and panaceas for whatever ails man.

In Tamkin there are undertones of the alter ego, the same device Bellow uses in the figure of Allbee in *The Victim*. At several points in the story there are strong hints that Tamkin is intended, at least on one level, to be a creature of Tommy's imagination; and it will be remembered that in Dostoevski's passage, it was suggested, for the lack of divine miracles, that man "was bound to create for himself a mess of new miracles, this time all his own." When Tamkin, the "confuser of the imagination" (93), but from whom "one could always get some truth" (63), tells Tommy of his dead wife, a suicide, he adds: "I tried everything in my power to cure her . . . my real calling is to be a healer. I get wounded. I suffer from it. I would like to escape from the sickness of others, but I can't. I am only on loan to myself, so to speak. I belong to humanity" (95).

And Tamkin belongs to that part of humanity that is Tommy. Tommy's revelation that all the time it was he who was carrying the burden of Tamkin, rather than Tamkin's carrying him, is appropriate to the discovery of the alter ego. We are reminded of Thoreau's townsmen who spent their lives pushing their "seventy-five foot by forty" barns down the "road of life," never doubting that their happiness depended on those barns, never discovering, as Tommy does, that the barn is their curse, even as Tamkin is Tommy's sickness.

There is a pattern to Bellow's alter egos: they always prevail over their counterparts to the degree that they are allowed to do so—and so it is with Tamkin. In the course of one of his wild stories, Tommy thinks, "if you encouraged Tamkin by believing him, or even if you refrained from questioning him, his hints [of his measureless experiences] become more daring" (80). At one point Tommy gets annoyed:

> "Damn it, Tamkin!" said Wilhelm roughly. "Cut that out. I don't like it. Leave my character out of consideration. Don't pull any more of that stuff on me. I tell you I don't like it."
> Tamkin therefore went no further; he backed down. (88)

Bellow is saying again that man controls his own existence, if he *will* control it and not leave it to the mercy of outer forces.

It is Tamkin who provides the irony of Bellow's title *Seize the Day*. Again and again, he urges Tommy to act on the moment. Within the first few pages, Tommy recollects some advice given by this financial wizard: "The whole secret to this type of speculation . . . is in the alertness. You have to act fast—buy it and sell it; sell it and buy in again. But quick! Get to the window and have them wire Chicago at just the right second. Strike and strike again! Then get out the same day" (8–9). And, when Tamkin explains economic efficiency, he says: "The spiritual compensation is what I look for. Bringing people into the here-and-now. The real universe. That's the present moment. The past is no good to us. The future is full of anxiety. Only the present is real—the here-and-now. Seize the day" (66).

Later Tamkin urges, "Be in the present. Grasp the hour, the moment, the instant" (90). The irony of such advice lies in its truth, but in a way that Tamkin never suspects. His counsel is founded on materialistic achievement, on making one's way in an envious, belligerent world.

At the end, Tommy discovers another meaning of the phrase, and the one Bellow intends: "Love that well which thou must leave ere long." Again, Bellow is stating a case seemingly beyond dispute—seize the day, for the night cometh. Man should choose dignity, live in harmony, and complete his own life: he should not waste it lamenting and suffering from past mistakes, from old and lost constructions (Dr. Adler), and from disillusioning new constructions (Tamkin).

Imagery

Ultimately, with Tommy's loss of hope in his father and with the realization of the nature of the tie between him and Tamkin, Tommy is thrown back on his own inner resources. He is now free. Bellow prepares for this moment all through the novel as he projects Tommy's struggle for survival through the use of the imagery of water. Within the first dozen lines of the book, the setting is imagistically formed: "the elevator sank and sank. Then the smooth door opened and the great dark red uneven carpet that covered the lobby billowed toward Wilhelm's feet. In the foreground the lobby was dark, sleepy. French drapes like sails kept out the sun" (3–4).

From this moment on, Tommy is in deep water; but, calling and reaching for help, he is unable to find a lifeline. Moreover, Tommy is not unaware of his situation: he feels as if he were drowning. Perhaps he is even in some strange way attracted to the idea, as if it were a deliverance. In any case, he remembers and pronounces beautiful and compelling the line from Milton's "Lycidas": "Sunk though he be beneath the wat'ry floor" (13). We do not say that Tommy has suicidal tendencies, only that vaguely and quite unconsciously he identifies himself with the drowned Lycidas.

Bellow even uses this imagery to trace the movements of his protagonist. After a violent scene with Dr. Adler, Tommy is made aware of the presence of Dr. Tamkin: "The sight of Dr. Tamkin brought his quarrel with his father to a close. He found himself flowing into another channel" (57). Here, however, the waters are equally dangerous, and he wonders shortly afterward, "But what have I let myself in for? The waters of the earth are going to roll over me" (77).

The reader feels the aptness of this water image when Tommy struggles but fails to establish some understanding and caring between himself and his world. In a particularly disagreeable scene with his father, his father asks, "What do you want from me? What do you expect?" To which Tommy cries: "'What do I expect?' He felt as though he were unable to recover something. Like a ball in the surf, washed beyond, his self-control was going out. 'I expect *help*'" (53).

Like anyone who is drowning, Tommy wants and expects help. Of course, he receives none from the merely annoyed Dr. Adler; and Tommy, leaving the scene, is "horribly worked up; his neck and shoulders, his entire chest ached, as though they had been tightly tied with ropes. He smelled the salt odor of tears in his nose" (55–56). Recalling Lycidas a second time, he wonders if it would not be better for him to sink beneath the watery floor: "would that be tough luck, or would it be good riddance?"[6]

Irony is evident in Bellow's imagery. Water is precisely the cure that Dr. Adler recommends for Tommy. He uses it himself, constantly lauding its beneficial affects: "there's nothing better than hydrotherapy when you come right down to it. Simple water has a calming effect and would do you more good than all the barbiturates and alcohol in the world." (44). Later the reader is told, "It was all he had to give to his son and he gave it once more. 'Water and exercise,' he said" (45). In the final scene with his father, Tommy is greeted with the question as to whether or not he has taken a swim yet (77). All of this water imagery, of course, has echoes of baptismal rituals, which, coming from his father, Tommy rejects as hopelessly useless. But Bellow depicts a kind of baptism as the setting for Tommy's rebirth. Tommy is at the funeral where he breaks down in great grief. As he looks down on the corpse of the stranger, "With great stifling sorrow, almost admiration, Wilhelm nodded and nodded" (117). As Tommy gazes with new understanding: "The flowers and lights fused ecstatically in Wilhelm's blind, wet eyes; the heavy sea-like music came up to his ears. It poured into him where he had hidden himself in the center of a crowd by the great and happy oblivion of tears. He heard it and sank deeper than sorrow, through torn sobs, and cries toward the consummation of his heart's ultimate need" (118).

Here, Tommy indeed sinks "beneath the wat'ry floor," sinking "deeper than sorrow" to the "Heart's ultimate need." And we might recall the line from "Lycidas"—"Sunk though he be beneath the wat'ry floor" with particular attention to the word "though." Obviously Milton intends that the drowned Lycidas shall rise spiritually, shall be reborn. So does Bellow intend that, though "the sea-like music came up to his ears" and though he "sank deeper than sorrow," Tommy is to have such a rebirth. For Tommy sinks *deeper* than sorrow—not to sorrow, but beyond—to a certain peace. Interestingly enough, then, one of the major themes in the novel might well lie in the single line from Milton's elegy.

In any case, Tommy's own tears supply the waters for this baptism. They come from deep within, from his own resources, from the personal and immediately heartfelt understanding that man in his mortality has little choice but to "seize the day." It would seem to be an ignominious condition, one in which all constructions turn to dust: but man in his subangelic power does have this choice—he can choose dignity to overcome the ignominy, along with Sisyphus, and live in harmony at least with himself. Tommy's revelation is Bellow's answer to the Dostoevskian dilemma, and it calls for a revision of the Horatian *carpe diem* theme. In his ode (I, 11), Horace urges that the day be seized because the future is unknown. Bellow makes the same plea, but for a very different reason: man should seize the day because the future *is* known.

Chapter Five
Henderson the Rain King

Millionaire Eugene Henderson, who is huge of frame and heavy of flesh, is world and life weary to the point of extreme irascibility: and he is one of a large group of fictive heroes who "light out for the territory"; in this case, Africa. As protagonist in Bellow's *Henderson the Rain King* (1959), Henderson states his case in the opening lines of the novel:

What made me take this trip to Africa? There is no quick explanation. Things got worse and worse and pretty soon they were too complicated.

When I think of my condition at the age of fifty-five when I bought the ticket, all is grief. The facts begin to crowd me and soon I get a pressure in the chest. A disorderly rush begins—my parents, my wives, my girls, my children, my farm, my animals, my habits, my money, my music lessons, my drunkenness, my prejudices, my brutality, my teeth, my face, my soul! I have to cry, "No, no, get back, curse you, let me alone!" But how can they let me alone? They belong to me. They are mine. And they pile into me from all sides. It turns into chaos.

However, the world which I thought so mighty an oppressor has removed its wrath from me.[1]

The final line should be noted. From it, Bellow seemingly intends his novel to be, superficially at least, a success story. That is, through whatever experiences are in the offing, his protagonist has evidently achieved some measure of peace and contentment. In this chapter, which has to do with that achievement, we shall see that Henderson's achievement is directly germane to Bellow's concept of man as sub-angelic. As a general guide for this discussion, the narrative will be followed; but its essentials can be stated quite briefly: first, Eugene Henderson relates the story of the dismal circumstances under which he left for Africa; he narrates his experiences with the natives of Arnewi and with the Wariri; then he recounts his departure for home.

Foundations for Alienation

First, however, since Bellow's point of view is extremely important to an understanding of his intentions toward his protagonist, it is helpful to see some likenesses between Swift's *Gulliver's Travels* and *Henderson the Rain King*. Both protagonists are interested in medicine (Gulliver is a physician; Henderson wants to be one); both are placed beyond civilization through unforeseen circumstances; both visit fanciful peoples in strange cultures; both have extended philosophical discussions with the kings, queens, and princes of these cultures; both suffer experiences that shake their established worlds; and both return home in a condition far removed from that in which they had set out.

These general parallels are by no means the only ones. Indeed, in order to clarify many of his final meanings, Bellow invades Swift like a monarch. For the moment, the importance of recognizing Swift as an influence lies in understanding that, even as the major meanings of *Gulliver's Travels* are to be found in the responses of Gulliver to his experiences, so do Bellow's intentions lie within the experiences of Henderson. As in Swift's work, the education of Bellow's protagonist has meaning only insofar as the reader brings his knowledge and insight to bear on the experiences of the protagonist, all of which should become clear in discussing this safari of the intellect.

In the opening passage of the novel, previously cited, the clear echoes of Melville's Ishmael serve as a general introduction to the motives behind Henderson's escape to Africa. As the chapter progresses, the likenesses between the two travelers become clearer. Henderson is suffering from the same social and philosophical maladies that motivate Ishmael to sign on board the *Pequod:* both are afflicted with a morbid depression of the spirits, or, as Ishmael explains, his "Hypos" had "the upper hand"; and, while Henderson does not exactly have a yen for "methodically knocking people's hats off" in the city of "old Manhatto," he does feel compelled to battle drunkenly with the state troopers of Danbury, Connecticut, as well as to argue unreasonably with his wife Lily, to alienate his son and daughter, to refuse his tenants heat during the winter, to fire his forty-five automatic at their cat, to shout over a petty disagreement in such a voice that the elderly maid succumbs to a heart attack, to raise pigs from which his only pleasure comes from their annoying presence to family and neighbors, and to continually harass in a dozen other ways family, friends, acquaintances, and community with his unpredictable, irrational, and often violent behavior.

While Henderson does not exactly join Ishmael in "pausing before coffin warehouses," his situation is much the same when he thinks of his "condition at the age of fifty-five . . . [and] all is grief": both men are desperate in their longing to find some meaning to a turbulent life that is seemingly without purpose and that is quickly passing them by. It has been a long search for Henderson. Within a few paragraphs of the end of the novel, when he tells of a job he had had as a boy that required him to ride a roller coaster with a bear named Smolak, he remembers his words to his boss: "We're two of a kind. Smolak was cast off and I am an Ishmael, too" (338). What could be more obvious?

Escape

Eugene Henderson, a rich, frustrated American, is running away from personal problems that soon assume implications of a well-recognized general condition that is far from original in literature: his is a search for meaning amid a life of plenty. This significance includes integrity, identity, utility, and purpose, which depend on place and function. Henderson, who recognizes his displacement, even regards himself as inferior in value to his pigs: "Taxwise, even the pigs were profitable. I couldn't lose money. But they were killed and they were eaten. They made ham and gloves and gelatin and fertilizer. What did I make? Why, I made a sort of trophy, I suppose. A man like me may become something like a trophy" (24). And he painfully searches for an answer to his feelings of uselessness:

What do you do with yourself if you have a temperament like mine? A student of the mind once explained to me that if you inflict your anger on inanimate things, you not only spare the living, as a civilized man ought to do, but you get rid of the bad stuff in you. This seemed to make good sense, and I tried it out. I tried with all my heart, chopping wood, lifting, plowing, laying cement blocks, pouring concrete, and cooking mash for the pigs. . . . It helped, but not enough. Rude begets rude, and blows, blows; at least in my case; it not only begot but it increased. Wrath increased with wrath. (23)

Henderson, trying to clean the Augean stables, attempts to purge himself of a violent spirit through violence. In any case, despite his recognition of his situation and all of his effort, there still seems to be no solution to his problem. His grief only flourishes.

All of this frustration would seem to point to Henderson as symbolic of a group whose immediate necessities—food, shelter, clothing, and general well-being—have been met, but whose need for peace of mind and sense of direction has not. As such, he is certainly representative of a segment of our nation. But that Bellow would not limit function so narrowly—that he would state Henderson's existence to be operative on a wider and deeper scale—is evident in the early part of the novel when he shows his protagonist to be the descendant of a rather select group of people. For example, Henderson imagines what bystanders are saying about him, as he sits on the beach idly shooting stones at bottles: "Do you see that great big fellow with the enormous nose and mustache? Well, his great-grandfather was Secretary of State, his great-uncles were ambassadors to England and France, and his father was the famous scholar Willard Henderson who wrote that book on the Albigensians, a friend of William James and Henry Adams" (7). And later, when he is accounting for the immense proportions of his nose, he recalls that "I was once a good-looking fellow . . . but it certainly is a nose I can smell the world with. It comes down to me from the founder of my family. He was a Dutch sausage-maker and became the most unscrupulous capitalist in America" (82).

Bellow indicates that his protagonist is a product of the auspiciously successful, and his success was based on such "high-minded" pursuits as politics, finance, science, history, and scholarship in general. However, lest Henderson be considered a phenomenon peculiar to this country, Bellow has his background include diplomats whose lives are closely related to people abroad. Furthermore, he is depicted as a world traveler, both as a soldier of World War II and as a civilian. He has lived in England, France, Italy, and Germany (15–18). To this point, then, Henderson is probably to be regarded as symbolic of affluent elements of Western culture, but it must be remembered that by "affluent" Bellow would describe lives relatively rich and comfortably secure in a variety of ways—intellect, prestige, talent, money, authority. Such affluence could easily persuade its possessor that only his approach to life is the answer to any spiritual despondency. Such affluence would tend to shunt into the background, and there lie festering, the fundamental and universal fact of man's existence—his mortality.

Aside from the main theme of *Henderson the Rain King*, but certainly related to that theme, is Bellow's concern with this seeming paradox—the spiritual malaise in an environment of sufficiency. In one of his book reviews, he states: "The lives of the Castros with their new wealth stand as a warning that the heart may empty as the belly fills . . . . now that technology extends the promise of an increase of wealth we had better be aware of a poverty of the soul as terrible as that of the body."[2]

This description seemingly relates to Henderson, who is a "graduate of an Ivy League university" (4) and the inheritor of millions. In spite of his wealth and distinction (he is a holder of various war medals for valor), he suffers just such a "poverty of the soul," as if the removal of want has brought about the removal of a meaningful reality. That is, once victory over basic needs is achieved, what is there left to fight for? What remains of real concern? All other wants, in the last analysis, are luxuries, which, like all luxuries, pale into insignificance upon the acquiring.

Henderson seems to be aware of this state, yet he does want. Again and again, he hears an inner voice that makes its demands: "there was a disturbance in my heart, a voice that spoke there and said *I want, I want, I want!* It happened every afternoon, and when I tried to suppress it it got even stronger. It only said one thing, *I want, I want!*" (24). What he wants, he does not know. He only knows that what he has, much as that is, is not enough.

In any case, because material things are in the saddle and ride mankind, Henderson, with Emersonian authority, leaves his wife and children to follow his genius. Africa is his destination; but "all travel is mental," says Henderson (167)—and his journey is no different. This Africa of the mind is the *Pequod* or Lilliput, where values can be reconsidered and reality subjected to new perspectives.[3]

A Curse on the Land

On the way to the land of the Arnewi, Bellow sets the scene for the deeper implication of his work. As Henderson and his native guide

Romilayu trudge through dry and barren land deeper into the heart of Africa, Henderson says: "I got clean away from everything, and we came into a region like a floor surrounded by mountains. It was hot, clear, and arid and after several days we saw no human footprints. Nor were there many plants; for that matter there was not much of anything here; it was all simplified and splendid, and I felt I was entering the past, no history or junk like that. The prehuman past" (46).

And, a little later when he remembers this period, "I was so sure that I had left the world. And who could blame me, after that trip across the mountain floor on which there was no footprint, the stars flaming like oranges, those multimillion tons of exploding gas looking so mild and fresh in the dark of the sky; and altogether that freshness . . . like autumn freshness . . ." (52–53). Bellow places in conjunction anthropological and geological pre-Adamic conditions, a fitting trail to follow if one is in search of essentials, and if one is trying to discover the roots of the soul's poverty.

As for the Arnewi village itself, Henderson comments again and again on its atmosphere of antiquity. He asks Romilayu, "How old is this place anyway? . . . I have a funny feeling from it. Hell, it looks like the original place. It must be older than the city of Ur" (47). His description of the landscape is significant, for he repeatedly uses such terms as "glitter," "gold," "light," "brilliant," "radiant," and "sparkling," as if he were looking upon a life newborn, trailing clouds of glory. When Henderson explains to Prince Itelo, "Your Highness, I am really kind of on a quest" (65), Bellow clearly means this quest to take place deep in the Edenic past at the time of man's first appearance.

Appropriate to the antiquity of these peoples, the Arnewi are cattle raisers. When Henderson enters their village, he finds them in tears and sadness, helplessly wringing their hands, because their water supply has been contaminated by the mysterious appearance of a multitude of frogs. Since their dying cattle are not only sacred, but also considered to be members of their families, their grief is deep. Romilayu explains the situation to Henderson: " 'Dem cry for dead cow,' he said. And he explained the thing very clearly, that they were mourning for cattle which had died in the drought, and that they took responsibility for the drought upon themselves—the gods were offended, or something like that; a curse was mentioned. Anyway, as we were strangers they were obliged to come forward and confess everything to us, and ask whether we knew the reason for their trouble" (50–51).

There are two points of significance within this passage: first, the statement that "a curse was mentioned" is meaningful to the allegory; for only a few pages earlier Henderson, lying drunk on a bench in the Danbury station, swears loudly that "There is a curse on this land. There is something bad going on. Something is wrong. There is a curse on this land!" (38). Although the specific nature of these curses is yet unknown, it is evident that the two are to be regarded as one. They are really the same curse, with the grief in Danbury having its roots in man's beginnings. Bellow draws the analogy when Prince Itelo and Henderson are examining the cistern. When they are through with the inspection, Henderson says: "As we turned away I felt as though that cistern of problem water with its algae and its frogs had entered me, occupying a square space in my interior, and sloshing around as I moved" (61).

The second point is that the natives, says Henderson, "were obliged to come forward and confess everything to us, and ask whether we knew the reason for their trouble." It is important here that the reader see beyond Henderson's interpretation of what is happening. Since Henderson chooses these words, which are clearly echoes of the confessional, his choice indicates a presumption of his possessing qualities of divinity. In this connection, his entrance to the village is significant: to announce his arrival, he, like God, sets a bush on fire with his cigarette lighter. The implications of the fact that *this* bush burns to a spot of ashes, unlike the one on Mount Sinai, are lost on Henderson; but Bellow intends the reader to see the mistaken pretensions and unlimited assumptions within the character of Henderson.

Among the Arnewi, Henderson meets Queen Willatale, who has achieved the high distinction of being named "woman o' Bittahness." When he exclaims that she hardly looks bitter in all her evident poise and comfort, with her huge mass obviously well cared for, Itelo explains: "'Oh, happy! Yes, happy—bittah. Most bittah,' said Itelo. . . . A Bittah was a person of real substance. You couldn't be any higher or better. . . . She had risen above ordinary human limitations and did whatever she liked because of her proven superiority in all departments" (75).

Henderson is highly impressed with the queen, and through his lavish descriptions she comes into focus as an Earth symbol:

> To me she was typical of a certain class of elderly lady. . . . Good nature emanated from her; it seemed to puff out on her breath as she sat smiling with many small tremors of benevolence and congratulation and welcome. Itelo indicated that I should give the old woman a hand, and I was astonished when she took it and buried it between her breasts. . . . there was the calm pulsation of her heart participating in the introduction. This was as regular as the rotation of the earth . . . my mouth came open and my eyes grew fixed as if I were touching the secrets of life; but I couldn't keep my hand there forever and I came to myself and drew it out. Then I returned the courtesy, I held her hand on my chest and said, "Me Henderson. Henderson." The whole court applauded to see how fast I caught on. So I thought, "Hurray for me!" and drew an endless breath into my lungs. . . . The queen expressed stability in every part of her body. (71–72)

The symbology of Queen Willatale is rather obvious, but what might be overlooked is the Adamic role of Henderson; the "endless breath" that he draws marks the beginnings of mankind.

But this man, who is plagued with problems, feels that the queen can help him:

> I believed the queen could straighten me out if she wanted to, as if, any minute now, she might open her hand and show me the thing, the source, the germ—the cipher. The mystery, you know. I was absolutely convinced she must have it. . . . It comforted me just to see her, and I thought I might learn to be sustained too if I followed her example. And altogether I felt my hour of liberation was drawing near when the sleep of the spirit was liable to burst. (79)

And Queen Willatale does indeed see to the roots of this newcomer's longings:

> "Grun-tu-molani," the old queen said.
> "Say, you want to live. Grun-tu-molani. Man want to live." [Itelo translates.]

"Yes, yes, yes! Molani, Me Molani. She sees that? God will reward her, tell her, for saying it to me. I'll reward her myself. I'll annihilate and blast those frogs clear out of that cistern. . . . Not only I molani for myself, but for everybody. I could not bear how sad things have become in the world and so I set out because of this molani. Grun-tu-molani, old lady—old queen. Grun-tu-molani, everybody!" (85)

With joyous gratitude, Henderson, in a moment of illumination, couples his desire to live with the necessity to eliminate the frogs from the cistern. He is now eager to start on what he considers his personal project. Feeling sure that he can help the Arnewi, he says to Itelo: " 'Itelo, you leave this to me, and [I] drew in a sharp breath between my teeth, feeling that I had it in me to be the doom of those frogs. . . . I realized that I would never rest until I had dealt with these creatures and lifted the plague" (61). The prince, who allows Henderson to do as he pleases, merely cautions him, "Mr. Henderson. . . . Do not be carry away." To which Henderson replies, "Ha, ha, Prince—pardon me, but this is where you happen to be wrong. If I don't get carried away I never accomplish anything" (88).

The remedy, to Henderson, is a home-made bomb which he fashions with almost childish enthusiasm. He is a practical man, and this job he can do. With Yankee ingenuity, he uses his shoelace as a fuse, lighter fluid on the fuse, powder from his bullets, and a flashlight case for the shell. And he blows the frogs out of the water with results that are godlike as well as manlike in their indiscriminate destruction—the end of the cistern is also blown out, and all the water escapes into the arid soil.

Henderson is overcome with grief and frustration. Once again his life stands revealed. He simply cannot understand his everlasting failure to achieve something of value. In tears he asks, "Why for once, just once! couldn't I get my heart's desire? I have to be doomed always to bungle" (111). Bellow is saying that this curse, born with Adam and traveling its course up to the present, leaving in its wake a poverty of the soul, is not to be lifted through the genius of scientific and technological achievement; that man in his prideful manipulation of the measurable is likely to be persuaded of godlike abilities that he does not possess; finally, that this blind and willful misapprehension of his limited potentialities can drive man, in spite of good intentions, to destroy the value of life itself, just as the water loses value as it soaks the Arnewi sands. Briefly, Bellow says that man is not God; and for him to mistake his human nature as deity can only result in a disillusioning and despairing sickness of the heart.

"I Want"

While these are the general implications of Henderson's battle with the frogs, Bellow intends a more specific statement. Henderson actually undergoes an existential experience. It will be recalled that the plague of frogs is analogous to the curse that Henderson feels to be his particular burden. The frogs in the water (a symbol of life) are the equivalents of the voices within Henderson's life that cry *"I want, I want."* The issue is the same: to rid life of its contaminating and frustrating elements, whether those elements be frogs or voices. But these frogs, and, by analogy, the voices, are a condition of life; and they belong where they are. Bellow points to the issue when his protagonist notes how the frogs seem to fit in their environment: "There really was a vast number of these creatures woggling and crowding, stroking along with the water slipping over their backs and their mottles, as if they owned the medium" (59–60). And again: "There in their home medium were the creatures, the polliwogs with fat heads and skinny tails and their budding little scratchers, and the mature animals . . ." (107).

Although it is difficult to state precisely what the frogs symbolize, Bellow gives a hint in a descriptive reference to "their emotional throats" (60, 88). In conjecture, they represent those elements within man that are the sources of his imaginative urgings, his intuitive quests, his cravings for extensions of self, his dreams and desires, as well as his memories of past wrongs, his despairs and frustrations, and, over all, the absolute negation of his deep longings for immortality. In any case, Henderson accepts the Arnewi fears of the frogs as his own problem, or he senses in them a symbol of his own problem; and he is most anxious to destroy them in the attempt to purge himself. What he learns, of course, is that man is finally defined by his human condition, which includes his mortality.

This illumination suggests an existential discovery, and Henderson's reactions to the catastrophe that he brings about are directly to the point:

The explosion had blasted out the retaining wall at the front end. The big stone blocks had fallen and the yellow reservoir was emptying fast. "Oh! Hell!" I grabbed my head, immediately dizzy with the nausea of disaster, seeing the water spill like a regular mill race with the remains of those frogs. "Hurry, hurry!" I started to yell. "Romilayu! Itelo! Oh, Judas priest, what's happening! Give a hand. Help, you guys, help!" I threw myself down against the escaping water and tried to breast it back and lift the stones into place. The frogs charged into me like so many prunes and fell into my pants and into the open shoe, the lace gone. . . . It was a moment of horror. . . . Romilayu waded up beside me and did his best, but these blocks of stone were beyond our strength. . . . Anyway, the water was lost—lost! In a matter of minutes I saw (sickening!) the yellow mud of the bottom and the dead frogs settling there. . . . Under me the water of the cistern was turning to hot vapor and the sun was already beginning to corrupt the bodies of the frog dead. (109–10)

The words "dizzy with the nausea of disaster" recall the terms of Sartre and Kierkegaard in their attempt to describe man's reaction to his discovery of his state of absurdity and, further, to describe the consequences of that realization. Henderson's cry of "Oh! Hell!" may be regarded as Sartre's "cry of *nauseé.*" Moreover, Henderson is "sickeningly" aware of the filth and corruption of the landscape and of the dead frogs around him—a state reminiscent of Sartre's description of the world as viewed through the eyes of the "absurd" man. Bellow's careful choice of the word "dizzy" is suggestive of Kierkegaard's term "the dizziness of freedom," which he uses to describe man's reaction to the responsibility that he inherits as a consequence of his discovery of freedom. If man is free, then he is responsible in his actions for no less than the fate of mankind. There are parallels in Henderson's case: he is specifically allowed the freedom to act in his decision to destroy the frogs, and his "dizziness" comes as a painful illumination of his responsibility to the Arnewi.

There are even echoes of Camus in this passage when Henderson fails to lift up the blocks of stone, as if in his present confusion he is not yet ready to enact the role of Sisyphus; and as will be seen, this failure has its sequel as the story progresses. Henderson's inability to estimate properly his mortal condition is reflected in a line of poetry that Henderson finds returning to his thoughts again and again, either in its entirety or in part: "I do remember well the hour that burst my spirit's sleep." He feels that the words are somehow indicative of and perhaps harbingers of this own awakening and release from his spiritual bondage. The line is from Shelley's "Revolt of Islam" (1. 31), a poem dedicated to a throwing off of customs and traditions that everlastingly exert a tyranny over the lives of mankind. Shelley uses this particular line as he explains how he felt when he first saw below the superficial mores of his society and beyond the hypocritical pretensions being passed on from generation to generation that would deny the facts of man's nature, one of which is his mortality. Although we shall later refer to Bellow's use of this line, in this instance the motto of Shelley's poem is especially to the point, not only to Shelley's work but to one of Bellow's major purposes in *Henderson the Rain King:*

> There is no danger to a man that knows
> What life and death is; there's not any law
> Exceeds his knowledge: neither is it lawful
> That he should stoop to any other law.

The first line and a half is of particular significance, for Henderson has yet to discover "what life and death is." His condition springs from the judgment that took place in the Garden of Eden, that man shall die, that he is mortal. That is the source of his human condition. It is not, however, the source of his curse; *he* is the source of that. Not fully aware of "what life and death is," he insists upon godlike illusions, refusing to come to terms with his human condition.

Bellow gives numerous instances of this unconscious arrogance that seems to be deeply imbedded within the character of Henderson. The incident of the burning bush has been cited. Then at another point Henderson relates how, in his opinion, Itelo sees him as a totem pole or as "a human Galapagos turtle" (66), both indicative of his illusions of extended durability. Again, he is given to threats that could only be carried out by Gulliver in Lilliput. When he and Romilayu are taken prisoners as they approach the Wariri lands, he says of his captors, "For a small inducement I would have swept them up in my arms, the whole dozen or so of them, and run them over the cliff" (118). And a few sentences later, "I could have grabbed his gun and made scrap metal of it in one single twist . . ." (119). His gift of a raincoat to Queen Willatale, which is also related to these illusions, is especially significant as it puts to use one of Bellow's favorite symbols—rain as "an emblem of the shared condition of all." Here, Henderson is establishing himself as a power that will protect Queen Willatale from the rain, or from that shared human condition—mortality.

Shelley's line of poetry, then, seems to be something of a still small voice that intermittently calls Henderson to reality, urges him to burst his spirit's sleep and to awaken to his role in the drama of man. Until he does so, he will chase phantoms of immortality which can lead only to a despairing negation of the powers he does possess and to a useless admiration of the less-than-human. That is, when he is continually confronted by the failure of his attainment of the ideal, there is the inclination to renounce the real, his humanity.

Such a result is evident as he relates his thoughts during this grief-filled period: "I had been very downcast, what with the voice that said *I want* and all the rest of it. I had come to look upon the phenomena of life as so many medicines which would either cure my condition or aggravate it. But the condition! Oh, my condition! First and last that condition! It made me go around with my hand on my breast like the old pictures of Montcalm passing away on the Plains of Abraham" (65).

What Henderson seems not to understand is that all of the medicines of human constructions will not cure him of mortality. Contrive and build as he will, compute and analyze as he might, the frogs will still be there. As for the frogs, it is little wonder that he envies them: "They say the air is the final home of the soul, but I think that as far as the senses go you probably can't find a sweeter medium than water. So the life of those frogs must have been beautiful, and they fulfilled their ideal . . ." (88). What Henderson fails to see is that the frogs have no ideal; therefore, they do not suffer the stretches of the imagination, constructing dreams of existence beyond their nature. "I should have been a pair of ragged claws," says Prufrock, with much the same envy of the less-than-human.

To this point, then, Bellow's protagonist acts as archetype for all men who have discovered that the victory over the realities of physical need is not the final battle; that there is another obstacle to an unsullied existence, to a life without frogs, and that that obstacle is the reality of death, the fact of which is ever a check upon the most triumphant moment. Moreover, unlike the reality of want, this reality, the "*I want*" reality of Henderson, is always victorious; it greets man each morning with the sun in spite of his magnificent achievements the day before and it leaves him in despair. More generally, of course, Bellow projects his protagonist in the role of all men in the process of examining their position in nature and coming to an existential illumination.

The Wariri

In the same way that Swift's meaning in *Gulliver's Travels* is complete only with Gulliver's several voyages, Bellow's purposes are dependent on both of Henderson's encounters in Africa, first with the Arnewi and then with the Wariri. The two experiences supplement each other. This connection between the two adventures is established by Bellow as soon as Henderson and Romilayu begin their long, hot journey to the land of the Wariri. Henderson's description of the landscape is significant: "Behind us the high mountains we had emerged from showed their crumbled peaks and prehistoric spines" (115). Ahead of them, however, "there was more wood on the mountains," and there are stone shapes of "towers and acropolises" (113), along with "giant spiders" whose webs are "set up like radar stations" (114).

With their arrival at the Wariri village, Henderson notes "bigger buildings, some of them wooden" (118), with flowers and fences a part of the scene. Moreover, the social organization is relatively sophisticated, with advisors, police chiefs, soldiers, ministers, and other kinds of officials that mark an advanced society. It is evident that Henderson is moving from a prehistoric culture, that of the Arnewi, to a culture that bears a greater resemblance to what is known today as civilization. And, while it is impossible to name, date, and locate this civilization, the use of such terms as "radar" would indicate that Bellow intends at least to include within his scope elements of contemporary civilization. In any case, the contrast seems to function in the interests of bringing Henderson's problems up to date and of offering new perspectives on the same issues.

Through a somewhat detailed analysis of the two major actions in Wariri land, Bellow's foremost aims may at least be conjectured. The first of these actions has to do with Henderson's appointment as the rain king when King Dahfu—with whom Prince Itelo had gone to college in Beirut, and of whom Itelo had spoken to Henderson several times—invites Henderson to be present at the rain ritual. The Wariri need water too, although not so desperately as the Arnewi. The ritual consists of two parts: first, Dahfu and a young lady play a nightmarish game of catch with two skulls which Henderson finds out later to be the remains of Dahfu's father and grandfather. While Henderson cannot help admiring the grace and skill exhibited by Dahfu and his opponent, he feels there is something ominous about the game. The main part of the ceremony is equally weird: a large number of wooden gods are placed in the center of an arena to be whipped, kicked, and subjected to all kinds of indignities by a large number of the Wariri people, much to the joyful shouts of the audience. Then, one by one, the figures are carried to another location some twenty feet away. Finally, only two figures are left: Hummat, the mountain god, and Mummah, the goddess of clouds. One of the local strong men manages to move Hummat, but he fails in his effort to budge Mummah, the larger of the two. Henderson offers and then even begs to be of assistance; he succeeds:

> I stood still. There beside Mummah in her new situation I myself was filled with happiness. I was so gladdened by what I had done that my whole body was filled with soft heat, with soft and sacred light. The sensations of illness I had experienced since morning were all converted into their opposites. These same unhappy feelings were changed into warmth and personal luxury. . . . My spirit was awake and it welcomed life anew. Damn the whole thing! Life anew! I was still alive and kicking and I had the old grun-tu-molani. . . . I went back to sit beside Dahfu's hammock and wiped my face with a handkerchief, for I was annointed with sweat. (192–93)

With this epiphany Henderson bursts his spirit's sleep. He is now Sungo, or rain king. And, with the use of the terms "sacred light" and "annointed with sweat," Bellow would have it understood that this is an experience of depth, a spiritual enlightenment of great significance. Bellow also intends a comparison between Henderson's failure with the Arnewi and his success with the Wariri. The differences are highly functional. In the case of Mummah, Henderson relies only on his own strength, contrary to his exhibition of technical ingenuity with the frogs. Obviously, Bellow is saying that the bursting of the spirit's sleep must be accomplished by man's own resources. "I had the old grun-tu-maloni," Henderson shouts, and he feels "life anew," but only because he of himself worked at it and did something of value.

There are other implications in this event. In the "Revolt of Islam," in the first several lines of the third stanza of the introduction, Shelley writes:

> Thoughts of great deeds were mine, dear
> Friend [Mary Godwin], when first
> The clouds which wrap this world from
> Youth did pass.
> I do remember well the hour which burst
> My spirit's sleep.

This awakening is precisely what has happened to Henderson, for Mummah is goddess of the clouds. Henderson moves the clouds which had wrapped his world in the same way that the world is wrapped or hidden from the child. He comes to an awareness much like Wordsworth describes in his Tintern Abbey ode when the poet explains, "For I have learned / To look on nature, not as in the hour / Of thoughtless youth. . . ." And, if for the moment we can return to the Arnewi, it is Queen Willatale who informs Henderson that he is still looking at the world as a child might. As Itelo translates it, "She say . . . world is strange to a child. You not a child, sir?" (84). But Henderson has lived the vision of a child; with his world wrapped in clouds, he has not known "what life and death is."

To this point, Henderson's experiences have been a clearing away project, a pushing aside of the dead wood that he has been stumbling over: the clutter and confusion of the mind of a man unwilling or unable to see himself without illusions and without the need for mad, furious constructions to support those illusions. And, when the rains come down in deluge, Bellow is once again depicting this purgation of confusion through a dramatization of the shared condition of humanity.

Henderson's triumphant happiness, however, is short-lived. No sooner is he appointed Sungo than he is subjected to indignities that completely shatter his spirit. He is stripped of his clothing, garbed in a few thin weeds, and forced to become a part of a wild, howling mob that dashes about the village. His bare feet are bruised and cut; he is lashed by blind, frenzied, and indiscriminate whips; and, finally, he is seized and thrown into a muddy, stinking cattle pond: "Nor was any humor intended. All was done in the greatest earnestness. I came, dripping stale mud, out of the pond. I hoped at least this would cover my shame, for the flimsy grasses, flying, had left everything open" (199).

Bellow's intentions are clear: he is saying that the first reaction of man upon the realization of his humanness is a feeling of pain, degradation, and shame in his spiritual nakedness, just as Adam and Eve felt a like reaction when their mortality was established. Henderson's arising from the ooze and mud is an obvious reference to man's origins, as well as an indication of Henderson's final immersion into the facts of his own existence. As he surveys the effects of his "life anew," these facts appear most brutal and discouraging:

> This is how I became the rain king. I guess it served me right for mixing into matters that were none of my damned business. But the thing had been irresistible, one of those drives which there was no question of fighting. And what had I got myself into? What were the consequences? On the ground floor of the palace, filthy, naked, and bruised, I lay in a little room. The rain was falling, drowning the town, dropping from the roof in heavy fringes, witchlike and gloomy. Shivering, I covered myself with hides and stared with circular eyes, wrapped to the chin in the skins of unknown animals.
> (203)

In a Lear-like setting, and certainly with Lear-like implications of the stripping of man to essentials, Henderson looks like nothing so much as a half-drowned tarsier, with its staring "circular eyes." He has reached the depths, but these are not the depths of understanding that confront Lear. It is the reader who sees while Henderson experiences. When Romilayu asks him, "Whu fo' you did it, sah?"—Henderson can offer no explanation: "'Oh, Romilayu . . . if I could explain that I wouldn't be where I am today. . . . The whole thing is so peculiar the explanation will have to be peculiar too. Figuring will get me nowhere, it's only illumination that I have to wait for.' And thinking of how black things were and how absent any illumination was I sighed and moaned again" (204).

Dahfu and the Lion

In any case, with the bursting of his spirit's sleep and with the shattering beginnings of his "life anew," Henderson turns to King Kahfu, who introduces him to the extensions of *grun-tu-molani*: "I know that Arnewi expression. . . . Yes I have been there, too, with Itelo. I understand what this grun-tu-molani implies. Indeed I do. . . . Granted, grun-tu-molani is much, but it is not alone sufficient. Mr. Henderson, more is required. I can show you something now— something without which you will never understand thoroughly my special aim nor my point of view" (217–18).

Thus begins another descent into the depths toward illumination, for Dahfu takes Henderson to a chamber deep in the underground where he keeps Atti, a lioness. Henderson is half out of his mind with fear, but Dahfu insists that he become friends with Atti. Many hours (and many pages) are spent in these surroundings, with Dahfu and Henderson philosophizing on the nature of man; but Dahfu is the instructor. Briefly, Dahfu contends that a man may become whatever he chooses. "It is all a matter of having a desirable model in the cortex. For the noble self-conception is everything. For as conception is, so the fellow is. Put differently, you are in the flesh as your soul is. And in the manner described a fellow really is the artist of himself" (268).

Day after day there follow *lion lessons* with Dahfu assuring Henderson that, if he acts like a lion, he will take on the attributes of the lion. He will achieve the fearless equanimity of Atti because, as he explains, "Observe that Atti is all lion. Does not take issue with the inherent. Is one hundred per cent within the given" (263). In spite of his doubts, Henderson gets down on his hands, posterior in the air, balances on his toes, and roars like a lion. Yet he never manages a great deal of faith: "I would never make a lion, I knew that; but I might pick up a small gain here and there in the attempt" (298). His admiration for Dahfu is the only thing that keeps him at his transformative efforts.

Henderson does indeed have a great deal of faith in Dahfu as a person because he faces the world and its reality without illusion and totally without fear—in short, with the courage of a lion: "Why . . . there's something about danger that doesn't perplex that guy. Look at all the things he has to fear, and still look at the way he lies on that sofa . . . But on the table near him he has those two skulls used at the rain ceremony, one his father's and the other his grandfather's" (277).

Dahfu seems to live the lesson that Henderson learned when he burst his spirit's sleep: in the midst of life, he is in death. Dahfu knows "what life and death is," and keeps ever-present reminders about as a part of that existence. It is the attitude of Atti, acting "one hundred per cent within the given," accepting precisely that which one is and no more. Yet, again, Bellow shows his protagonist as a doubtful student; he simply cannot share Dahfu's confidence: "But then what could an animal do for me? In the last analysis? Really? A beast of prey? Even supposing that an animal enjoys a natural blessing? We had our share of this creature—blessing until infancy ended. But now aren't we re-quired to complete something else—project number two—the second blessing? I couldn't tell such things to the king, he was so stuck on lions" (288).

To understand the full significance of the lion symbology, we must recall that the Wariri system of political progression is based on this animal. As Dahfu explains, when Henderson is envying him all of the attention he receives from his many wives,

> These same ladies, so inordinate of attention, will report me [when he has lost his youthfulness and strength] and then the Bunam who is chief priest here, with other priests of the association, will convey me out into the bush and there I will be strangled. . . . I am telling you with utmost faithfulness what a king of us, the Wariri, may look forward to. The priest will attend until a maggot is seen upon my dead person and he will wrap it in a slice of silk and bring it to the people. He will show it in public pronouncing and declaring it to be the king's soul, my soul. Then he will re-enter the bush and, a given time elapsing, he will carry to town a lion's cub, explaining that the maggot has now experienced a conversion into a lion. And after another interval, they will announce to the people the fact that the lion has converted into the next king. This will be my successor. (157)
> Well, then . . . this very young animal, set free by the Bunam, the successor king has to capture it within a year or two when it is grown. (209)

Dahfu's authority—indeed, his very existence—is founded upon the contrived relationship between him and lions. And so taken is he with this relationship that his only real pleasure seems to come from the strengthening of it. Dahfu seems to regard his people with extreme indifference, even his mother, whom he rarely bothers to see. In fact, at times he shows only disdain for those about him.

In view of all the winding philosophical discussions between Dahfu and Henderson concerning man and his life and destiny, Bellow's purposes are apt to get lost in the confusion. But essentially what Bellow has in mind with Dahfu and his lions is the same thing that Swift depicts in the relationship that evolves between Gulliver and the Houyhnhnms. Gulliver, too, reaches the point at which humanity seems inferior to the animal—horses, in his case. And, like Gulliver, Dahfu attempts to imitate and even to become the animal. What Bellow does, however, is to introduce a healthy doubt as to the efficacy of this animal-human relationship, although, as Henderson says, he "might pick up a small gain here and there."

In order to understand more clearly the position of Dahfu in this story, it is necessary to go into some detail concerning the lioness Atti and Dahfu's final days. Atti is persona non grata to all of the Wariri except Dahfu. She is an imposter, not the lion that holds the spirit of Dahfu's predecessor. However, Dahfu will not forego her companionship because he feels that she is largely responsible for his strength of spirit and for his ability to live "one hundred per cent within the given." Toward the end of the novel, the lion that is thought to hold the "right" spirit is located; and when Dahfu must try to capture it, he invites Henderson to share the extremely dangerous venture. Finally, perched on a precarious strip of wood, high above the trap into which this lion is driven, Dahfu prepares the net with which he is to make the capture. Henderson, alongside Dahfu, relates the scene:

Then, at the very doors of consciousness, there was a snarl and I looked down from this straw perch—I was on my knees—into the big, angry, hair-framed face of the lion. It was all wrinkled, contracted; within those wrinkles was the darkness of murder. The lips were drawn away from the gums, and the breath of the animal came over me, hot as oblivion, raw as blood. I started to speak aloud. I said, "Oh my God, whatever You think of me, let me not fall under this butcher shop. Take care of the king. Show him Thy mercy." And to this, as a rider, the thought added itself that this was all mankind needed, to be conditioned into the image of a ferocious animal like the one below. I then tried to tell myself because of the clearness of those enraged eyes that only visions ever got so hyperactual. But it was no vision. The snarling of this animal was indeed the voice of death. And I thought how I had boasted to my dear Lily how I loved reality. "I love it more than you do," I had said. But oh, unreality! Unreality, unreality! That has been my scheme for a troubled but eternal life. But now I was blasted away from this practice by the throat of the lion. His voice was like a blow at the back of my head. (306–7)

This voice is the voice of reality—the voice of truth that Henderson has always felt comes in blows (23, 213). This lion is death itself, not an Atti ("Compared with this creature, Atti was no bigger than a lynx" [307]) that one plays games with, deceiving himself that he is living with the truth well in hand. And the idea that mankind should for one moment allow itself to be cast into such an image horrifies Henderson. Even Dahfu could not completely know *this* vision of reality. How ironic that he places such a high value on Atti, who turns out to be just another construction to shield him from the fact itself, and ironic too when he urges Henderson to learn from Atti: "The poet says, 'The tigers of wrath are wiser than the heroes of instruction.' Let us embrace lions also in the same view" (260). When Dahfu is killed by this lion in an embrace of lightning-clawed murder, Bellow is saying that to base one's existence and position on the fiction of a claimed animal nature can only result in death. Besides, it turns out that the lion isn't the right one anyway. So perhaps Bellow intends the reader to understand that the whole Wariri system is a fiction through which Dahfu is deceived into destroying himself.

To bring the story to a close, Dahfu, as he is dying, tells Henderson that as Sungo he is the next king. But he and Romilayu manage to escape this fate; and, after several days of agonizing travel on foot and of subsisting on worms and locusts, they return to civilization. Before leaving the Wariri, however, Henderson insists on taking the lion cub that was staked out by the corpse of Dahfu, the cub that is supposed to hold within it the soul of the dead king. Bidding Romilayu good-by, Henderson, with his cub, flies toward home. On the plane he makes friends with a small boy, a refugee, an orphan "bound for Nevada with nothing but a Persian vocabulary" (339). The boy, who is going to live with some people who are adopting him, and the lion cub are Henderson's only companions. When the aircraft lands briefly—significantly, in Newfoundland—Henderson playfully and joyfully takes the boy on his back and runs, leaping and laughing, around the plane: "And the lion? He was in it, too. Laps and laps I galloped around the shining and riveted body of the plane. . . . The great, beautiful propellers were still, all four of them. I guess I felt it was my turn now to move, and so went running—leaping, pounding, and tingling over the pure white lining of the gray Arctic silence" (340–41).

A Success Story

Henderson's two visits in Africa really make for a whole as far as Bellow's intentions go. If understood as a whole, it seems that once again Bellow puts his protagonist through experiences that suggest the subangelic position of man. First, we see through Henderson's life with the Arnewi that man is not divinity, is not God. On the other hand, as Henderson lives with Dahfu and the Wariri, it is clear that neither is he animal. Man cannot become an animal any more than he can become God. Perhaps there is a little of both in man, as Bellow seems to hint when he gives to Henderson as companions the cub and the boy who, Henderson sees, is "still trailing his clouds of glory." But Henderson adds to this observation, "I dragged mine on as long as I could till it got dingy, mere tatters of gray fog. *However, I always knew what it was* [italics mine]" (339), as if to say that, while he has been divested of painful and hopeless illusions of immortal divinity, he has not been reduced to the animal state that denies all the implications of these "clouds of glory"—perhaps his godlike reason, his imagination, and most of all his ability to love. For within the last few paragraphs, he asserts, "Once more. Whatever gains I ever made were always due to love and nothing else" (339).

In any case, the optimism of Bellow can be seen if the return of Henderson is compared with that of Gulliver. Swift's protagonist, who is shattered beyond repair, has seen his yahoo nature and cannot recover from the vision. His only salvation lies in becoming like the Houyhnhnms, the impossibility of which drives him beyond peace and sanity. Henderson is exposed to the same dismal vision of himself as he suffers the consequences of bursting his spirit's sleep. Like Gulliver, he is almost drawn into this animal world, first by Dahfu's educative efforts and then through the laws of the Wariri. But through his own strength, and with much suffering, he walks away from and out of this fate. He returns to his home with an attitude completely contrary to that of

Gulliver. As he tells the airline stewardess: "You know why I'm impatient to see my wife, Miss? I'm eager to know how it will be now that the sleep is burst. And the children, too. I love them very much—I think" (335).

The story of *Henderson the Rain King,* then, is a success story of a man who achieves peace and contentment (or at least "the world has removed its wrath" from him) through an illumination of his subangelic nature, an illumination not to be confused with knowledge—Bellow leaves that to the reader. Henderson does know, however, that "there is justice. I believe there is justice, and that much is promised. Though I am not what I thought" (328).

Chapter Six
Herzog

As the novel *Herzog* (1964) opens, protagonist Moses E. Herzog is strolling around the grounds of his neglected, weather-beaten house in the mountains of Massachusetts. He is pale, weak, and distracted. Yet, as he enjoys the details of his natural surroundings, there is an air about him that hints at convalescence; it is as if, in spite of his distraction, his life has taken on a certain tranquillity, a new meaning, a promising expectancy. The narrator observes that, "though he [Herzog] still behaved oddly, he felt confident, cheerful, clairvoyant, and strong."[1] And within a few pages it is clear that Herzog is now indeed in a realtively healthy state, for this hopeful beginning is juxtaposed to a backward flight in time that depicts the slough of despair from which he has just emerged.

From these hints of well-being at the beginning of the novel, Bellow intends this work to be another depiction of man's subangelic possibilities: we can anticipate that the protagonist, after confrontations that call for intensive soul-searching examinations, will reach a viable position from which he can live a life founded on a measure of dignity and integrity.

This chapter considers the three levels of meaning of *Herzog*: at the first level, the protagonist plays the role of the innocent in the time-honored plight of illusion versus reality, of naivete versus experience; on the second he assumes the figure of the intellectual who is suffering from self-doubts concerning his own social relevance; on the third, he acts as a symbol of a general human condition. Each level may be evaluated in terms of its meaningfulness to the form of the novel as a whole as well as to the extent that it satisfies a rounded interpretation of Bellow's hero. These levels constantly overlap in the actual working-out of the novel; but, in the interests of clarifying the author's intentions, we shall attempt to see them as entities.

Some light must be shed on the condition of the protagonist as Bellow sets the backward action in motion. Moses E. Herzog lives in a small apartment in New York City. In the evening he teaches a couple of adult classes. In a state of emotional and intellectual chaos, he spends much of his time in random, disconnected thought that often takes its form in imaginary letter writing. Small wonder that he has much to think about: he has been twice married; twice divorced; turned out of his own house by his second wife Madeleine, adulteress; betrayed by his best friend Gersbach, adulterer; deprived of his young daughter; ignominiously bullied and used by his psychiatrist, his lawyer, and his doctor; pitied by his family and friends; unable to pursue his academic profession; and financially desperate. It is understandable, then, that "Late in spring Herzog had been overcome by the need to explain, to have it out, to justify, to put in perspective, to clarify, to make amends" (2).

Herzog cannot make any sense of his present situation nor of the forces that brought about his situation when his career was still largely before him and when he was settled in his personal life with his first wife Daisy. Herzog, clearly bewildered, offers only vague information: "What actually happened? I gave up the shelter of an orderly, purposeful, lawful existence because it bored me, and I felt it was simply a slacker's life" (103). Herzog, the innocent, has lost himself in deep woods: with a full heart he has wandered out of his element and has caught the full force of a reality that challenges his sanity. The conflict is Herzog versus the world and its ugliness. Time and again, Bellow's protagonist finds himself face to face with walls of brute fact, as when he learns of the deceptions of Madeleine and her mother, or when he discovers the affair between Gersbach and his wife, or again in the courtroom scene when as a casual observer he leaves the room in a sickened state because of his insight into man's inhumanity and into the callous workings of the law.

Almost every character that Bellow introduces into his work becomes for Herzog a source of what is often a very painful illumination. His is a case of the instructor instructed, with one of the high points of irony arising when one of the professor's students, his baby-sitter Geraldine Portnoy, assumes the role of instructor and teaches him of the infidelity of his wife. In her letter, Geraldine also feels it necessary to explain to Herzog the psychology of his relationship to Madeleine, not to mention a few lines concerning child psychology in the interest of his young daughter. This constant exposure to brutality is too much for Herzog. He comes to regard life as his personal instruction in reality, even bitterly giving the name of "reality instructors" to his many teachers.

Herzog, the romantic, cannot cope with a world based on principles alien to his own heartfelt visions and to his own orderly view of life. This man, who "practiced the art of circling among random facts to swoop down on the essentials" (10), finds that the facts are blinding and that the essentials are lost in the dark. But, paradoxically, he cannot relinquish his private view of the world. In one of his many desperate letters he refutes the apocalyptic implications of his recent experiences, "Very tired of the modern form of historicism which sees in this civilization the defeat of the best hopes of Western religion and thought . . ." (106). In spite of the indignities to which he is subjected, Herzog cannot take on the worldly cynicism that seems to surround him. He insists, like Augie, on a better fate.

While Bellow's novel is clearly concerned with the theme of innocence versus worldliness, any consequent resolution can end only in a partial vision, or worse, in a distorted one. This theme bypasses the storm that rages within Bellow's protagonist—and this storm is what the novel is about. Such a theme ordinarily takes place in the struggles of the protagonist with the world; in Bellow's novel, that struggle fails to lend itself to any sustained development. The reason is simple: though Herzog is an innocent and though he does confront reality, the confrontation occurs for the most part within the protagonist.

Self-doubt

The understanding of a broader scope in *Herzog,* however, depends to some extent on seeing in the first chapter Bellow's indications that his protagonist is going through a form of psychoanalysis. It is not an accident that the backward action begins with Herzog lying on a sofa and ends on the last page of the book with Herzog lying on his Recamier couch. Over and over Bellow repeats the description of his hero's physical position in connection with his self-examination:

Lying on the sofa of the kitchenette apartment he had rented on 17th Street, he sometimes imagined he was an industry that manufactured personal history, and saw himself from birth to death. (3)

He went on taking stock, lying face down on the sofa. (3)

Satisfied with his own severity, positively enjoying the hardness and factual rigor of his judgment, he lay on his sofa. (5)

Herzog from his sofa in New York now contemplated. . . . (8)

In his posture of collapse on the sofa, arms abandoned over his head . . . .
(10–11)

Obviously Bellow wants the reader to see Herzog in the position of a mental patient who is trying to create some order out of personal chaos. Thus Herzog's mind is the setting for the action, much of it backward moving. Many of the events, scenes, and characters are thus, in terms of good psychiatric dogma, abstractions or symbols of forces that play upon his mind. For example, Daisy, in all her orderliness, is a symbolic reflection of his life at the university. If the novel is a study of man's mind, as indeed it is, the reader is forced to interpret what goes on in that mind. The difficulty of such examination is compounded by the fact that the mind is in a state of rebellion, a condition symbolically established when the reader is told that Herzog carries in his pocket a copy of Pratt's *History of the Civil War* (105).

The scope of the novel broadens if we are to recognize that Bellow is projecting the image of an intellectual (humanist, writer) who, because he cannot reconcile his own existence with the world in which he lives, suffers a sense of noninvolvement as he comes to doubt his relevance to life around him. These self-immolating feelings of inutility to which the intellectual often subjects himself are precisely responsible for Herzog's view of himself as "leading a slacker's life" at the university. Bellow makes this conflict clear in a number of ways. For example, when Herzog was finishing work on his volume *Romanticism and Christianity*, the "heavy silence" he feels is representative of his demeaning self-appraisal: "Of course a wife's duty was to stand by this puzzling and often disagreeable Herzog. She did so with heavy neutrality, recording her objections each time—once but not more. The rest was silence—such heavy silence as he felt in Connecticut when he was finishing *Romanticism and Christianity*" (127).

Herzog issues a like judgment on his own value through another incident that takes place when he returns to his long-vacated house in

Massachusetts: "Someone came in the night and left a used sanitary napkin in a covered dish on his desk, where he kept bundles of notes for his Romantic studies. That was his reception by the natives. A momentary light of self-humor passed over his face . . ." (48–49). Herzog cannot help contrasting the bluntly realistic function of the napkin, and its immediate utility, with the role of his own work, whose content is transcendental by nature and whose utility seems to be far from immediate. At least his own personal life hardly offers itself in support of the value of a romantic, idealistic interpretation of existence.

Then in other ways Bellow makes clear Herzog's felt isolation. The "greased tracks, power, efficient black machinery" of the elevator that Herzog hears (26) suggests to him a denigrating contrast to his own endeavors: the elevator is functional; there is no doubt as to its value and place in society. So it is with the construction work going on outside his window: "They were demolishing and raising buildings. The Avenue was filled with concrete-mixing trucks, smells of wet sand and powdery gray cement. Crashing, stamping pile-driving below, and, higher, structural steel, interminably and hungrily going up into the cooler, more delicate blue. . . . He had to get to the seashore where he could breathe" (32).

In this active world, things are happening, tangible things of a value that all society recognizes and pays homage to; but such is not the case in Herzog's world. His value, he feels, is in serious doubt. His book which "younger historians" have praised for the way it looks "at the past with an intense need for contemporary relevance" (5) provides us with an excellent clue to Bellow's symbolic intent. The phrase "an intense need for contemporary relevance" is a clear, appropriate description of Herzog's insecurity—and, incidentally, a good one of the contextual framework of the novel itself. Wherever Herzog looks, indeed whatever he senses, regardless of whether his attention is given to the past or to the present, he feels an alienation and, even worse, a uselessness, as if his life were an activity of wasted and misplaced effort.

This second level approach has other merits, not the least of which is the exposition of the dilemma that often comes from an intellectual suspension of judgment, an attitude not without its value but also one that at times leads to a passivity of purpose, a loss of the name of action, reminiscent of a Hamlet personality.[2] When Herzog goes to his lawyer for advice, he is bullied into buying an insurance policy; he allows Ramona, his mistress, to lecture him endlessly, in spite of his annoyance; in silence, he passes over the rudeness of a store clerk. The sharpest instance of his quietude is shown when he allows Gersbach to take Madeleine's diaphragm to Boston, where she is visiting. Herzog is aggressive enough to question her later about the incident, but he has nothing to say when she tells him that he is unworthy of an answer.

One of Bellow's meanings, then, concerns the intellectual who lacks confidence in the value of self. By nature, Herzog is passive, unable or unwilling not only to express his own importance to himself in meaningful terms but to define his value in a society that does not pay him what he feels to be his due respect. All of his work and all of his ideals seem at odds with the activity and the facts of the world about him. When Herzog leaves the university, when he becomes so irascible and unstable that Daisy leaves him, his self-doubts are at the bottom of his anxiety. Briefly, his trouble lies in a lack of self-definition, which leads to a confusion that can find an outlet only in an ironic view of himself. In this view he sees himself as something like a patient etherized upon a table:

> That [had] brought him to consider his character. What sort of character was it? Well in the modern vocabulary, it was narcissistic; it was masochistic; it was anachronistic. His clinical picture was depressive. . . . Resuming his self-examination, he admitted that he had been a bad husband—twice. Daisy, his first wife, he had treated miserably. . . . To his son and his daughter he was a loving but bad father. To his own parents he had been an ungrateful child. . . . To his brothers and his sister, affectionate but remote. With his friends, an egotist. With love, lazy. With brightness, dull. With power, passive. With his own soul, evasive. (4–5)

Herzog—the noncommitted intellectual, the observer, living in no man's land, the self-loving egotist—keeps on drinking and cursing the light, half believing that by nature his case is hopeless.

Bellow develops this theme of the socially maladjusted intellectual or humanist by projecting Herzog through a series of experiences that culminate in purging his mind of distractions. These experiences, for the most part, consist of confrontations with characters who act out their roles in the forms of these distractions: they are symbols of forces that lead Herzog into his confused state. These confrontations, which occur throughout the novel, serve as appropriately placed stepping stones to the next level of meaning.

Contradictions

Herzog as a universal figure represents, on the third level of meaning, a struggle that has been operative since man's beginnings. This struggle is particularly evident today when, owing to all kinds of developmental knowledge and to a runaway population, man seems to be especially subjected to a thwarting, masochistic, disintegrative self-examination that often leaves him as nothing more substantial than a few cents worth of chemicals, which are already a drug on the market. Specifically, this ultimate theme is built upon man's inability to come to terms with his own nature; and Moses E. Herzog, acting as Everyman, is torn between elements, "more or less stable, more or less controllable, more or less mad" (16). This old theme goes back to the medieval debates between body and soul, and even further back to the dramatic agonies of the Greeks. On this third level, Bellow projects his protagonist through three stages: first, he accounts for Herzog's disturbed condition; second, he renders the manifestations of that condition; and, third, he offers a resolution which provides a release from that condition.

To understand what Bellow intends concerning the wellsprings of Herzog's conflict, we should recall that the story may be envisioned as a psychiatric venture, as an accounting for motives through a search into Herzog's past. As Herzog recreates his experiences, the reader has to interpret them and make them meaningful. For example, as the backward action begins, Bellow carefully specifies (through Herzog as narrator) the academic accomplishments of his hero; in so doing, Bellow establishes his thesis:

> He had made a brilliant start in his Ph.D. thesis—*The State of Nature in 17th and 18th Century English and French Political Philosophy*. He had to his credit also several articles and a book, *Romanticism and Christianity* . . . . The Narragansett Corporation had paid him fifteen thousand dollars over a

number of years to continue his studies in Romanticism. The results lay in
the closet, in an old valise—eight hundred pages of chaotic argument which
had never found its focus. It was painful to think of it. (4)

A few paragraphs later, Herzog explains one of his motives in moving to
Ludeyville, Massachusetts:

> In the peaceful Berkshires where he had friends (the Valentine Gersbachs)
> it should be easy to write his second volume on the social ideas of the
> Romantics.
> Herzog did not leave academic life because he was doing badly. On the
> contrary, his reputation was good. His thesis had been influential and was
> translated into French and German. His early book, not much noticed when
> it was published, was now on many reading lists, and the younger generation
> of historians accepted it as a model of the new sort of history, "history that
> interests *us*"—and looks at the past with an intense need for contemporary
> relevance. As long as Moses was married to Daisy, he had led the perfectly
> ordinary life of an assistant professor, respected and stable. His first work
> showed by objective research what Christianity was to Romanticism. In the
> second he was becoming tougher, more assertive, more ambitious. There was
> a great deal of ruggedness, actually, in his character. He had a strong will
> and a talent for polemics. . . . But he couldn't deceive himself about this
> work. He was beginning seriously to distrust it. His ambitions received a
> sharp check. Hegel was giving him a great deal of trouble. Ten years earlier
> he had been certain he understood his ideas on concensus and civility, but
> something had gone wrong. He was distressed, impatient, angry. At the
> same time, he and his wife were behaving very peculiarly. She was dissatis-
> fied. (5–6)

These few representative passages show how the author intends Herzog's past *in general* and the academic side of it *in particular* to mirror the
causes and effects of his rebellion and subsequent condition.

Bellow sets his universal conflict in motion through the implications
of the titles of Herzog's thesis and book. These two works are representative of the mind of his protagonist. First, the thesis directly suggests a
life of the reason and intellect. Second, and in manifest opposition, the
book clearly implies an impulse of the emotions and of the heart. These
counterclaims make for Herzog's struggle, and the everlasting struggle
of all men. But, if we set aside Herzog's academic work and concentrate

upon Bellow's development of his protagonist as a universal figure caught between reason and emotion, we find that the conflict is in Herzog's life itself.

In the feelings of Herzog toward his mistress Ramona, he is fully aware of the biological phenomena involved in his sexual encounters with her. When she enters from her bedroom to her living room, she is greeted with a kind of eager passivity: "She knew what she was up to. The warm odor, the downy arms, the fine bust and excellent white teeth and slightly bowed legs—they all worked" (16). Herzog is contemptuous of himself for being a part of this biology, for being drawn to an activity that he knows holds no answers for him, that in fact only seems to demean him. He feels compelled to speak to her on this subject in an imaginary letter: "You are a great comfort to me. . . . It's true. I have a wild spirit in me though I look meek and mild. You think that sexual pleasure is all this spirit wants, and since we are giving him that sexual pleasure, then why shouldn't everything be well?" (16). In spite of his knowledge, there is no escaping Ramona's appeal. At the end of the novel, Ramona visits him in Ludeyville: "as almost always, he heard the deep, the cosmic, the idiotic masculine response—quack. The progenitive, the lustful quacking in the depths. *Quack. Quack*" (237).

Through the medium of sex Bellow is showing Herzog to be deeply bewildered and genuinely disturbed by forces that drive him to activities that are, in the last analysis, everlastingly unsatisfying. This clear debate between the body and soul, between the reason and the emotions, is a struggle that is reminiscent of the dilemma of Prufrock, who, too, is captivated and repelled by "downy arms." Herzog, like Prufrock, is feelingly aware of his plight: "When he jeered in private at the Dionysiac revival it was himself he made fun of" (186).

In other instances of these contradictions, he looks with disdain upon the underworld, the hoodlum element with its crime czars; but, attracted by their power, he confesses that he is flattered to be in the company of one who is on the fringes of that world (35). Herzog is repelled by violence, but he feels its strong pull almost to the point of murdering Gersbach and Madeleine. Against his better judgment, this man of the intellect and heart admires physical strength and raw power.

Herzog does not always see the source of his chaos so clearly. There are those *felt* cases in which an irony of circumstances infringes on his consciousness but does not gain the focus of his attention. At one point, for example, his cab is stopped in a district in which a wrecking crew is working. Reflecting upon the world's anarchic condition, he desperately insists in one of his letters, " 'Reason exists! Reason. . . .' He then heard the soft dense rumbling of falling masonry, the splintering of wood and glass" (165). This image of destruction indicates Herzog's inner sense of doubt concerning the viability of what he stands for. In the same ironic vein, Bellow's hero feels or at least senses the irony of a cold, distant institution such as the Narragansett Corporation that subsidizes studies in romanticism. What Herzog senses is a charitable gratuity, a pat on the head from this machine, that makes a man subconsciously doubt his value.

It is easily understandable that in his projected study Herzog fails to find a focus and fails to make coherent the social ideas of the romantics, for his personal failures lie in his inability to integrate *himself* into a social coherence. It is equally understandable that he no longer understands Hegel, the master synthesizer. Herzog once understood him, ten years ago at the university, when "objective research" was possible. But with the completion of his book *Romanticism and Christianity* together with his thesis, the opposing armies—the mind and the heart—clashed in "heavy silence"; and now all he knows about Hegel's dialectic is that, like prayer for Huck Finn, it does not work out for him. Yet exactly what he cries out for is a positive relationship between the mind and the heart, between thought and action. There is a heartfelt urgency to his jotted parody, "What this country needs is a good five-cent synthesis" (207).

Through his protagonist, then, Bellow projects the image of a man who lacks a self-definition. Much like Hawthorne's Young Goodman Brown, Herzog has discovered seemingly contradictory truths about himself and is thrown into depths of self-doubt through that discovery. Bellow's Everyman has feelings of love, sex, and power that affront his intellect; he has ideals that are subjected to sharp modifications and even blunt denials. He cannot stand the inconsistency, and he insists that there must be some breakthrough into an existence that reconciles these warring elements and brings them working together in harmony. The vision of such a utopia, or rather the frustrated longing for such a utopian existence, is what leads Herzog into rebellion; and, when the backward action begins, he is seeking within himself for some meaning for his failure to achieve that reconciliation after his rebellion.

Symbols of the Mind

In the first chapter of the novel, Herzog goes to see Dr. Emmerich for a physical examination. Dr. Emmerich says, "I heard of your divorce—who told me? I am sorry about it." Herzog replies aphoristically in a quick note, "looking for happiness—ought to be prepared for bad results." Then the narrator states, "Emmerich put on his Ben Franklin eyeglasses and wrote a few words on the file card" (14). So Poor Herzog's Almanac takes shape. Herzog leaves his "orderly, purposeful, lawful existence" to look for the synthesis that will bring him happiness; in so doing, he is confronted by events that lead him to his sofa in his New York apartment, feeling much the same, no doubt, as Johnson's Rasselas feels at the end of his journey: to look for happiness is to chase the horizon. And Herzog does chase—Wanda, Sono, Zinka, Madeleine, Ramona. "(What a lot of romances! thought Herzog. One after another. Were those my real career?)" (166). "A strange heart," he scribbles of himself. "I myself can't account for it" (14). "Winning as he weeps, weeping as he wins. Evidently can't believe in victories" (16).

Herzog's life after he has left the university is intended by Bellow to reflect the twisting and turning search of man as he seeks a higher self, a synthesis. Each of his confrontations with other characters represents a segment of that search. But we must remember that Herzog's mind is being examined and that each of these characters may be properly thought of as extensions of that mind. Daisy is therefore a reflection of his academic life; in this sense, she is a part of Herzog's condition:

His early book . . . was now on many reading lists, and the younger generation of historians accepted it as a model of the new sort of history . . . [it] looks at the past with an intense need for contemporary relevance. *As long as Moses was married to Daisy, he had led the perfectly ordinary life of an assistant professor, respected and stable* [italics mine]. His first work showed by objective research what Christianity was to Romanticism. (5–6)

The line italicized that describes Herzog's domestic life seems to be out of context, placed as it is within an account of Herzog the scholar. But with this strategic juxtapositioning the author encompasses his intentions that Herzog's relationship to Daisy and Herzog's intellectual endeavors are to be regarded as pieces of a whole, a state of mind. And, if we read closely in the following passage, it is possible to recognize in the description of Daisy the characteristics from which Herzog is escaping:

> She was childishly systematic about things. It sometimes amused Moses to recall that she had a file card . . . to cover every situation. . . . When they were married she put his pocket money in an envelope, in a green metal file bought for budgeting. Daily reminders, bills, concert tickets were pinned by thumbtacks to the bulletin board. Calendars were marked well in advance. Stability, symmetry, order, containment were Daisy's strength . . . . *By my irregularity and turbulence of spirit I brought out the very worst in Daisy. I caused the seams of her stockings to be so straight, and the buttons to be buttoned symmetrically. I was behind those rigid curtains and underneath the square carpets* . . . Of course a wife's duty was to stand by this puzzling and often disagreeable Herzog. She did so with heavy neutrality, recording her objections each time—once but not more. The rest was silence—such heavy silence as he felt in Connecticut when he was finishing *Romanticism and Christianity*. (126–27)

"Stability, symmetry, order, containment" are not only Daisy's strength but the elements of the protected and orderly existence that stir Herzog to rebellion. Then, when he states that it was he who was behind her idiosyncrasies, Bellow intends just that. Daisy and all she stands for are a part of Herzog's mind; and Bellow depicts in this relationship the thesis that man can stand only so much reason and order; that he longs for subjective research, to stretch himself, to flee from a world cold with intellect alone. After all, man is also a creature of the heart—certainly Herzog is.

After Herzog's escape from old barren reason, a meaningful pattern develops. He turns to Sono (he had been seeing the Japanese girl even before his divorce), who is the precise antithesis to Daisy: she is warm, loving, subservient, admiring ("T'es philosophe. O mon Philosophe, mon professeur d'amour. T'es tres important. Je le sais"); and she caters to all of his moods: "But often he sat morose, depressed, in the Morris chair. Well, curse such sadness! But she liked even that. She saw me with the eyes of love, and she said, 'Ah! T'es melancolique   c'est tres beau' " (170).

But Sono takes care especially of his sensory needs: "She loved massages, believed in them. She had often massaged Moses, and he had massaged her. . . . She had a tender heart . . ." (167). Bellow's implications are varied, but they are centered around a retreat into romantic melancholy and sensualism. The massages are direct appeals to the senses. As Herzog recalls Sono, he writes, "To tell the truth, I never had it so good. But I lacked the strength of character to bear such joy." And then he reflects: "That was hardly a joke. When a man's breast feels like a cage from which all the dark birds have flown—he is free, he is light. And he longs to have his vultures back again. He wants his customary struggles, his nameless, empty works, his anger, his afflictions and his sins" (169). Sono, symbolic of Herzog's sensual nature, fails to content Herzog, the man. Happiness, the great synthesis, is not to be found in the indulgence of the senses. By nature, man is restless, and must push on from the lotus eaters: "she didn't answer my purpose. Not serious enough" (103).

With Madeleine, Herzog moves in another direction to look for happiness; and, as he says, he ought to have been prepared for bad results. Madeleine serves a complex function in Bellow's work, but her central purpose is to represent the object of man's pursuit and adoration of what is nebulously called "success." In fact, she is described as a bitch so often and by so many various people in the novel[3] that we can only conclude that Bellow has in mind the proverbial "bitch-goddess" of success. Certainly her personality supports the idea. Everyone admires her great beauty; she is vain, demanding everyone's admiration and attention; she insists on dominating every situation. Deceitful and nasty to those in her power, she is always looking for new recruits to her standard. She is especially anxious to attract those who are ambitious: "Should he have been a plain unambitious Herzog? No. And Madeleine would never have married such a type. What she had been looking for, high and low, was precisely an ambitious Herzog. In order to trip him, bring him low, knock him sprawling and kick out his brains with a murderous bitch foot" (93). Indeed, this "bitch" has made her mark on most of the people around Herzog. Dr. Edvig the psychiatrist is taken with her, as are Sandor Himmelstein, the Monsignor, Gersbach, and even Herzog's student Geraldine Portnoy, who speaks favorably of Madeleine even as she tells Herzog of his wife's infidelity.

Like success, Madeleine moves from object to object, and from interest to interest: "But when all was said and done, Madeleine didn't marry in the Church, nor did she baptize her daughter. Catholicism went the way of zithers and tarot cards, bread-baking and Russian civilization. And life in the country" (118). For, as she angrily asks Herzog, "What makes you think I intend to have a life-long affair with you?" (116). Her complete irresponsibility with money also bears mentioning; she spends outrageous sums on everything, from maternity clothes to cigarette boxes (56).

Appropriately enough, Madeleine takes everything that Herzog can give her—his name, money, reputation, and even his learning; and, when he can give nothing more, she moves to Gersbach, that "public figure" of a man, "that loud, flamboyant, ass-clutching brute . . ." (102). "He started out in educational radio, and now he's all over the place. On committees, in the papers. He gives lectures to the Hadassah . . . readings of his poems" (196). But Gersbach, too, will go the way of all flesh. As Herzog tells Phoebe, Gersbach's wife, toward the end of the novel, "He'll lose his value to Madeleine as soon as you withdraw. After the victory, she'll have to throw him out" (263).

Through the sequence of Daisy, Sono, and Madeleine, Bellow intends that with man's disillusion in his intellect and emotions, he turns to the pursuit of worldly success—fame, money, position—only to find that its achievement is barren. Happiness is not here, and the lesson is long, costly, and painful, one not too easily survived.

Ramona, the object of Herzog's final pursuit, represents another retreat, this time from the ego-shattering experience with Madeleine. Ramona is an earth-goddess (she runs a floral shop) who "had made herself into a sort of sexual professional (or priestess)" (17). She is more than willing to salve all of Herzog's wounds, to reassure him of his intelligence and masculinity, his virility and value: "Nonsense—why talk like that! You know you're a good-looking man. And you even take pride in being one. In Argentina they'd call you *macho*—masculine" (15).

Under Ramona's tutelage Herzog goes shopping for new clothes, a coat of crimson and white stripes and a straw hat, reminiscent of the 1920s and reflective of Herzog's retreat. Ramona does take good care of this sick Herzog, offering him "asylum, shrimp, wine, music, flowers, sympathy, gave him room, so to speak, in her soul, and finally the embrace of her body" (199). Her sexual antics attract him, but they also bewilder him: "It was odd that Ramona should sometimes carry on like one of those broads in a girlie magazine. For which she advanced the most high-minded reasons. An educated woman, she quoted him Catullus and the great love poets of all times. And the classics of psychology. And finally the Mystical Body. And so she was in the next room, joyously preparing, stripping, perfuming. She wanted to please" (202).

Ramona, Bellow intends, is another aberration of Herzog's mind. As such, the similarity in the attitudes of these two life-beaten people should be noted: "She was thirty-seven or thirty-eight years old, he shrewdly reckoned, and this meant that she was looking for a husband. . . . She wanted to give her heart once and for all, and level with a good man, become Herzog's wife and quit being an easy lay" (17). Herzog writes in his imaginary letters to her: "Dear Ramona, you mustn't think because I've taken a powder, briefly, that I don't care for you. I do! I feel you close about me, much of the time. And last week, at that party, when I saw you across the room in your hat with flowers, your hair crowded down close to your bright cheeks, I had a glimpse of what it might be like to love you." Herzog shows signs of Ramona's desperate resignations: "He exclaimed mentally, Marry me! Be my wife! End my troubles!" but then he catches himself "and was staggered by his rashness, his weakness, and by the characteristic nature of such an outburst, for he saw how very neurotic and typical it was" (66).

What Herzog comes to discover through all of these experiences—his love affairs, which Bellow intends to be reflective and subjective, inclinations of personal gratification—is that he will never be content or at ease with himself through his misguided efforts to exploit a part of his nature, nor will he find a viable life through a denial of any other part of his nature. On one level he is trying to do the impossible—to find happiness through outer sources—to supplement himself, so to speak, through these love affairs. But on a deeper, universal level, these

attachments and attractions are symbolic of elements to be found in all
men, and all men will find that their ease of heart will come from
within themselves if it comes at all.

A Definition

This lonely truth is brought home to Herzog when he dashes to
Chicago to protect, he tells himself, his daughter from Gersbach and
Madeleine, who are living together. As Herzog sneaks up to the house
and looks through the bathroom window, he is greeted by a scene that
goes far to dispel his mistaken pretensions of self and his misinformed
idea of his relation to others. When he sees the hated pretender
Gersbach tenderly and affectionately giving his daughter a bath and
little Junie delighting in the scrubbing, Herzog looks at Gersbach and
thinks:

> The hated traits were all there. But see how he was with June, scooping
> water on her playfully, kindly. . . . The child jumped up and down with
> delight. . . . Moses might have killed him now. . . . There were two
> bullets in the chamber. . . . But they would stay there. Herzog clearly
> recognized that. . . . Firing this pistol was nothing but a thought. [Herzog
> writes a quick note] The human soul is an amphibian, and I have touched its
> sides. [And then he thinks] Amphibian! It lives in more elements than I will
> ever know; . . . I seem to think because June looks like a Herzog, she is nearer
> to me than to them. But how is she near to me if I have no share in her life?
> Those two grotesque love-actors have it all. And I apparently believe that if
> the child does not have a life resembling mine, educated according to the
> Herzog standards of "heart," and all the rest of it, she will fail to become a
> human being. . . . As soon as Herzog saw the actual person giving an actual
> bath, the reality of it, the tenderness of such a buffoon to a little child, his
> intended violence turned into theater, into something ludicrous. . . . Lin-
> gering in the alley awhile, he congratulated himself on his luck. His breath
> came back to him; and how good it felt to breathe! It was worth the trip.
> (257–58)

Herzog realizes that he has been using his daughter in much the same
way he has been using his affairs with women—as an imagined source of
happiness. He had thought that little June needed him, that she was
even a part of him. Obviously he is mistaken. It is even more important

that he loses his intense hate of Gersbach and Madeleine; hence, as Bellow intends, Herzog no longer hates in himself those elements for which these two actors stand. Herzog is released from a self-imprisoning self-hatred of elements in his own nature.

But Herzog, since he still wants custody of his daughter, goes straight to the house of Phoebe Gersbach and urges her to divorce her husband; for the consequence may be that any scandal revealing Gersbach's infidelity may yet bring June back to him. But he is bluntly told the direction he must take when Phoebe refuses to do anything about Gersbach's affair with Madeleine: "'Why do you come to me [Phoebe asks], if you want custody of your daughter? *Either do something by yourself or forget it* [italics mine]. Let me alone, now Moses.' [Herzog admits] This too, was perfectly just. . . . 'You're right. This was an unnecessary visit'" (264).

With this last effort that is so obviously ill-conceived, Herzog returns to his house in Ludeyville, where he faces himself, finds his synthesis, and writes: "Why must I be such a throb-hearted character. . . . But I am. I am, and you can't teach old dogs. Myself is thus and so, and will continue thus and so. And why fight it? My balance comes from instability. Not organization, or courage, as with other people. It's tough, but that's how it is. On these terms I, too—even I!—apprehend certain things. Perhaps the only way I'm able to do it. Must play the instrument I've got" (330).

All men must come to terms with their nature. Herzog realizes that in the past he has been victimized by that nature because of his inability to define it and accept it for what it is. He is beginning to understand himself as man: "And terrible forces in me, including the force of admiration or praise, powers, including loving powers, very damaging, making me almost an idiot because I lacked the capacity to manage them" (326). Herzog, who now puts all of the blame for his problem squarely on himself, faces the fact that he is a human being subject to "terrible forces"; but he also realizes that he is only at their mercy if he fails to understand them.

It is little wonder that, as the story opens with Herzog back in Ludeyville, he states in the first line, "If I am out of my mind, it's all right with me" (1). And, at the end of the novel, the line is repeated (315). The importance of this remark far exceeds its seeming casualness, for Bellow intends it to be interpreted literally, at least in a sense: for Herzog's mind has failed to manage these "terrible forces." Furthermore, with the concluding scene, which finds Herzog closely involved with nature, Bellow intends that Herzog is *out of his mind* [italics mine]: he is no longer subject to the "terrible forces" of the mind, and he has found his place in the natural order of things:

> Then he thought he'd light candles at dinner. . . . But now it was time to get those bottles from the spring. . . . He took pleasure in the vivid cold of the water. . . . Coming back from the woods, he picked some flowers for the table. He wondered whether there was a corkscrew in the drawer. . . . A nail could be used, if it came to that. . . . Meanwhile, he filled his hat from the rambler vine, the one that clutched the rainpipe. . . . By the cistern there were yellow day lilies. He took some of these, too, but they wilted instantly. And, back in the darker garden, he looked for peonies; perhaps some had survived. But then it struck him that he might be making a mistake, and he stopped. . . . Picking flowers? He was being thoughtful, being lovable. How would it be interpreted? (He smiled slightly.) Still, he need only know his own mind, and the flowers couldn't be used; no, they couldn't be turned against him. So he did not throw them away. . . . Walking over notes and papers, he lay down on his Recamier couch. . . . At this time he had no messages for anyone. Nothing. Not a single word. (340–41)

Significantly, this is the first time in the novel that Herzog has left his position as an observer of nature, which he is throughout the book, to become a participant. And then there is the observation on the part of Herzog—not a knowledgeable conclusion, but an illumination— that he too must remain in nature, like the flowers, if he is to prosper. The novel ends as the backward action begins, with Herzog's lying on a couch. Only this time it is the couch of reason, a "Recamier couch," much like the one, no doubt, upon which Madame Recamier reclined when the French classicist David painted her likeness. Bellow implies that his protagonist is recovering his balance and is entering a world of the reasonable.

And perhaps Bellow's entire novel is to be interpreted in the light of the classic dictum, *know thyself*. At least Moses E. Herzog, "a solid figure of a man" (9), has learned its importance. In any case, "at this time" there will be no more attempts to define himself through

communication with the world, no more insistent intellectualization of
the world or of his relationship to it. For now he is content to
be—Moses E. Herzog. He writes his last letter: "But what do you
want, Herzog? But that's just it—not a solitary thing. I am pretty well
satisfied to be, to be just as it is willed, and for as long as I may remain
in occupancy" (340). We might even say that Herzog has attained a
state of *sweet* reasonableness.

The Faust Legend

Bellow often uses the images of actors and theaters in order to convey
the idea that "all the world's a stage, and all the men and women merely
players." In *Herzog,* Bellow casts his protagonist into the dramatic
tradition of Faust, which allows us to interpret Herzog's experiences
and dilemmas through the Faustian myth, and further, to see Herzog as
representative of the intellectual development of man since the
Renaissance.

Bellow provides an endless variety of hints that point to his protagonist as Faust. For example, Herzog writes a letter to himself: "Dear
Moses E. Herzog, Since when have you taken such an interest in social
questions, in the external world? Until lately, you led a life of innocent
sloth. But suddenly a Faustian spirit of discontent and universal reform
descends on you. Scolding, Invective" (68).

Within the first few pages, he is describing his studies: "His first
work showed by objective research what Christianity was to Romanticism. In the second he was becoming tougher, more assertive, more
ambitious. . . He had a strong will and a talent for polemics, a taste for
the philosophy of history. . . . digging in at Ludeyville, he showed a
taste and talent also for danger and extremism, for heterodoxy, for
ordeals, a fatal attraction to the 'City of Destruction'" (5–6). Here is
Faust with his ambition, polemics, philosophy, and tastes, and certainly his "fatal attraction" to Bunyan's "City of Destruction." Herzog
is a university professor who is, in his words, as "bored" as Faust was.
The flight that Herzog takes while in Poland is reminiscent of Faust's
travels under the will of Mephistopheles: "They flew through angry
spinning snow clouds over white Polish forests, fields, pits, factories,
rivers dogging their banks, in, out, in and a terrain of white and brown
diagrams" (32). And the geography of Herzog's trip is significant

because it encompasses the area in which Faust was operative, the Eastern European area, where Herzog lectures "in Copenhagen, Warsaw, Cracow, Berlin, Belgrade, Istanbul, and Jerusalem" (7), and specifically in Cracow, where there "was a frightening moment . . . when the symptom appeared" (24), just a "little infection he had caught in Poland" (13). In Goethe's work, Cracow is the precise setting for Faust's teaching and for his bargain with Mephistopheles. And Herzog feels Mephistopheles inside himself when he writes, "There is someone inside me. I am in his grip. When I speak of him I feel him in my head, pounding for order. He will ruin me" (11).

Bellow intends that, as in the case of Faust, Mephistopheles be seen as a creature of Herzog's imagination; and, when Herzog says, "I do seem to be a broken-down monarch of some kind" (39), it is with the idea that this spirit is a part of Herzog. And then, keeping in mind the view that the other characters in the novel are symbolic of forces within Herzog, Bellow has his protagonist say:

> Take me, for instance. I've been writing letters helter-skelter in all directions. More words. I go after reality with language. Perhaps I'd like to change it all into language, to force Madeleine and Gersbach to have a *Conscience* [italics in original] . . . . If they don't suffer, they've gotten away from me. And I've filled the world with letters to prevent their escape. I want them in human form, and so I *conjure up a whole environment and catch them in the middle. I put my whole heart into these constructions. But they are constructions* [italics mine]. (272)

This passage contains the clear indication that Bellow would have the reader see his work as an exposition of a psychological condition. This condition, he intends figuratively and dramatically, is the result of diabolic forces. It will be remembered that Herzog decides Madeleine would never have married an unambitious person: "What she had been looking for, *high and low* [italics mine], was precisely an ambitious Herzog" (93). She had "the will of a demon," he says (102). So Madeleine is an extension of the Mephistophelean spirit in Herzog, as is Gersbach: "He's a ringmaster, popularizer, liaison for the elites. He grabs up celebrities and brings them before the public. And he makes all sorts of people feel that he has exactly what they've been looking for" (215). And, even as Mephistopheles suggests to Faust that he could peacefully lead a sensuous existence, so does Ramona try to convince Herzog that life with her would be ideal.

In addition to the aptness of the Faust legend as a description of the mental condition of Herzog, Bellow intends that the myth be seen as part of the resolution to his novel. Herzog states the case when he tries to explain his work to Zelda: "Herzog tried to explain what it was about—that his study was supposed to have ended with a new angle on the modern condition, showing how life could be lived by renewing universal connections . . . revising the old Western, Faustian ideology . . ." (39).

In Goethe's drama, Faust finds his contentment in social usefulness. He creates a vast area of productive land out of the swamps, where people can live in freedom and in pragmatic activities. Through this achievement he finds peace and harmony. At one time Herzog has similar ideas. He thinks about giving his land and house in Ludeyville to a utopian group (48). The idea remains with him, but he finally decides against it.

This house, "an old ruin of a place but with enormous possibilities" (48), suggests the condition of Herzog, as Bellow implies when his protagonist sees "the shadow of his face in a gray, webby window" (2). And when Herzog tells his brother Will at the end of the story that "I could go to work and become rich. Make a ton of money, just to keep this house" (331), he does so with the illumination that he himself is worth saving, that the first and most important step is to work with himself, which means knowing and enjoying himself in his human condition. Although this condition is admittedly beset with many limitations and countless liabilities, it is also one with "enormous possibilities." Through his hero, Bellow seems to be saying that man's earthly salvation is not to be gained in social movements, utopian visions, political nostrums, scientific investigations (and this compulsive activity is what Herzog's letters are all about), but in learning to live with himself as he exists in the subangelic position of man.

Chapter Seven
Mr. Sammler's Planet

With the publication of *Mr. Sammler's Planet* (1970) Saul Bellow adds one more alienated hero to the six he has presented in as many novels. This time it is Mr. Artur Sammler, a seventy-four-year-old Polish Jew who is partially blind in one eye. Except for a few crushing events during World War II, his history is sketchy. In the 1920s and 1930s he served in London as a correspondent for Polish papers and journals, and was a member of a cultural circle presided over by H. G. Wells. Just prior to World War II, he and his wife and daughter Shula returned to Poland where his wife became a victim of a genocidal mass murder, with Sammler barely escaping. When the novel opens, he and his daughter have been living in New York for over twenty years, both completely dependent upon the physician Elya Gruner who is a nephew to Sammler, but only a few years younger. It was Dr. Gruner who lifted them out of a displaced persons' camp just after the war and brought them to New York. For all these years, then, Sammler has had little to do but live simply, read extensively, and play the role of the detached, observing philosopher.

Mr. Sammler is not a recluse. Quite the opposite. He has friends who continually seek him out for his wit, conversation, and counsel, and who confess their lives to him, almost beyond his patience. If it is not his friends, then occasions, events, or facts confront him and demand his attention. The world gets in his way, with questions that confuse Sammler. He knows that he seldom has any acceptable answers for people, occasions, or for himself. Or what answers he has seem irrelevant. During a lecture to a university group, a militant student routs him with obscenities; Wallace, the hyperactive son of Dr. Gruner, out to make his fortune and thereby gain his freedom, easily dismisses injunctions on family love and loyalty; sensuous and sexually active Angela, daughter to Gruner, is extremely impatient with advice from anyone so hopelessly dried-up, especially advice on her problems; even

Shula, Sammler's daughter (now forty years old), does not take him too seriously and at times treats him almost as if he were a child, although she nags him constantly to continue his definitive memoir on H. G. Wells that bogged down many years ago. As the novel opens, even Sammler doubts his relevancy: "Shortly after dawn . . . Mr. Artur Sammler . . . took in the books and papers of his West Side bedroom and suspected strongly that they were the wrong books, the wrong papers."[1] However, there is Dr. Gruner, who lies dying in the hospital. By him, Sammler feels needed. To him, Sammler feels he has something to say. Early in the book Sammler visits Elya briefly, but because of interventions—people, occasions, facts—he experiences great difficulty in returning to his nephew. He finally arrives, but not in time to see Elya alive.

Setting and Symbol

Bellow's settings are consistently symbolic, and such is the case in this novel. Sammler lives in a city imaged in the yellows of sickness, disease, and contagion. The entire New York landscape gives forth odors of fear and decay. Everyone seems to be cursed with an anguish of spirit, frantically building personal utopias out of old and worn-out materials that have failed again and again to bring any peace. It is the stock market for Elya, a shrewd financial coup for Wallace, a woman's arms (preferably plump) for Walter Bruch, the H. G. Wells memoir for Shula. And so it goes. New York is a mad city, filled with hippies, muggings, mini-skirts, wild business enterprises, obscenities, riots, rallies, and determined sexual somersaults. Yet, we are not too many pages into the novel before it becomes apparent that New York is only a symbol for a world-wide condition. When Sammler is anxiously looking for a telephone to report a pickpocket, he finds that "most telephones were smashed, crippled. They were urinals, also. New York was getting worse than Naples or Salonika. It was like an Asian, an African town" (7). With these widening horizons, Sammler assumes the dimensions of a world citizen or an Everyman, a characterization that Bellow consistently projects through his protagonists.

In typical Bellow fashion, with added breadth comes added depth, and we find that the immediate action of three days in the life of

Sammler is only a mirror for deeper significances whose meanings lie in various stages of the past. It is important at this point to understand that Bellow is actually writing several stories in one, with each story progressively set more deeply in historical implications. That is, Sammler is a character in his own right; but through his actions and through his mind we are witness to a cyclical view of man's intellectual growth and development since the thirteenth century. Extremely complex in the unfolding, this view is based on at least four time referents—the three days' action of the novel, some several years prior to this action, Sammler's earlier life in England, and ultimately a time span that goes back to the Renaissance. Since Bellow structures his novel within these cycles of history, we would expect to find a recurrence of events, which is exactly the case. To illustrate this recurrence, and for later referential purposes, it is necessary first of all to trace one of the major threads of the story.

As the novel opens at dawn on the first day, Sammler awakens in a state of anxiety. Thinking back to events of the past few days, he fears that he has been discovered seeing too much because he recently caught the eye of a huge Negro pickpocket at work on a city bus. At that time, the old refugee tried to call the police from a telephone booth, but he could not find one that had not been vandalized. He called when he arrived home, but the police were not interested. They already had too many such reports. As the morning wears on, Sammler leaves home and again catches the pickpocket brazenly robbing an old man. In fear of reprisal, he tries not to be seen watching; but the thief follows him home, backs him up against the wall and silently exhibits his own genitalia to Sammler, as if in warning.

That night and into the second day, Sammler ponders this experience, but does nothing about it. The student Lionel Feffer, however, knows exactly what to do. He will catch the thief in the act with his miniature camera. On the third day, after several delays, Sammler is on his way to the hospital to see Elya Gruner. He stops the car when he sees his pickpocket with a stranglehold on Feffer, forcing him back against the bus and silently struggling for the camera. Sammler pleads uselessly for help from the gathering crowd, but he finally has to call upon Eisen who has only recently arrived in New York. (In Israel, Eisen was Schula's husband, but he beat her so much that Sammler brought her to

New York.) At first, Eisen refuses to help, but then he strikes the Negro almost senseless with a baize pouch of medallions bearing religious inscriptions. Sammler is horrified at the violence and leaves the scene immediately, impatient to return to Elya at the hospital. Learning that Elya has already died, Sammler insists over staff objections on seeing the body of his nephew. In the final lines of the novel Sammler delivers an intercession for the soul of Elya.

Wider Issues

We will return to the events of these three days, but for now we must look to the wider time referent of the last several years through Sammler's reading. His studies have been endless. Darwin, Kierkegaard, Freud, Milton, Dickens, Shaw, Proust, Rousseau, Nietzsche, Saint-Just, Malraux, Sartre, Camus, Kant, and Schopenhauer just begin the list. At one point, the narrator, who as often as not speaks from Sammler's position and point of view, lists Sammler's readings:

. . . Toynbee, Freud, Burckhardt, Spengler . . . historians of civilization—Karl Marx, Max Weber, Max Scheler, Franz Oppenheimer. Side excursions into Adorno, Marcuse, Norman O. Brown, whom he found to be worthless fellows. Together with these he took on *Doktor Faustus, Les Noyers d'Altenbourg,* Ortega, Valery's essays on history and politics. But after four or five years of this diet, he wished to read only certain religious writers of the thirteenth century—Suso, Tauler, and Meister Eckhardt. In his seventies he was interested in little more than Meister Eckhardt and the Bible (37).

(As an aside for the moment, it should be noted that Spengler and Toynbee are represented here—both well known for cyclical interpretations of history that see civilizations organically rising and falling.)

Again before returning to the thread of the story, we must recall the even longer time span of the 1920s and 1930s when Sammler was an avid disciple of H. G. Wells. In those days, utopian hopes were high, as Sammler describes them to a group of university students: "the project [of H. G. Wells] was based on the propagation of the sciences of biology, history, and sociology and the effective application of scientific principles to the enlargement of human life . . . a service . . . based on a rational scientific attitude toward life" (41).

Cyclical Failures

Now, going back to the action of the three days, we can follow the recurrence of a particular event through three of the four time cycles. When Sammler is filled with anxiety over the fear of reprisal from the pickpocket, he seeks help through the telephone and the police—both symbols of institutions (science and law) man has constructed in the name of progress and human betterment. For Sammler, these institutions are failures. The first recurrence is evident in the reported reading. Over the past few years, Sammler had been giving his time to historians of civilization and political polemicists, to fictional projections on the nature of man, and to essayists on history and politics. He had been looking to "authorities" who could bring him some understanding, and, hence, some peace of mind; but somehow they do not offer him an image of man that allows him to rest easily. He turns away from science and the law in the case of the pickpocket. (The fact that he now reads only the Bible and the writings of Meister Eckhardt will be discussed later.) We find the second recurrence in the time referent that embraces Sammler's life in England where the utopian constructions of H. G. Wells, based on rationalistic scientific principles, also failed to bring about an Edenic existence for Sammler. World War II taught him that scientific principles need not bring happiness. Witness the Nazi horrors founded on such principles. It is little wonder that the memoir on H. G. Wells lies neglected. The point is, in each of these time spans, Sammler repeats the same mistake. He counts upon institutional constructions based on reason and deduction to assuage his feelings of anxiety.

The significance of this cyclical dramatization of history will be brought into focus later, but at this point let us suggest that Bellow's main theme in *Mr. Sammler's Planet* centers partially on the recurring failure of man to devise ways through which he may live a life of tranquillity. The theme in its entirety may well be found in the writings of Alfred North Whitehead whom "Sammler admires so much" (29). In his *Science and the Modern World*, Whitehead states: "When we consider what religion is for mankind, and what science is, it is no exaggeration to say that the future course of history depends upon the decision of this generation as to the relations between them. . . . We have here the two strongest general forces . . . which

influence men, and they seem to be set one against the other—the force
of our religious intuitions, and the force of our impulse to accurate
observation and logical deduction."[2] *Mr. Sammler's Planet* is the story of
a man who finds himself in a world of mad encounter caused by an
imbalance between these two forces of science and religion. Over the
years man has increasingly centered his hopes for happiness on "impulses to accurate observation and logical deduction" and has lost sight
of the truths that lie in "religious intuitions." For example, we have
accepted in principle the ideas of H. G. Wells that we will find peace
and contentment if we sit down and figure out, rationally and scientifically, a "correct" social, political, and economic structure. Or, we feel
we will live more equably if we just learn more about our animalistic
nature—perhaps through Freud. Again, it is reasonable to believe that
a proper distribution of wealth will solve our problems. Karl Marx will
help us here. Sammler finds that such hopes consistently fail and leave
despair in their wake because equally strong forces that are born of deep
human intimations, not founded on rational scientific reasoning, demand their share of our attention. The felt idea of immortality cannot
be demonstrated in a laboratory, nor supported with logic and reason;
nevertheless, that idea is more strongly necessary to our sense of
well-being than any theory of government or any image of man
formulated along rational lines by "authorities." Bellow's novel is both
a history and a prophecy concerning this conflict between science and
religion.

Character as Symbol

It was said that the fourth time referent sweeps back in history to the
thirteenth century. In this time zone, Bellow uses Sammler's readings as
a projection of man's intellectual development over these years, but he
also turns to characterizations in order to concretize that development
and its contemporary results. Bellow accounts for today's despair by
personifying certain ideas that have their roots in the Renaissance. For
example, the black pickpocket is a composite man. He goes about his
business robbing us, wrapped in ideologies designed by Nietzsche,
Rousseau, Darwin, and Freud. We sense a variety of Darwinisms (man's
animality, survival of the fittest, man's descent) whenever the thief

appears: "He no more spoke than a puma would" (49); his "face showed the effrontery of an animal" (5); he looked like a "great black beast . . . seeking whom he might devour" (14); looking at him "Sammler felt an immediate descent" (46). Then, Rousseau's noble savage makes his French appearance: "The dark glasses, the original design by Christian Dior" (10); "Sammler believed he could smell French perfume from the breast of the camel's-hair coat" (10); he was "mad with an idea of *noblesse*" (294); "a certain princeliness" (294); "he wore a single gold earring" (14). Nietzsche's superman makes his entrance in the camel's-hair coat that the pickpocket always wears (the Persian, Zarathustra). He wears a homburg (German, as was Nietzsche) hat, and "the black eyes [had a] super candor" (50). He possesses all of the silent assurance, strength, super power, barbaric law-unto-himself of Nietzsche's great criminal. Finally, when he exposes himself to Sammler, he is asserting Freud's thesis on the primacy of sexual power.

Bellow extends the roots of this image back to the Renaissance by continually reminding us that the Negro boards the bus at Columbus Circle. Almost too pat, considering the novel's date of publication (1970), we are told that "he operates between Columbus Circle and Seventy-second Street . . ." (121).

Through this figure, Bellow intends us to see that out of the Renaissance came vague ideological panaceas that were born in the vacuum left by the Renaissance negation of our earlier "religious intuitions" and by our concurrent exaltation of "accurate observation and logical deduction" (to use Whitehead's terms). These panaceas slowly developed, always in answer to man's search for a satisfying image of self-definition, until they finally took shape in a figure that frightens and degrades us. We have been taught that the figure is in our image, and we are filled with despair to the point of surrendering to that image.

Eisen is another such figure. He functions as both history and prophecy. Clearly another Nietzschean superman with his great strength and violent-prone personality, he reminds us of the strength-through-joy idiocy of Hitler when we see him always smiling or laughing, even when he describes his own war sufferings (24). (How ironic that the Nietzschean superman manifests itself in two of the most maligned and downtrodden races—the Negro and the Jew; but one of Bellow's favorite observations is that ideas, in one form or another, work their ways throughout the whole of society.) Toeless owing to amputation during the war, with a shuffling gait in the familiar image of William Butler Yeats's beast in his "The Second Coming," Eisen says, "I have come to America to make myself a new career" (168). And the narrator comments: "On his mutilated feet he had learned to move fast. Ingenious adaptation" (167). Bellow points to the future when he shows Eisen standing in the crowd around Feffer and the pickpocket: "He was waiting to be discovered" (287). (Or perhaps Bellow intends, with Sammler as contemporary man, that we have already called upon this figure of violence to solve our problems. The evidence is abundant that we have done just that.)

In any case, Sammler, as contemporary man and as a character in his own right, confronts these personified ideas that have been inflicted upon him by "authorities" who learned to write powerfully enough to bring to life these distorted images. Sammler explains to Govinda Lal, a Hindu biophysicist who has plans to colonize the moon (reminiscent of H. G. Wells), that we were "scribbled" into this fear and trembling by cure-all "ideological hashish" (213):

. . . you see what I mean—people become authoritative and plebians of genius elevate themselves first to nobility and then to universal glory, and all because they had what all poor children got from literacy: the ABCs, the dictionary, the grammar books, the classics. Until, soaring from their slums or their little petit-bourgeois parlors, they were addressing worldwide millions. These are the people who set the terms, who make up the discourse, and then history follows their words. Think of the wars and revolutions we have been scribbled into. (213)

Both the pickpocket and Eisen are creatures that intellectuals have conjured up over the past few centuries. We have allowed these busy thinkers to narrow our self-definitions to such an extent that we fail to recognize our own complexities and potentialities. Eisen's rationalization of his violent behavior is an example. It was noted before that Sammler regrets asking Eisen for help, but he is especially saddened to hear Eisen's logic:

"You can't hit a man like this just once. When you hit him you really must hit him. Otherwise he'll kill you. You know. We both fought in the war. You were a partisan. You had a gun. So don't you know?" His laughter, his logic, laughing and reasoning at Sammler's absurdities, made him repeat until he stuttered. "If in—in. No? If out—out. Yes? No? So answer." It was the reasoning that sank Sammler's heart completely. "Where is Feffer?" he said, and turned away. (291–92)

Sammler feels in Eisen's words the same "gut-level" jungle reasoning that he had experienced in World War II. When he stops Eisen from the stroke that would have killed the helpless pickpocket, he must have been reminded of the time when in the name of such reason he killed an unarmed German soldier who was begging for his life. Eisen's rationale is seductive in its simplicity and attractive in its logic; but behavior based on an "all-or-nothing" attitude is bound to project man along a single path that denies the complexities of being a man. It is the attitude of a fanatic and one that parallels the long course of man's increasing rejection of "religious intuition" for the single-visioned acceptance of scientific ideological panacea. Weaving its way from the Renaissance to the present, it is also an attitude that accounts for, reflects, and counterpoints Sammler's three futile attempts in the twentieth century to calm later tides of anxiety. Sammler leaves the scene because Eisen's argument leaves nothing to say. Where such logic prevails, there is nothing to discuss, no room to move in. "Damn these—these occasions! he was thinking. Damn them, it was Elya who needed him. It was only Elya he wanted to see. To whom there was something to say. Here there was nothing to say" (292). He hurries on toward the hospital.

Sammler as Priest

The incident between Feffer and the pickpocket is only one of a series of delays that the pilgrim Sammler encounters on his progress toward Elya Gruner and religious affirmation. There are other Vanity Fairs and Sloughs of Despair. Yet, finally, he looks down upon the body of his nephew and whispers an intercession for his soul. Sammler assumes priestly duties here, and we may suppose that he sees himself in the role of Meister Eckhardt; hence, at first it seems that Sammler is withdrawing from the world only to seek sanctuary in another institution—the church. But Bellow is not describing a religious experience in the traditional sense. To see what Bellow does intend, we must know that

Meister Eckhardt, a thirteenth-century priest, was judged a heretic for advocating substantive changes in church doctrine, which, in a sense, is what Bellow advocates in his fictional examination of the conflict between science and religion. The point can be made through a further thought of Whitehead's: "Religion will not regain its old power until it can change in the same spirit as does science. Its principles may be eternal, but the expression of those principles requires continual development."[3] Several times throughout the novel, there are indications that Sammler's progress represents just such a spiritual development. For example, Sammler holds fast to religious principles—duty, obligation, responsibility, love, deep and abiding feeling for immortality, desire for eternal peace, and lasting hope for salvation; but Bellow de-institutionalizes these impulses when he indicates key modifications through the words of Sammler: "But being born one respects the powers of creation, one obeys the will of God—*with whatever reservations truth imposes*" [italics mine] (220). One such reservation is Sammler's implicit understanding that there may well be no personal immortality but that there is a "spark" (in German, the word *sammler* means "storage battery") that leaps from man to man, from age to age, uniting humanity in an immortality that expresses itself in a will to live and to endure—a will ("That inner creative fury of the world" (209), as Sammler describes it) that is stronger than any idea of man conjured up by "authorities" who insist that we accept as truth their own narrow, finite, and often degrading images of man.[4]

The Enduring Debate

Bellow dramatizes this struggle between science and religion through the lengthy dialogue between Mr. Sammler and Dr. Govinda Lal, an Indian biophysicist who has completed a manuscript entitled *The Future of the Moon,* in which he describes technological coups that will allow us to inhabit space and, consequently, solve some of our problems here on Earth. He explains:

After 1776 there was a continent to expand into, and this space absorbed all the mistakes. . . . Europe after 1789 did not have the space for its mistakes. Result: war and revolution, with the revolution ending up in the hands of madmen. . . . We are crowded in, packed in, now, and human beings must feel that there is a way out, and that the intellectual power and skill of their own species opens this way. . . . Not to accept the opportunity would make this earth seem more and more a prison. If we could soar out, and did not, we should condemn ourselves. We would be more than ever irritated with life. As it is, the species is eating itself up. (218–19)

Sammler has silent reservations about this, but he is listening. He then speaks: "Well, if as you say we are the kind of creature which is compelled to do what it is capable of doing, it would follow that we must demolish ourselves. But isn't that up to the species?" To which Dr. Lal replies, "I believe you intimate that there is an implicit morality in the will to live. . . ." He points out to Sammler that there is no "duty" in biology: "We please ourselves in extracting ideas of beauty from biology" (220). And so it goes—with Dr. Lal scientifically, rationally justifying an escape, and Mr. Sammler maintaining that answers are to be found here, on Earth, within ourselves. Outward is no answer—peace lies in the other direction.

All of this does not mean, however, that Mr. Sammler does not value the thoughts of Dr. Lal, for he occasionally agrees with him and is hard put to answer. In these moments, he tells Dr. Lal, "Inability to explain is no ground for disbelief. . . . All is not flatly knowable" (236). The point is that with Mr. Sammler and Dr. Lal we do not have uncompromising adversaries who refuse to understand the ground of the other. What is happening in this dialogue is that through Mr. Sammler and Dr. Lal, Bellow is talking to himself. In the end, Bellow as Mr. Sammler holds to his moral, ethical, even mystical ground; but he has given just space to the other side of his thinking.

The whole episode is steeped in irony, for we are witnessing what we think of as an unlikely confrontation—between an Indian rationalist and a Jewish intellectual mystic. Sammler is aware of his personal development:

The scene, for such a conversation, was itself curious—the green carpets, large pots, silk drapes of the late Hilda Gruner's living room. Here Govinda Lal, small, hunched, dusky, with his rusty-gilt complexion, his full face and beard, was like an Oriental ornament or painting. Sammler himself came under this influence, like a figure in Indian color—the red cheeks, the spreading white hair at the back, the circles of his specs, and the cigarette smoke about his hair. To Wallace he had insisted that he was an Oriental, and now felt that he resembled one." (220)

Here, Bellow brings us the haloed figure of an Eastern mystic, a figure with whom Sammler feels some affinity.

Finally, if in *Mr. Sammler's Planet* Bellow is using a cyclical view of history as set forth by Spengler and Toynbee, he parts company with their conclusions. Neither man nor his civilizations need be swept away by monstrous forces, for man creates those forces and he can control them by turning inwardly, to the depths of self, and cultivating other images of himself based on religious principles. Then, prophetically, Bellow proposes cycles that have narrowed in time sequence to a mere three days. Perhaps a course has been run, and we are ready to move with Sammler back to that point in history when we first discarded the better image of man, back to the thirteenth century when science and religion were in dubious battle, and, through a reinterpretation of religious intuitions, to strike a more equable balance between the two forces.

There is more to be said about this book: Bellow's characterizations offer extensive commentary on contemporary sociological events; an exploration of the many ironies Bellow sets in motion illuminates his use of ideological tensions. Then, there is much to support a reading of Elya Gruner as a Gatsby-like figure whose death symbolizes the passing of an age. We should say, however, that *Mr. Sammler's Planet* marks a new direction in Bellow's fiction, as I indicate in other places in this book (chapters 1 and 10). As round and as complete as *Herzog* and his other novels are, Bellow could not be contained within those created worlds. One can guess that on looking back he found them too round, their resolutions too complete for the needs of the human spirit; too much at ease in Zion, given today's world with its paralyzing uncertainty about place and value for the individual and for mankind. Tommy Wilhelm, Henderson, and Herzog rest easily after their adventures; but the human spirit asks for more. *Mr. Sammler's Planet* initiates the search for this "more"; and Bellow's next novel, *Humboldt's Gift,* continues the seeking.

Chapter Eight
Humboldt's Gift

For reasons that will become clear, we must begin our discussion of *Humboldt's Gift* (1975) with a few words in review of our comments on *Mr. Sammler's Planet.*[1] We found that Mr. Sammler acts as a figure of Western thought that reaches back to the thirteenth century and makes its way to the present through a series of ideological cycles. We suggested that the purpose of this journey is to trace the historical ascendancy of science over religion and that Mr. Sammler, at the end of these cycles, is Bellow's advocate for a redress in the balance which Bellow feels would make possible a less despairing vision of man than the reign of science has been able to afford. Then, owing to Mr. Sammler's intermittently repeated praises for the work of the philosopher Alfred North Whitehead, to the specific exclusion of a host of other thinkers since the Middle Ages, we turned to the work of Whitehead and found the central issue dramatized in *Mr. Sammler's Planet.* In his *Science and the Modern World,* Whitehead sets the following thesis:

When we consider what religion is for mankind, and what science is, it is no exaggeration to say that the future course of history depends upon the decision of this generation as to the relations between them. . . . We have here the two strongest general forces . . . which influence man, and they seem to be set one against the other—the force of our religious intuitions, and the force of our impulse to accurate observation and logical deduction.[2]

Religion will not regain its old power until it can change in the same spirit as does science. Its principles may be eternal, but the expression of those principles requires continual development.[3]

In this chapter we will have several occasions to look back at these statements, for Whitehead's thinking reaches through *Mr. Sammler's Planet* and on into the heart of *Humboldt's Gift.*

Character as Figure

Von Humboldt Fleisher and Charlie Citrine, the two central figures in *Humboldt's Gift,* are dual protagonists; they represent almost the same historical and metaphysical forces. We may think of them as distinct but inseparable manifestations or currents of the Hegelian World Historical Spirit, which we may briefly describe here as a universal force that drives our world toward some metaphysical cosmic significance. As such a current, Humboldt sweeps from ancient Greece to the present, a period of time that is established early in the novel when Charlie as narrator says, "To follow Humboldt's intricate conversation you had to know his basic texts . . . Plato's 'Timaeus,' Proust on Combray, Virgil on farming, Marvel on gardens, Wallace Stevens' Caribbean poetry, and so on."[4] These entries are significant in that they reflect the history of Western culture indicated by representative texts from ancient Greece, Rome, the Renaissance, and the immediate setting of Humboldt's rise and fall, the 1920s, 1930s, and 1940s. But Bellow has something else in mind here, too. These "basic texts" have at least one thing in common: they are all examples of how Western aesthetics have brought to bear the power of the fanciful and the imaginative on the physical, material world in the effort to make that world metaphysically significant. It is a tradition that Humboldt forsakes when he is distracted to the point of destruction by the magnetism of success in the here-and-now; and a tradition that Charlie, after his own confrontations with this success, manages to build on.

It is probable also that Bellow intends Humboldt to represent still another movement within our cultural history. He did publish ballads; and Bellow, in his opening sentence, is careful to say just that: "The book of ballads published by Von Humboldt Fleisher in the Thirties was an immediate hit." Then Bellow adds, "Humboldt was just what everyone had been waiting for" (1). It is odd at best that Bellow should choose ballads as a vehicle for Humboldt's success, unless he is pointing to a particular role for Humboldt. It is likely that Bellow intends his figure to stand for the first currents of the romanticism of the later eighteenth century, a period that brought a revival of the ballad. Tired of neoclassic achievements, everyone was waiting for a change. And we have already described Humboldt's "basic texts" as works that are founded on what is basically the romantic tradition: the use of the fancy and the imagination on the material world. Humboldt, in one of his roles, is the romantic tradition that lost its imaginative power to see the world in terms of that power, and surrendered to, or was destroyed by, realism, which is ultimately based on the idea that accurate observation and logical deduction is more relevant to our lives than is our romantic intuition. Certainly to see Humboldt as such a figure is consistent with Bellow's overall thesis.

The Failure of Humboldt: The Rise of Charlie Citrine

With the year 1952, it is time for Charlie's ascendancy, and Humboldt's fall. Charlie describes his friend: "Very different from the young poet with whom I went to Hoboken to eat clams, he was now thick and stout. . . . His handsome face has thickened and deteriorated" (20). As they approach Humboldt's rundown country shack, Humboldt echoes King Duncan: "This castle hath a pleasant seat. Also, The heaven's breath smells wooingly here" (23), and we can anticipate the future with young Charlie playing out the role of Macbeth, yet unconscious of his part in the drama. Charlie is in the process of assuming Humboldt's role, with his roots in Humboldt, growing out of Humboldt, "his protégé" (15), hence a force whose seeds are in the past, but whose fruition is of the present and future. Referring to Humboldt's "basic texts," Charlie says, "I knew what they were. . . . One reason why Humboldt and I were so close was that I was willing to take the complete course" (17). So we can think of Charlie as a kind of "cultural point-man."

On one of its levels, then, this novel, like *Mr. Sammler's Planet,* is a tracking of our cultural history, its present state and future. Moreover, while in this essay we will deal only peripherally with the subject, the novel also has a great deal to do with the more narrow matter of the history and state of Western art. The two lines of culture and art often overlap in the telling, for Bellow sees art as a reflection of culture, and too often ignominiously subject to it. Charlie explains one of the reasons for the failure of his friend the poet: "He consented to the monopoly of power and interest held by money, politics, law, rationality, technology" (155). Yet through Humboldt, Bellow is also describing a wider condition than that existing only in art. Certainly we all seem to have given the same consent that causes Humboldt to fail.

Through Charlie's success (his drama about one Von Trenck is adapted into a Broadway hit) and through Humboldt's continuing decline, the two friends are estranged, largely through the envy of Humboldt; and Charlie, now suffering from the distractions of his own success, tries to move away from a cultural establishment that finds its only reason for being on what we have seen to be Whitehead's analysis: our impulse to accurate observation and logical deduction. More and more, Charlie entertains the other side of the equation, our religious intuitions. Through his own frustrating and confusing experiences with money, sex, marriage, fame, status, etc., and certainly through the disintegration of his friend Humboldt, "a wonderful man [but] overawed by rational orthodoxy" (363), Charlie begins to see what can happen when we are caught in a culture whose behavior is dictated by the consequences of a victorious science, whose ideologies and even its art have consented to the victory, and whose spirit feels that our human significance ends with death. After one of Charlie's metaphysical flights, his mistress Renata states the thesis: "I prefer to take things as billions of people have done throughout history. You work, you get bread, you lose a leg, kiss some fellows, have a baby, you live to eighty and bug hell out of everybody, or you get hung or drowned. But you don't spend years trying to dope your way out of the human condition. . . . I believe I live in nature. I think when you're dead you're dead, and t at's that" (430–31).

Although scientific observation would seem to agree with Renata, Charlie finds such a thesis dispiriting, destructive, and even boring. It all adds up to an absurd nada. He explains to her, of course without success, that "ignorance of death is destroying us. . . . No honorable person can refuse to lend his mind, to give his time, to devote his soul to this problem of problems. Death now has no serious challenge from philosophy, religion or art" (350). As our "cultural point-man," Charlie takes on this role of challenger; but first, like his fellow Wisconsinite Houdini, that "Great Jewish escape artist" (435), he, too, must escape— in this case, from a world that believes in and behaves on the certainties of Renata.

The Great Escape

But escape is not easy. Charlie must disengage himself from a number of strong ideological and emotional attachments, all of which take the form of characters too numerous to list here. However, his ex-wife Denise, the jaded gangster Cantabile, and Renata are interesting examples, since through them we can see Bellow's technique of projecting certain contemporary conditions into their historical inceptions. It will help to keep in mind that while these three figures are characters in their own right, they function as reflections of Charlie's mind, as many of the other characters do. In a sense, Charlie is disengaging from ideas buried deeply in himself, ideas that he (and Bellow, too, one supposes) feels have become worn-out.

In Denise we see what has happened to all that Athena once stood for. This goddess of war and wisdom has now become a carping, vindictive nag, "pelting me [Charlie reports] with the ammunition she stored up daily in her mind and heart" (227). Her voice was "militant" (224); "and she had an intensely martial personality" (40). And we catch a vague image of the once stately, beautiful, Trojan-helmeted, fully-armed Athena in the now deteriorated beauty of one who in her "top-heaviness" is now merely "very intelligent" (57), as opposed to being the embodiment of wisdom. Of significance are the mundane uses to which she puts her intelligence—for status, prestige, connections with the great—the Kennedys and the Javitses. This failing Athena "was a speed reader and covered every detail of world crisis under the [hair] dryer. . . . To prepare for the White House, she mastered *Time, Newsweek,* and *The U.S. News and World Report*" (57). Of course, as a figure of the intellect, she is heavily derisive of Charlie's religious intuitions, his Steiner studies in anthroposophy, and of his relationship with the sensual Renata—"All symptoms of a mental and physical decline" (227), she accuses. But she claims it is not too late; she can still save Charlie: "We should become reunited" (228). But Charlie gets a divorce from this life of the mind; for "despite her intelligence, she had been bad for my idea" (44), an idea that we can guess has to do with Whitehead's religious intuitions.

Cantabile must be cast off, too. This enfeebled, anxiety-ridden would-be ganglord with his "daggerbrows" (83) who "had cast himself as an expert on the underworld" (79) is all that is left of Satan, or of a Goethean Mephistopheles. The "smoky-souled Cantabile" (88) had fallen on bad times: "His large feet and dark eyes also hinted that he aspired to some ideal, and that his partial attainment or non-attainment of the ideal was a violent grief to him" (87). In his faded Satanic role, he forces Charlie to accompany him to the heights of a

half-constructed high-rise, and later offers to act as his procurer. Like
Denise, he is going to do a lot for Charlie, mainly bring him great
wealth, if only Charlie will join him and do as he says. "I've prepared a
paper that I want you to sign" (454), Cantabile says (in sound Mephistophelean procedure), referring to a contractual arrangement he had
drawn up that gives him an interest in a script left by Humboldt to
Charlie, which, until now unknown to Charlie, has been made into a
highly successful movie. But Charlie refuses to sign, and is at least
partially saved. Again, as with Denise, Charlie manages to disengage
from this attachment. At the end, Charlie declares to Kathleen,
one-time mistress to Humboldt, "My own romance with wealth is
over" (478).

Charlie's most painful disengagement comes when he parts from
Renata. Like Denise and Cantabile, she is a decaying spirit of the past.
She is what remains of, what we have made out of, the pulsating power
and energy of Aphrodite. This failing goddess of the sea, the embodiment of love and beauty, hence youth, is introduced in the first few
pages, as Charlie reminisces of an occasion in her bed: "About my low
cholesterol Renata was well informed. . . . I repeated to her the
doctor's comments about my amazingly youthful prostate and my
supernormal EKG. . . . She gazed at me with love-pious eyes. . . . I
inhaled her delicious damp" (9). She too tries to convince Charlie that
his future is with her. "I've kept your sex powers alive," she claims
(328). Not only does she promise him a life of the senses, there will be
other rewards: "You can always make money, plenty of it. Especially if
you team up with me" (349). In spite of his strong feelings for Renata,
Charlie has some reservations about their future. Who will push his
wheelchair when he is on "the border of senility, his back hooked and
feeble? . . . Renata? Not Renata. Certainly not" (9).

Charlie has the power to break his attachments to Denise and
Cantabile; not so with Renata. It is she who leaves him, as her kind of
sensualism and beauty ever does. Fulfilling her role of Aphrodite, she
marries Flonzaley, an undertaker, and modern embodiment of Aphrodite's husband, Hephaestus, ancient god of fire and the volcanic underworld. Flonzaley as a weakened Hephaestus now gets his power from
his wealth, drawn from a world that tries to solve its death problems
with money. When Renata marries him she leaves her small son Roger

in Spain with Charlie, who was hoping to live with Renata there. She tells Charlie, "It's him you need now, not me" (432). Aeneas is the son of Aphrodite, and Roger plays that role. At least Charlie has someone to lead him to an Eternal City. But soon the Senora, Renata's mother, an ancient, plotting crone, comes and takes Roger away, and Charlie is alone. He must find his own way without a guide.

Renata: The Failure of Beauty

As one of Bellow's most complex figures, Renata carries several philosophic and metaphysical implications. After losing her to Flonzaley, Charlie, in a calmer mood, thinks on his affair with this goddess of love and beauty: "In taking up with her I had asked for trouble. Why? Maybe the purpose of such trouble was to turn me deeper into realms of peculiar but necessary thought" (433). And we assume that Charlie is now ready to climb higher on the Platonic ladder, toward a more cosmic attachment. If we are to understand Bellow's further intentions, we must see Renata's role in terms of what seems to be, again, Bellow's reading of Whitehead.

The quality of beauty that Renata represents is directly associated with the victory of science and our impulse to accurate observation and logical deduction. That is, we have confined our idea of beauty to earth-bound definitions, since we see no further than our earthly existence. Moreover, we can never experience more cosmic definitions until we move beyond that vision. In his *Adventures of Ideas,* Whitehead has a section entitled "Civilization" (which at its broadest is the stretch of Bellow's novel) wherein he proposes five requisites of a civilized society—Truth, Beauty, Adventure, Art, Peace.[5] In his discussion of beauty, Whitehead makes it clear that we must look beyond nature, beyond the material world, for the quality of beauty that will offer us a timeless human significance. Nature, or the material world, is by definition cyclically repetitive, hence lacking this significance. Whitehead says, "This is the Beauty realized in actual occasions which are the completely real things in the universe."[6] Infinite repetition of such "occasions" is, of course, one definition of boredom; and here we get some insight into Charlie's constant concern with boredom. At one time he even has a plan to write a "master essay" on the subject (108).

Whitehead's ideas on beauty come to life when Charlie recalls just such an occasion as Whitehead describes. Charlie is taking a trip through France with, significantly, Renata:

Renata pointed to the landscape and said, "Isn't that beautiful!" I looked out, and she was right. Beautiful was indeed there. But I had seen Beautiful many times, and so I closed my eyes. I rejected the plastered idols of Appearances. These idols I had been trained, along with everybody else, to see, and I was tired of their tyranny. I even thought, The painted Veil isn't what it used to be. . . . The damn thing is wearing out. We crave more than ever the radiant vividness of boundless love, and more and more the barren idols thwart this. A world of categories devoid of spirit waits for life to return. Humboldt was supposed to be an instrument of this revival. This mission or vocation was reflected in his face. The hope of new beauty. The promise, the secret of beauty. . . . It was consistent that Renata should direct my attention to the Beautiful. She had a personal stake in it, she was linked with Beauty. (16–17)

"A new beauty"—that is what Charlie is looking for; but he knows he will not find it in nature, in the material world, so he closes his eyes, something he is unable to do for the time being while looking at Renata. His training had been too thorough, his attachment too strong. Her beauty, like the landscape, has its perfection; but it is a lower type of perfection since it is finite, repetitive, and lacking in metaphysical significance. Hence, "The damn thing is wearing out." Whitehead describes the problem through the example of the growth and decay of the ideal of perfection invented by the ancient Greeks:

The [Greek] race was awakened into progress by a great ideal of perfection. This ideal was an immense advance upon the ideals which the surrounding civilizations had produced. It was effective and realized in a civilization which attained its proper beauty in human lives to an extent not surpassed before or since. Its art, its theoretic sciences, its modes of life, its literature, its philosophic schools, its religious rituals, all conspired to express every aspect of this wonderful idea. Perfection was attained, and with the attainment, inspiration withered. With repetition in successive generations, freshness gradually vanished. Learning and learned taste replaced the ardour of adventure.[7]

There are at least two points to be observed here. First, there is an obvious parallel between Whitehead's matter and that "occasion" of Charlie's trip with Renata. What Whitehead reports happened to the Greek ideal of perfection is happening to Charlie's ideals. The other point: Whitehead says that this type of perfection "was effective and realized." The key word is "realized," for that which is realized is necessarily closed, finite; hence, again, failing in metaphysical significance. Obviously what we are looking for, what Charlie is sensing a need for, must be infinite, enduring, a perfection or ideal that exceeds the conditions set by nature. Charlie must learn to look beyond Renata, as he does at the end when he comes to terms with this attachment:

The beauty of a woman like Renata was not entirely appropriate. It was out of season. Her physical perfection was of the Classical Greek or High Renaissance type. And why was this sort of beauty historically inappropriate? Well, it went back to a time when the human spirit was just beginning to disengage itself from nature. Until that moment it hadn't occurred to man to think of himself separately. He hadn't distinguished his own being from natural being but was a part of it. But as soon as intellect awoke he became separated from nature. As an individual, he looked and saw the beauty of the external world, including human beauty. This was a moment sacred in history—the golden age. Many centuries later, the Renaissance tried to recover this first sense of beauty. But even then it was too late. Intellect and spirit moved on. A different sort of beauty, more internal, had begun its development. This internal beauty, manifested in romantic art and poetry, was the result of a free union with the spirit of nature. So Renata was really a peculiar phantom. My passion for her was an antiquarian passion. She seemed to be aware of this herself. Look at the way she swaggered and clowned. Attic or Botticellian loveliness doesn't smoke cigars. . . . I couldn't say that *I* had the new sort of internal beauty. . . . But I had heard of this beauty, I got advance notice of it. What did I propose to do about this new beauty? I didn't know yet. (433–34)

Renata represents the Greek ideal of perfection of beauty in its decayed state, as that ideal clings to Charlie, hence to our culture. There are other implications to her role, too, too many to take up here. But when she writes her final letter to Charlie, she says, accusingly, "You put me in the whore position" (429); and there seems to be some truth here (as

Charlie might say), since our culture is now using love and beauty as weapons of merchandising. Of course, Whitehead would point to such practices as what happens to perfection if we stand on its achievement too long. He would not be astonished at Charlie's report that our contemporary Aphrodite now smokes cigars.

Worldly Success and the Failure of Peace

We recall that each of the figures we have discussed—Denise, Cantabile, and Renata—claims to be indispensable to Charlie's future. All together they promise fame, status, power, money, love, beauty, youth, and no doubt other guarantees. Of course it all adds up to worldly success, the very thing that destroys Humboldt. In the opening pages, Charlie describes the catastrophe: "That charming fluent deeply worried man to whom I was so deeply attached, passionately lived out the theme of Success. Naturally he died a Failure. What else can result from the capitalization of such nouns" (6). A few pages later, Charlie recalls an afternoon with Humboldt: "The subject that afternoon was Success. I was from the sticks and he was giving me the lowdown. Could I imagine, he said, to knock the Village flat with your poems and then follow up with critical essays in the *Partisan* and the *Southern Review?* He had much to tell me about Modernism, Yeats, Rilke, Eliot. . . . I have vertigo from success, Charlie. My ideas won't let me sleep. . . . It'll happen to you, too. I tell you this to prepare you" (12). The young Charlie is flattered, "madly excited," he reports. "Of course I was in a state of intense preparation and hoped to knock everybody dead" (12). He has yet to experience this success.

Now all of this seems like just so much cliché—money, power, fame, etc., do not bring happiness. But there are, again, metaphysical implications. The issue is still the conflict between science and religion, with the desire for success consequent to our impulse to accurate observation and logical deduction. When Whitehead comments on the nature of peace in a civilized society, he discusses one of the adjuncts of success, the desire for fame. He maintains there can be no peace within a society whose aims are not beyond the personal, that peace is only possible through a transcendence of the personal. He speaks of this desire for fame as an "inversion of the social impulse,"[8] by which he means that while a civilization at its highest depends on the individual impulse toward social worth and status, when that impulse becomes egotistic and self-serving, hence finite since the individual is so, the necessary impulse toward the impersonal higher aims of that civilization are turned against themselves. He states that such "an inversion of the social impulse . . . involves the feeling that each act of experience is a central reality, claiming all things as its own. The world then has no justification except as a satisfaction of such claims."[9] And even with their satisfaction, such claims must end in despair since they are founded on finite principles. Whitehead says that our goals must be based on "an appeal beyond boundaries,"[10] which necessitates a vision of self as "one of a series," as Charlie puts it (383).

There is another interesting parallel between the thought of Whitehead and Bellow. Whitehead says, and here we should keep Humboldt in mind, that "such a pathology [the desire for fame] consists in the destruction of the audience for the sake of fame."[11] Again and again, Charlie describes Humboldt as a pathological case, specifically at one point, "a classic case of manic depression" (7). After Humboldt publishes his ballads and achieves his success, he thrives on audience, whether it be Charlie, Kathleen, his lawyers, or the admiring patrons of the White Horse Tavern. "Humboldt could really talk" (4), Charlie says. On one level, Bellow has in mind here the successful artist and his inclination to desert his art for fame and other like goals. We have all seen and heard the creative mind, after his aesthetic or intellectual achievement, become an omnipresent figure on radio, television, in magazines, newspapers, and journals, and on the inevitable lecture circuit. Yet ultimately we are all involved because we too have accepted this definition of success, finite though it be. In the face of this desire for fame, the destruction of the audience or the world means nothing, even if we are part of that worldly audience. As the young Charlie says in his excitement to knock everybody dead, "I didn't really care how many people bit the dust" (14). It is little wonder that Bellow, the Nobel Prize winner and gatherer of many other awards, has often voiced his own fears toward such fame.

Spain and a Legacy of Peace

In one way or another, Charlie finally disengages from all his attachments. He is alone in Spain, and running out of money. Then, as he reports, he "came into a legacy" (6) which "wiped out many immediate problems" (10). Of course he is referring to Humboldt's gift, which solves his financial difficulties. Yet there are far more important implications here; and since we will be dealing with them, some review might help. Humboldt does not intend to do so, but he actually leaves two gifts to Charlie. First, there is an outline for a film scenario, "kid stuff" that together they had tossed off "in a vein of humor" while at Princeton (453). Charlie had even forgotten about it. This scenario deals with the seriocomic adventures of one Caldofreddo who by turning cannibal survives being stranded on an expedition to the Arctic, an expedition that, given all the jealousy and bickering, must have been consequent to the desire for fame. He ends up in a Sicilian village, an "amiable old gent, the ice cream vendor who is loved by the kiddies" (461). Yet as Humboldt explains in his letter to Charlie, "But that is not my gift to you. After all, we collaborated, and it would be chintzy of me to call it a gift. No, I have dreamed up another story and I believe it is worth a fortune" (342).

This second story line (Humboldt labels it "Treatment" [343]) is about a man named Corcoran who takes his exotic mistress to romantic far-off places. "Returning, [Humboldt says,] Corcoran writes a marvelous book—a book of such potency and wit that it must not be kept from the world." The only trouble is—"He cannot publish. It would hurt his wife and destroy his marriage" (344). So he decided to try for everything—money, love, fame, success, happiness, etc.—by taking his wife on a duplicate journey, this time secretly filming the trip, and publishing that trip, as well as selling the film rights. He does so, and his personal life is a disaster. The project is a great success, but both his wife and mistress leave him quite alone with his success.

Humboldt points out that he intends this second story as a comment on Charlie's life (347), and Charlie is not unaware of the parallels: he too is alone with his success, such as it is. Humboldt, still the teacher, is trying to minister to Charlie through this "Treatment." It all amounts to a pursuit for salvation through art, or as Charlie puts it, a hope for "redemption through art," a subject we must take up later.

In the first story, with Caldofreddo's rescue from the icefloe, there are meaningful echoes of Gulliver's escape from the Houyhnhnms. In both stories, the protagonists go somewhat mad on the rescue vessels, since they are unable to recover from their past: Gulliver cannot forget his "ideal" Houyhnhnms; Caldofreddo cannot forget the horror of his cannibalism. But then Bellow leaves his parallel and points to distinctions: we must remember that Gulliver's madness prevails since he blindly maintains his deformed ideals; but Caldofreddo survives in peace because he is willing to forsake his fruitless desire for fame and to take up a truly idyllic life in the Sicilian village. From what we have already said, we can see that Bellow uses the Gulliver story to warn us what can happen when we stay with ideals that are not operative, and to show us that with a reevaluation of self and place, we can live in peace. In the Caldofreddo story, further implications are clear: when man is freezing (figuratively) and alone, in complete despair, without hope for the future, he becomes a cannibal. Personal existence is all. (And we remember Whitehead's contention that the desire for fame, probably one of the goals of Caldofreddo as he set forth on his expedition, leads to the destruction of the audience, hence to a kind of cannibalism.) Things change, however, when man is at peace, as Caldofreddo is, in Sicily; he is able to think beyond the personal. He is able to cope with slings and arrows. When a reporter suddenly appears, threatening to expose Caldofreddo's past, Caldofreddo pushes a huge rock down a hill toward the reporter; but, no longer a cannibal thinking only of self, he warns the reporter just in time. Then Caldofreddo confesses his past to the village and the story ends "with a choric scene of forgiveness and reconciliation" (465).

Bellow's intentions toward these stories certainly exceed the few remarks I have made; but the central point at this time is that contrary to Humboldt's intentions it is the *first* story, of Caldofreddo, rather than the second, that solves Charlie's "Immediate problems." It is, Charlie discovers, this "kid stuff" that has been made into a film which the world is standing in line to see. Although Bellow may have other reasons for this irony of intention, more than likely he is following a kind of script himself. In further delineation of the nature of peace in a civilized society, Whitehead states: "The experience of peace is largely beyond the control of purpose. It comes as a gift."[12] Given Bellow's obvious interest in Whitehead, as well as the clear parallel between Whitehead's contention and the best laid scheme of Humboldt, it is most likely that Bellow got his title, *Humboldt's Gift,* right here.

Certainly the money from the Caldofreddo story, which makes possible a kind of peace for Charlie, was not the result of Humboldt's purpose, nor Charlie's, who had quite forgotten the "kid stuff." And as Charlie says of the now-dead Humboldt and the legacy, "He came from left field" (34). The World Historical Spirit works in mysterious ways, even to itself.

Free of parasitical attachments, and with some money, Charlie takes up a more peaceful existence. But it is difficult for us to understand a state of peace that comes to us only through accident. We are used to such language as "the pursuit of peace." We say it is one of our goals. And certainly we do not ordinarily define peace in terms of a man's chasing his own private horizons, as Charlie is able to do with the money from the Caldofreddo film. He now plans to spend some time at the Swiss Steiner Center of Anthroposophy at Basel, continuing his studies. We can, however, get a clue as to what is *not* meant by this peace when Whitehead says that it "is not the negative conception of anaesthesia";[13] and we recall Charlie's frustrated cries against this kind of false peace: "But . . . we sleep. Just sleep, and eat and play and fuss and sleep again" (226–27). This is the false peace that comes with what we earlier referred to as the perfection of an ideal. There is a great temptation to rest content within that perfection, as did the Greeks and Romans within their perfections, and as we seem to be doing within our perfected, that is, concluded, ideas of man based on accurate observation and logical deduction. Ultimately, exhaustion sets in, and anesthesia masquerades as permanence until decay becomes impossible to live with. Charlie recalls to Naomi, his childhood sweetheart, his own earlier condition: "As I was lying stretched out in America, determined to resist its material interests and hoping for redemption through art, I fell into a deep snooze that lasted for years and decades" (306).

Charlie's Women: Tracking the Past

At its widest, *Humboldt's Gift* is the story of mankind.[14] Charlie's attachments to Naomi Lutz, Demmie Vonghel, Denise, and Renata recount man's progress from his existence in a state of nature, his slow withdrawal from that state as he discovers intellect, and finally, his development of aesthetic impulses. Altogether it is a history of mankind.

Naomi as Charlie's sweetheart represents the mind in its state of nature, when man saw himself as a part of nature, without distinctions wrought by intellect. Charlie recalls to the now mature Naomi, "I loved you cell by cell. To me you were a completely nonalien person. Your molecules were my molecules. Your smell was my smell" (302). And again Charlie says, "When I loved Naomi Lutz, I was safely *within life*" (76). He also tells her, "I've often thought . . . that I lost my character altogether because I couldn't spend my life with you. . . . If I had been able to hold you in my arms nightly since the age of fifteen I would never have feared the grave" (213). Certainly this is true because our fear of death came with our separation from nature and the development of intellect. In connection with this account of Charlie's relationship with Naomi, Bellow uses Old Testament names and places to set this condition of our state in nature in deep history: Naomi, Jacob, Laban (214), Asher (290). Then Naomi's last name is Lutz, almost a duplicate of the place Jacob named Beth-el, but which was formerly called Luz.

Demmie Vonghel, Charlie's second love, represents that twilight zone in which man is partly in but withdrawing from nature through the development of his intellect. Bellow models Demmie on the earth-goddess Demeter whose daughter, hence part of herself, was abducted and taken to hell. It will be recalled that during the day Demmie works (she teaches Latin, scrubs her own floors—naked); during the evening she can be quite sophisticated; but late at night she has nightmares of hell. She awakens screaming, "I know there is hell. There is hell—there *is*" (20). Her father was one of the "last of the old-time Fundamentalists" (19). In one myth, Demeter's father is Zeus, perhaps another old-time fundamentalist. Demmie as figure works on other levels that we will not go into here since our present purpose is to see her only as figure for a particular time in the history of man. Demmie, like Demeter, is agrarian: "Hers was the sort of face you might have seen in a Conestoga wagon a century ago, a pioneer face" (19). As frontier figure, she is nature on the frontiers of intellect. Demmie dies in a plane crash; it is time for Demeter to return to earth.

Denise, as we said earlier, enters in the role of Athena, representing man's development of intellect. George Swiebel describes her as "a great beauty but not altogether human" (40); and Charlie admits, "I'm still afraid of Denise. She still wields a certain power" (56). Yet Charlie

leaves her since, as we suggested earlier, "she had been bad for his idea."
That idea needs powers beyond those of intellect because it is based on
Whitehead's religious intuitions aiming for metaphysical significance.
As adversary to Denise as Athena, we have Charlie's next attachment,
Renata as Aphrodite. The feud between these two is an extension of that
event ages ago involving Paris and the apple. But to our point here,
Charlie's life with Denise and Renata overlaps. He takes up with Renata
while still married to Denise, but in the process of divorce, a situation
that is quite appropriate if we keep in mind figurative roles. As a
consequence of man's discovery of intellect (Charlie's marrying Denise),
he also discovered aesthetics that moved him closer to metaphysical
longings; hence Charlie's move to Renata who, as the shadow of
Aphrodite, embodies these longings. Significantly, in the story the
divorce from Denise is never concluded. Man does not escape intellect
so easily. As Charlie says, "She still wields some power." Through these
four figures—Naomi, Demmie, Denise, and Renata—Charlie progresses through the whole of human history. Further evidence that
Bellow intends such wide-ranging perspective is made clear through a
passage we cited earlier in this chapter, showing Charlie, at the end of
the novel, rationalizing his broken relationship with Renata, as well as
her present irrelevance to his life, in terms of man's intellectual and
aesthetic development.

While Bellow does intend these figures as projections of world
history, he also intends them to act out the history of the United States.
The pattern of growth and development is clear: Naomi as our religious
beginnings; Demmie as our agrarian years; Denise and Renata as fallen
ideals, as the failure of the American dream, showing the misplaced
uses to which we have put our intelligence and our aesthetics. Further,
on this level, we can see Humboldt as Gatsby when we see him "in a
checked sport jacket and strap-fastened polo boots" (20), and even as F.
Scott Fitzgerald when Charlie comments that "Humboldt spoke won-
derfully of the wonderful, abominable rich" (14). In any case, as we
have used them, neither our intellect nor our aesthetics, brought to
perfection in ancient Greece and presently manifested in abused and
misused forms, will serve metaphysical purposes. Both have tried, and
exhaustion has set in. Charlie, as our "cultural point-man," moves
beyond these figures on his journey toward limitless beauty and lasting
significance, hence toward a durable peace. This journey makes for the
kind of peace that Charlie finds. Unknown to him even at the end, since
he is still ignorant of his precise future, and still somewhat distracted,

Charlie is going in the "right" direction, unencumbered by attachments to old, worn-out ideas. He has achieved what Whitehead calls the "zest for Adventure,"[15] as he is willing and eager to test new ideas in his search for his metaphysical significance. It is an endless, infinite adventure; one in which, as Whitehead says, we see ourselves as "process,"[16] as opposed to seeing ourselves in terms of Renata's theory of "when you're dead you're dead, that's that." But we must not mistake Bellow: Renata has some truth. As Charlie says, speaking of Houdini's death, "So you see, nobody can overcome the final fact of the material world" (436). There is no personal, physical immortality. We must find our significance beyond the material, within World Historical forces of the metaphysical. As Humboldt in his last days of lucidity writes to Charlie, "Last of all—remember: we are not natural beings but supernatural beings" (347).

Hope for Charlie Citrine and Civilization

Humboldt's Gift ends with Charlie's attendance at Humboldt's second funeral. His body was moved from "far out in Deathsville, New Jersey, one of those vast necropolitan developments," to "Valhalla Cemetery" (438). Evidently, we are to see this second burial as a just reassessment of the role that Humboldt played, and is yet playing. He is now a hero with a continuing existence; for as Charlie says, "His soul [is] in some other part of creation, there where souls waited for sustenance that only we, the living, could send from the earth, like grain to Bangla Desh" (462). Yet if we remember the figurative role of Humboldt, we understand that this reassessment is intended to be a contemporary understanding that the past fought its battles, accomplished what it was destined to accomplish, and is to be respected for its effort and achievements. As Charlie says, it is up to us, the living, to not let this past wither into a state of nonbeing, much as Lincoln advises in his Gettysburg Address. Humboldt as figure still stands, like the Roman Republic. Whitehead makes the point: "In one sense, the Roman Republic declined and fell; in another sense, it stands a stubborn fact in the universe. To perish is to assume a new function in the process of generation."[17] And Bellow is asking us to see ourselves and our civilization in just such terms.

What it all amounts to is an escape from history in order to connect with the infinite. Charlie sees the situation. He tells Kathleen, "Now I begin to understand what Tolstoi was getting at when he called on mankind to cease the false and unnecessary comedy of history and begin simply to live" (477). Certainly for Charlie there will be no more visions of himself as a World Historical Figure, shaker of the world, yet always at the mercy and whims of the World Historical Spirit, as was Humboldt. Now we can understand why he tells Kathleen that while following his Steiner studies he would be perfectly happy to serve as an extra in her projected film (478). Further, we can guess that there will be no more biographies from Charlie about such figures. He will live simply, and "listen in secret to the sound of the truth that God puts into us" (477), a sound that affirms our intuition of immortality, or at least a measure thereof. Can we manage this? There is the Bellowian optimism in Humboldt's last letter to Charlie: "This morning . . . the sun was bright. For certain of the living it was a very fine day. Though without sleep for several nights I remembered how it used to be to bathe and shave and breakfast and go into the world. A mild lemon light rinsed the streets. (Hope for this wild combined human operation called America?)" (341). We are surely to see Charlie Citrine manifesting that mild *lemon* light, and offering hope for our culture.

Philosophy and Art

The novel closes here, but a few more words might be helpful. Philosophical elements have always been a part of Bellow's work and have been widely recognized. Indeed, in the last two novels, much to the discomfort of some readers, Bellow threatens to become the philosophical essayist. But it is the late metaphysical bent that has drawn the most attention. The question usually takes some such form as—does he mean it?—all this business of the soul and an afterlife, and especially about Steiner and his anthroposophy. Yes, Bellow does—at least figuratively. As far as Steiner is concerned, he is a figure for an illustration of Bellow's contention, through Charlie, that we must try new ideas, even ideas that are unscientific, and hence, that tend to inhibit us.[18] Whitehead says that "Peace is the removal of inhibition."[19] At the end of the novel, in spite of the many derisive attacks on his anthroposophical studies, and in spite of his own doubts—"There were passages in Steiner that set my teeth on edge" (439)—Charlie triumphs over his inhibitions and is able to go ahead with his irrational studies. One more point: Whitehead says that "a great civilization interfused with Art presents the world to its members clothed with the Appearance of immortality."[20] And that is precisely why Charlie says: "At this moment I must say, almost in the form of deposition, without argument, that I do not believe my birth began my first existence. . . . On esthetic grounds, if on no others, I cannot accept the view of death taken by most of us, and taken by me during most of my life—on esthetic grounds therefore I am obliged to deny that so extraordinary a thing as a human soul can be wiped out forever" (141). The key words are "on esthetic grounds." If we are to have a great civilization we must *feel* our permanence, even if we cannot *think* it. Only then will we be at peace. Whitehead says, "Peace is. . . the intuition of permanence."[21] Such is the direction of Charlie Citrine as character in his own right, and as "cultural point-man." More narrowly, it is the direction that Bellow would have the artist take, for, as Whitehead suggests, art has a role to play here. We can better understand that role if we keep in mind Whitehead's term that we called on before to explain in part the peace Charlie finally experiences: that is, an intuition of all things, including ourselves, as "process."[22] Charlie voices his intuition of this idea several times. To Kathleen he says, "The question is this: why should we assume the series ends with us? The fact is, I suspect, that we occupy a point within a greater hierarchy that goes far beyond ourselves" (479). The individual within a civilized society sees himself as an individual, but also a part of the "greater hierarchy" of his civilization in a continuum. And Whitehead says that that is the business of art: "This is exactly what we find in great Art. The very details of its compositions live supremely in their own right. They make their own claim to individuality, and yet contribute to the whole. Each such detail receives an access of grandeur from the whole, and yet manifests an individuality claiming attention in its own right."[23] So, great art in its delineations of man will escape the narrow, distorted, imbalanced vision that is confined within the here-and-now, confined to the singular instance and occasion, and depict man as part of a whole, as "one of a series." Whitehead uses the example of Chartres, the Gothic cathedral, wherein "each detail claims a permanent existence for its own sake, and then surrenders it for the sake of the whole composition."[24] Civilization at its highest demands that kind of composition from its artists. But to create such a composition, in art or in life, we need what Charlie calls a "different scale" (479), by which he means a metaphysical scale, one that will allow us an intuition of our lives as a part of an infinite composition. Therein lies our metaphysical significance—and our peace.

It will not be easy. Certainly it will not set easily on those who are still attached to their impulse to accurate observation and logical deduction, and Charlie Citrine knows why: "As none of this is Scientific, we are afraid to think it" (10).

Chapter Nine
Other Works:
Shorter Fiction and
To Jerusalem and Back

Mosby's Memoirs and Other Stories

Of the dozen or so short stories Saul Bellow has given us, six have been collected under the title of *Mosby's Memoirs and Other Stories* (1968). This volume has been justly praised, and the stories merit their increasingly frequent inclusion in standard literature anthologies, although one supposes those inclusions are partly owing to Bellow's wider reputation as a novelist. In any case, the stories stand on their own. Of added interest to the reader of Bellow's novels is how these tales parallel and, in many cases, look forward to the matter of his longer works.

The first selection, "Leaving the Yellow House," is a good example. We are given old Hattie, "not exactly a drunkard, but she hit the bottle pretty hard," living forty miles from the nearest town in a barren desert setting that is a fit metaphor for what her life has become. She is surrounded by five or six friends who reluctantly help her and who, Hattie knows, would be better off without her. Through her reminiscences we learn that life for Hattie has been one long series of mistakes and disappointments, but she is not ready to give up: "It's looked bad many a time before, but when push came to shove I made it. Somehow I got by."[1] The latest indignity is a broken arm, which further threatens her proud, independent spirit, since she must rely even more on those around her. Hattie ends up with only one thing she can call her own, an old yellow house she recently inherited. Given her age and health, she knows she should prepare for death, and make out a will assigning this house, but this she cannot bring herself to do: "I am not ready to give up on this. No, not yet. And so I'll tell you what, I leave this property, land, house, garden, and water rights, to Hattie Simms Waggoner. Me! I realize this is bad and wrong. Not possible, yet it is the only thing I really wish to do, so may God have mercy on my soul" (42).

In spite of a life seemingly not worth living and certainly one that cannot last much longer, Hattie refuses to call it quits, and she can no more give up her house than she can give up on life. This story was originally published in 1957, some seven years before Herzog; and in that novel we remember that Bellow uses the house as a metaphor for Herzog's commitment to life. Herzog decides to keep his all-but-ruined house, and start anew. Like Herzog, and all Bellowian protagonists, Hattie will play the phoenix. As the narrator tells us, "She was not one to be miserable for long; she had the expression of a perennial survivor" (15).

Dr. Braun in "The Old System" looks ahead to the character of Mr. Sammler in Bellow's Mr. Sammler's Planet. Toward the end of a long life, and appropriately at the end of the year on a cold December day, Dr. Braun tries to think his way through to some meaning, some use for this life, even as old Sammler spends his declining years. Also like Mr. Sammler, Braun lives in an existential knot: with a clear prehension of cosmic indifference, he struggles with a day-to-day world in which there *are* such things as "childhood, family, friendship, love [even though they] were stifled in the grave" (82). How does one deal with such contradiction? Braun has no sympathy for the separatist. He says, "Every civilized man today cultivated an unhealthy self-detachment. Had learned from art the art of amusing self-observation and objectivity. . . . It made him [Braun] sad to feel that the thought, art, belief of great tradition should be so misemployed" (48). In his fiction, Bellow often dramatizes the position that we have misused our traditions, knowledge, and imagination. On one level, the character of Humboldt in the later novel *Humboldt's Gift* is guilty of such debasement. and later on in this chapter we will meet the character of Dr. Mosby who "cultivated an unhealthy self-detachment," and must suffer the consequences.

But Dr. Braun in "The Old System" has a more immediate problem: should he meet his dying sister Tina's adamant condition that he pay her a large sum of money to see her a last time. They have been quarreling a long time, but her demand is ridiculous. Nevertheless, he pays; she then refuses the money and embraces him. And then, "These tears! When you wept them from the heart, you felt you justified something, understood something. But what did you understand? Again, *nothing*! It was only an intimation of understanding. A promise that mankind might—*might*, mind you—eventually, through its gift which might, *might* again—be a divine gift, comprehend why it lived. Why life, why death" (82–83). And again we are looking ahead to *Humboldt's Gift*, for the gift that Humboldt passes on to Charlie Citrine is just such a gift that we must use to continue our search for meaning. The name of the gift? The imagination. If in our search for meaning, the facts of life and death stand in our way, we must imagine our way through those facts. In the following story, "Looking for Mr. Green," we see the thesis dramatized again.

"Looking for Mr. Green" explores a theme Bellow examines in much greater depth some twenty-five years later. Existential in its implications, it centers on the idea that meaning comes from one's search, and that the nature of the search is often at odds with the values and beliefs of society. The story is set in the depression years. George Grebe, thirty-five years old, finally manages to get a job in his native Chicago, delivering relief checks in the Negro district. George is a well-educated man, "a university man," and his liberal studies of the rise and fall of civilizations make him aware of just how little his present activity means in historical perspective. He is captivated daily with the evidence right in Chicago "where cycles were so fast and the familiar died out, and again rose changed" (105). In spite of this chaos, George feels, or chooses to feel, that he *must* succeed in delivering a check to the ephemeral Mr. Green. This mission embodies the biblical injunction Bellow sets before the story: "Whatsoever thy hand findeth to do, do it with thy might."

The neighbors in the ghetto area give George no help at all, for they suspect his motives: he might be a cop or a process server. Then perhaps they really do not know Mr. Green, or maybe Mr. Green does not even exist. Eventually, George finds the name Green below a shattered mailbox, and he exultantly rings the bell, only to be confronted by a drunken naked woman reeling downstairs, mouthing obscenities that are directed, one supposes, to a partner she has just left. At first, George refuses to hand her the check, having been warned of such deception on this job. But he finally gives in and has her sign, for "Though she might not be Mrs. Green, he was convinced that Mr. Green was upstairs.

Whoever she was, the woman stood for Green, whom he was not to see this time" (109).

In the face of all the change and ruin that the world offers, and that George lives with in Chicago, he repeatedly ponders problems of appearance and reality. In the midst of all this floating chaos, what is real? What can we count on? What abides? Such abstract, weighty philosophical questions are brought to a point in George's search for Mr. Green when George answers in an act of faith: Mr. Green does exist. Yet he berates himself: "Well, you silly bastard . . . so you think you found him. So what? Maybe you really did find him—what of it?" But a stronger feeling prevails: "It was important that there was a real Mr. Green whom they could not keep him from reaching because he seemed to come as an emissary from hostile appearances" (109). George Grebe has several ancestors in Bellow's novels including the characters of Henderson, Herzog, and Charlie Citrine, all of whom end their stories with acts of faith that challenge prevalent thought and opinion.

"The Gonzaga Manuscripts" makes no claim of Jamesian depths, but here Bellow does depict the innocent, idealistic American clashing with European culture. The young, romantic Clarence Feiler comes to Spain on a "quest," as he thinks of it, to track down some of the unpublished poetry of the dead poet Manuel Gonzaga. Clarence owes a lot to Gonzaga. He explains, "I was just killing time in graduate school till I came across Gonzaga. . . . I felt right away . . . that I was in touch with a poet who could show me how to go on, and what attitude to take toward life. . . . Gosh! There should be someone trying to find those posthumous poems. They ought not to be given up. They must be marvelous" (112–13). Given such language, along with a few examples of the poetry of the deep-thinking Gonzaga, as well as with several clichéd, cross-purposed, and learned literary pronouncements from Clarence, we are not surprised when Clarence runs into trouble. It is not Spain: "Clarence loved Spanish cities, even the poorest and the barrenest, and the capitals stirred his heart as no other places did" (112). He loves the scenery, the culture, the history, the traditions. Unfortunately, he has to do business with the people if he is to locate the poems, and they have no understanding or sympathy for his quest. He is shuffled from one family to another, having to endure what he reads as insults to America and snide innuendos concerning the great Gonzaga, this even from a close friend of the dead poet. Clarence's quest comes to a bitter end when he reaches what he thinks is his goal only to discover that the interest shown in him by his latest guide, one Alverez-Polo, rests on the assumption that he has come to Spain to finance a uranium mine. The poems? They were buried with the countess to whom Gonzaga had made love. "Oh, damn! Oh, damn it! And didn't he [your uncle] leave you anything in that collection of papers that has to do with Gonzaga? No journals, no letters that mention Gonzaga? Nothing?" To which his last hope Alverez-Polo answers, "He left me these shares in the mine. They're valuable. Not yet, but they will be if I can get capital" (141).

At the beginning of the story we are told that Clarence had been to Spain twice before, when he was a graduate student studying Spanish literature and again to see the ruins of the Civil War. But "this time he came, not as a tourist, but on a quest" (112). Yet he is mistaken, at least partially, since there is something very touristy and very American about Clarence, in his worship of the past as he understands that past, and in his disturbed feelings about the gritty present. Clarence joins a list of Bellowian characters who desperately try to use art to solve their own problems of relevancy or as a messianic instrument with which to instruct the world. This list goes back as far as the secondary figure of John Pearl in *Dangling Man* and continues through the central characters of Herzog, Mr. Sammler, Humboldt, and Charlie Citrine. All meet with failure.

"A Father-to-Be," the shortest story in the collection, centers on a mystery that engages Bellow throughout his fiction: the pull of sex and the triumph of sex, against all reason. Rogin, a thirty-one-year-old research chemist, is taking the New York subway to have dinner with his fiancée Joan who shares an apartment with another woman. As with all of Bellow's protagonists, Rogin has problems, mainly with a younger brother he is putting through college, a mother who also needs money, and his fiancée Joan who has debts he is trying to pay off. Joan is "beautiful, well-educated, aristocratic in her attitude," but she is unable to find "suitable work" (144). As fast as Rogin pays her bills, she spends, and as he rides toward her apartment he grows increasingly disturbed by these thoughts. He is determined to take control. But what further strengthens this determination is that seated on the subway next to him is a man about forty years old who looks like Joan, and who, Rogin imagines, might be a preview of some future son of his.

He does not like the looks of this man. He and this man obviously have nothing in common. Is this what his life is all about? Is this why he worries and works "only to become the father of a fourth-rate man?" (151). He is resolved to make a few things clear to Joan. But Rogin is defeated by sensual forces that bury all his resolve when Joan, treating him like a child, insists on giving him a shampoo. She "pressed against him from behind, surrounding him, pouring the water gently over him until it seemed to him that the water came from within him, it was the warm fluid of his own secret loving spirit, green and foaming, and the words he had rehearsed he forgot . . ." (155).

The invincible sensuousness of women, with the implications of iron-bound human survival, against all argument or reason, is a common theme in Bellow's work. Even in the first novel, *Dangling Man,* Joseph has his Kitty. More notably, Herzog has his Ramona and Charlie Citrine of *Humboldt's Gift* his Renata.

Dr. Willis Mosby of "Mosby's Memoirs" is not the usual protagonist found in Bellow's fiction, since he seems to have had the world pretty much as he wished it. As he writes his memoirs, isolated on a mountain just outside the town of Oaxaca, Mexico, his reflections give no hint of regrets or disillusionments, no heartfelt confessions of mistakes nor painful memories of failures and rejections. Oh, some of his students had disappointed him, but "you cannot grow a rose in a coal mine." And he had been fired by Princeton University, "because his mode of discourse was so upsetting to the academic community." And of course "Mosby was invited to no television programs because he was like the Guerrilla Mosby of the Civil War. When he galloped in, all were slaughtered" (176). Just so did Mosby see himself.

When the story opens he is reminding himself, as he writes his memoirs, to "avoid the common fate of intellectuals" by, one supposes, getting too serious; and to this point his survey has been rather weighty, tracing his fundamentalist background and a wide variety of his intellectual achievements. For comic relief, he decides to center his attention on a true schlemiel, one Lustgarten, a chronic loser who was intermittently a part of Mosby's life. When he dispenses with the Lustgarten episode, it is time for Mosby to join a tour to visit some temple ruins.

"Mosby's Memoirs" is the story of a man afflicted with one of the seven deadly sins—pride. In this case, intellectual pride. For the telling, Bellow uses Dantean thought and imagery. The mountain Mosby lives on is Dante's mountain in Purgatory and the ruined tomb Mosby visits provides him with a vision of Hell. Then it is appropriate to Dantean thought that Mosby was in Mexico on a Guggenheim grant, that he chose to be there, and to do what he was doing. Just so did Dante describe the role of free choice in divine punishment. Toward the end of the story, as Mosby follows the guide toward the tomb, we are told that "Mosby was going once more through an odd and complex fantasy. It was that he was dead. He had died. He continued, however, to live. His doom was to live to the end as Mosby" (182). Writing his memoirs was Mosby's doom, his purgatory, to relive every step of his life, wading in intellectual pride until he could stand the sin no longer—again, just as Dante conceived the cleansing process of Purgatory. Deep in the tomb, "his heart was paralyzed! His lungs would not draw! Jesus, I cannot catch my breath!" Then, like many other Bellowian heroes, Mosby has had enough of this past, this intellectual quagmire, and he turns back toward the bit of daylight at the entrance of the tomb. "I must get out," he told the guide. "Ladies, I find it very hard to breathe" (184).

"The Silver Dish"

Not included in the above volume is Bellow's recent short story, "The Silver Dish," published in the *New Yorker* (25 September 1978). We cited in a footnote to our discussion on *Humboldt's Gift* Alfred Kazin's remark that Bellow "invented himself again and again in book after book." He does so here. Woody Selbst ("self" in German), a sixty-year-old tile setter, somewhat successful, reminisces on his youth and on the recent death of Morris, his father. Woody's memories of his youth remind us of Augie March in Chicago, when we see Woody surviving contrary forces in his life, the heavily straight, religious forces on his mother's side and the catch-as-catch-can life of his father Morris, a thief, a con artist, deserter of his wife and children, a lusty "hard-bellied" man in pursuit of what the day will bring. One day, it brings him a silver dish that he steals from Woody's benefactor, Mrs. Skogland. This, after he has conned Woody to take him to her house to beg for money which, Woody knows, he will bet on horses. Henry James's *The Golden Bowl* is the study of moral turpitude, and Bellow's "The

Silver Dish" is centered on the same issue; for Woody is attached to his father, perhaps likes him, but knows his moral flaws as he knows himself. Of course that is the point. Bellow is both Woody and Morris, and when Woody lies down beside Morris in the hospital, as Morris is dying, and tries to restrain the old man from detaching the life-preserving tubes, it is Woody who is clinging to life. But Morris deliberately slips away: "You could never put down that self-willed man. When he was ready to make his move, he made it—always on his own terms." Here we are listening to Woody speak of his father; but we could be hearing about that wanderer Augie March or about Saul Bellow himself as he looks at his past work and decides it is time to move on—as Bellow has already declared (see below, chapter 10). For Bellow readers, "The Silver Dish" is familiar territory in its characters, its Chicago setting, its style, and its concerns with the cycles of life and death. It will take on added significance as the cycles of Bellow's career develop.

To Jerusalem and Back: A Personal Account

During the 1967 Arab-Israeli War (The Ten Days' War), Saul Bellow went to Israel as a reporter for *Newsday* magazine. In 1975, along with his wife Alexandra, he went back, this time to stay for several months. *To Jerusalem and Back: A Personal Account* (1975) is a record of that trip. In form a journal, this book takes us from London to Israel, back to London, and finally home to Bellow's Chicago; the content is an account of Bellow's observations and reflections on life in Israel, focused on her struggle for survival in the Middle East. Having said that much, however, further generalization is difficult because the book becomes so many things: it is a political primer setting forth the multisided positions and issues of the Arab-Israeli conflict; at times it becomes a polemic as the note of persuasion in Bellow's voice is heard; it is also a philosophical exercise with comment sweeping from the particular to the universal; it is a personal pilgrimage with Bellow's returning to a cultural home to make connections; perhaps at its best, it is a sketch book evoking events, people, places, scenes, and moods. All of these strands run together, at times abruptly and without transition; for Bellow never allows the particular moment nor the immediate event to restrain a provoked thought.

The arrival in Jerusalem is typical. Bellow finds himself at a dinner attended by notables such as Mayor Teddy Kollek and Isaac Stern. Also present is Michel Tatu, foreign news editor of *Le Monde*. Tatu's presence calls forth memories, and Bellow's mind wanders from the clink of glasses and buzz of conversation to a letter he had sent some time before to *Le Monde*, outlining his hopes that France would not return to what Bellow sees as an anti-Semitic thread in French history. "The letter was never acknowledged," Bellow notes abruptly,[2] then details his further complaints against proterrorist positions taken by *Le Monde*. No further mention is made of the party; and with only the narrowest of textual spacing we are suddenly in another time, another place, looking down on the Dead Sea, a piece of nature that Bellow observes through Emersonian eyes: "I look downward toward the Dead Sea, over broken rocks and small houses with bulbous roofs. The color of these is that of the ground itself, and on this strange deadness the melting air presses with an almost human weight. Something intelligible, something metaphysical is communicated by these colors. The universe interprets itself before your eyes. . . . Elsewhere you die and disintegrate. Here you die and mingle" (10).

This dual perspective engaging the old and the new, the past and present, is one of the book's unifying elements. Bellow's sense of history is always lurking under the surface of the moment, ready to sweep us back to biblical times, or as often, to add a more immediate reflection, as when he comments on a discussion concerning the Middle East power struggle: "I have been hearing conversations like this one for half a century. . . . What is wrong with it is that the discussants invariably impart their intelligence to what they are discussing. Later, historical studies show that what actually happened was devoid of anything like such intelligence" (78).

Throughout the book, Bellow's mind repeatedly wanders to the world of art, and especially to the question of how the imagination fares, indeed how it survives, in an existence so necessarily taken with the reality of the moment, with the "butcher problems of politics" (80). In this world, art seems almost a luxury. Bellow grieves over the poet Berryman's suicide, "but it wasn't senseless grief. Something else mingled with feelings of heaviness. The transforming additive: the gift of poetry. . . . I am thinking that some of the politicians I meet are admirable, intelligent men of strong character. But in them the marvelous additive is lacking. It is perhaps astonishing that they aren't demented by the butcher problems, by the insensate pressure of crisis" (80). But art is necessary if politics are to mean anything. Bellow recalls two Russian writers: "Before he died of cold, hunger, and exhaustion in Siberia, Osip Mandelstam recited his poems to other convicts, at their request. Andrei Sinyavsky, in his prison journal, concentrates on art. Perhaps to remain a poet in such circumstances is also to reach the heart of politics. Then human feelings, human experience, the human form and face, recover their proper place—the foreground" (22).

From time to time, we hear direct echoes of Bellow's fiction, especially in his characterization. To be sure, we do not get the full-blown, larger-than-life figures we are used to, for these people are real; but we do catch elements of the Bellowian style. At the dinner party we spoke of earlier, Bellow quickly sketches one of the guests, an Armenian archbishop: "The Archbishop is, to use an old word, a portly man. His cassock, dark red, swells with the body. On his breast two ball-point pens are clipped between the buttons. He has a full youthful clever face; a black beard; small and tidy. The eyes are green" (5). Such a figure might well be found on horseback wending his way toward Canterbury, or, in *Herzog*.

Not only in style are we reminded of the novelist; some ideas found in his fiction are also restated in the journal. At one point, Bellow looks with apprehension at a trend he sees developing in the capitalistic countries: "The free countries are curiously lethargic about their free-dom. . . . Many exult over its [capitalism's] approaching death. Tired of old evils, they long for the new thing and will not be happy until they've had it. Baudelaire writes . . . that life is a hospital in which each patient believes that he will recover if he is moved to another bed" (84–85). As we suggested in our discussion of *Seize the Day*, this futile compulsion to change beds is precisely the force that drives Tommy Wilhelm to attach himself to Dr. Tamkin.

Mr. Sammler's Planet offers a wider parallel. In that novel Bellow has Mr. Sammler repeatedly make the point that understanding is best gained through our making distinctions, and not through everlasting explanations: "One had to learn to distinguish. To distinguish and distinguish and distinguish. It was distinguishing, not explanation, that mattered. Explanation was for the mental masses. Adult educa-tion." This idea is voiced so often in the novel, one can judge that Bellow feels the power of the point to be quite instructive. In any case,

To Jerusalem and Back is built around that same idea. Most of the book rests on distinction, on points and counterpoints, one view as opposed to another. When Bellow returns to Chicago, he responds to a university colleague: "Janowitz asks me how I assess the situation in Israel, and what I would recommend. I answer that I don't think my judgment has much value. I am simply an interested amateur—a learner. I can, however, tell him what I have heard from intelligent and experienced observers" (164).

Although the center of this book concerns life in Israel under seige, we cannot take the space here to examine military and political issues; they are far too complicated.[3] But Bellow talks and listens to a wide spectrum of people, to those high in council, to his friends, to the cab driver and the masseur. The opportunities for enlightenment are everywhere: "Here in Jerusalem when you shut your apartment door behind you you fall into a gale of conversation—exposition, argument, harangue, analysis, theory, expostulation, threat, and prophecy. . . . I listen carefully, closely, more closely than I've ever listened in my life, utterly attentive, but I often feel that I have dropped into a shoreless sea" (25). During these exchanges, Bellow never disputes. As he says, "I have come to listen, not to differ" (113). Yet with the writing of the book, with recollection in greater tranquility, he sets his differences and agreements within the text.

It should be said that after all the miles and all the talking, Bellow ends in frustration. The problems of the Middle East simply overwhelm him: "Trying to put it all together, 'to come to clarity,' as one of my professors used to say. What a nice thing to come to. But the subject resists clarification. . . . Instead of clarity, one is infected with disorder" (175). As for the future and the chances for peace, Bellow draws from one of his most respected authorities, Elie Kedourie: "Kedourie says nothing off the top of his head. His judgments are thoroughly considered. And he is not optimistic" (145).

To Jerusalem and Back ends in sadness, as Bellow ponders the world and its killing—in Lebanon, in Cambodia, wherever: "What is the meaning of such corpse-making? In ancient times the walls of captured cities in the Middle East were sometimes hung with the skin of the vanquished. That custom has died out. But the eagerness to kill for political ends—or to justify killing by such ends—is as keen now as it ever was" (182).

Chapter Ten
Looking Backward

Part of Saul Bellow's achievement, of course, comes from his ability to bring form and content into a keenly balanced and effective relationship; and while it is not possible here to discuss in full this ability, we can point to examples as they appear in one novel or another. We will be looking at his use of character; his use of distance and point of view; his sense of the comic; his urban settings. Finally, we will explore thematic patterns throughout his work, and then make suggestions for what we might expect from Bellow in the future.

Characterization

Bellow's writing can be very deceptive: every story—indeed, every page—is so dominated and controlled by the thoughts and actions of the central character that the casual reader might well imagine that Bellow is interested mainly in character development. Of course he is not. He uses character in the old allegorical tradition: to dramatize a preconceived idea. His protagonist is invariably an Everyman whose primary function is to embody the progress of a state of mind, and his supporting characters are foils that clarify the state of mind. Hence, Bellow's novels are never about anyone; they never really probe the depth and breadth of anyone. What they do is explore thoroughly a particular human condition through character. For example, the central meaning of *Seize the Day* is not found within the person of the protagonist, Tommy Wilhelm, but through Tommy insofar as he represents man in search of identity and purpose. So it is with many of the supporting characters: the meaning of Einhorn in *Augie March* lies in what he represents—literary and social forces of the 1920s.

Both of Bellow's early novels, *Dangling Man* and *The Victim,* are contemporary statements: they lack the historical intentions of his later work. The protagonists, Joseph and Asa Leventhal, may be seen as modern men caught in dilemmas produced by a mass urban society; the supporting characters, as foils to make clear those dilemmas. The character of Schlossberg in *The Victim,* however, is an exception that points to one aspect of Bellow's development. Schlossberg, an embodiment of Victorian attitudes, is the first of a long line of characters whose purpose is to set Bellow's meanings into historical perspective. While Schlossberg is not fully developed and makes only a brief appearance, he is the direct ancestor of the much more complex figure of Madeleine in *Herzog,* in that both of them are manifestations of Victorianism.

After *The Victim,* Bellow is no longer content to limit his vision to contemporary issues. Beginning with *The Adventures of Augie March,* he always assigns his protagonists, and many of his other characters, multilevel roles, one of which projects his thematic implications back into history. When we read of the experiences of Augie March, Tommy Wilhelm, Eugene Henderson, and Moses Herzog, we are examining the dilemmas of modern man; but we are also looking at the wellsprings of those dilemmas.

From time to time throughout this study, these symbolic extensions have come into focus; but Bellow's use of the four women in the life of Moses Herzog offers the best example. Bellow sets Daisy, Sono, Madeleine, and Ramona in a meaningful sequence so that they represent certain cultural and literary influences on Herzog. In this light, Herzog may be seen as contemporary man who looks back upon the forces that have shaped his present. Allegorically, his progress from one to the other of these women is largely motivated by many of the same impulses and pressures that were the cause of the changes in these literary and cultural movements.

During the discussion of the multilevel meanings in *Herzog,* much is said of Daisy and Sono to support this historical approach to interpretation (see above, chapter 6). Hence briefly at this point, Daisy's "stability, symmetry, order, and containment" are neoclassical attributes, while Sono's appeal to the senses and the concern with the person, as well as her specific admiration for the melancholy disposition of Herzog, show her to be a figure of the romantic temperament. In more detail, now, Madeleine follows as a representative of the Victorian period. Her personality shadows forth the *bitch-goddess success* reigning in those days, the corruption and greed. She images the deception and hypocrisy of the time. Bellow points specifically to her place in history as he describes the setting in her apartment:

The fixtures were old-fashioned in this place. These had been luxury apartments in the 1890's. The broad-mouthed faucets ran a shattering stream of cold water. She dropped her pajama top so that she was bare to the waist, and washed herself with a cloth, purifying herself with angry vigor. . . . Silent, barefooted, wearing his trench coat as a robe, Herzog came in and sat on the edge of the tub watching. The tiles were a faded cherry color, and the toothbrush rack, the fixtures, were ornate, old nickel. . . . His open curiosity, the fact that he familiarly shared the bathroom with her, his nakedness under the trench coat, his pallid face in this setting of disgraced Victorian luxury—it all vexed her. (110)

Here is Madeleine, the Victorian, in the act of compromise. Unmarried, she has stayed the night with Herzog; in the morning, as she prepares herself for church, she blames Herzog for her moral duplicity. She is angry at him for what she feels to be a betrayal of her better self, and hence is a mirror for many of the same feelings of self-betrayal that Herzog experiences. One of the most effective scenes in the book depicts Madeleine in the act of self-transformation, as if—through this change, which Bellow shows through a detailed description of Madeleine putting on her makeup—she could live two lives (110–12).

Through Ramona, Herzog's final attachment, Bellow reflects the modern concern for sex as a panacea for the life without focus or direction. Sex is Ramona's stated road to happiness. She attempts to teach Herzog, to persuade him that his salvation lies within her vision of existence. But it is significant that Ramona is somewhat jaded and somewhat frightened; and she is looking for a husband, by which Bellow intends that the contemporary concern with the physical is an escape from desperation that has seen its day.

Through these women as symbols, Bellow clarifies the present state of contemporary man by pointing to his cultural backgrounds, and setting forth directions for his future. At the end, Herzog realizes his debt to these influences, but he rejects them as definitive of him. Such is the case with Mr. Sammler whose progress includes a number of symbolic encounters; and certainly the case of Charlie Citrine, who traces the past, present, and even the future dimly seen, through figures that encompass nothing less than the history of Western civilization.

Since Bellow's figures act as symbol, they possess certain "flat" characteristics that point toward stereotypes. For instance, with the exception of Augie March, who is a peripheral case, all of Bellow's protagonists play the role of a troubled innocent searching out his own identity. Then, and this includes Augie, they are stereotyped by their predictability. Asa Leventhal of *The Victim* establishes a pattern of puzzlement and rage whenever he encounters his antagonist, Allbee; we come to expect Augie March to "move on" regardless of his station at a particular time; we know that Madeleine, Herzog's wife, will keep on posturing for others and lying to herself.

Finally, Bellow stereotypes his people through caricature; their every action and every word, and, in the case of his protagonists, their thoughts, are struck on canvases bigger than life. They cry harder, laugh louder, shout more often, hurt more deeply, anger more quickly, and, in general, live more intensely than any normal person. Bellow magnifies their manners and physical characteristics, as in the case of the lawyer, Sandor Himmelstein, in *Herzog*:

> Himmelstein sat in his wing chair, his feet tucked under his short belly. His eyes were moist, the color of freshly sliced cucumbers, with fine lashes. He chewed a cigar. His ugly nails were polished. He has his manicure at the Palmer House. (82)
> This fierce dwarf with the protruding teeth and deep lines in his face. His lopsided breast protruded from his green pajama top. (86)

Sandor is a stereotype of jaded dissipation and misguided energies.

It would be a distortion of Bellow's technique, however, to let the matter of characterization rest here: for these figures have a vitality that refuses to be contained within the definition of a stereotype. They burst out of such a definition and become people in their own right. Dr. Tamkin of *Seize the Day* does represent a variety of gods of contemporary materialism—he is a figure in what is essentially a morality play—yet he comes alive. Grandma Lausch in *The Adventures of Augie March* represents Victorian mores; but she, too, has in her the breath of life. This list could go on, but the fact that Bellow creates believable people needs little support: some of his characters have already achieved a kind of life beyond art—Herzog is the outstanding example.

It is always difficult to say just how an author brings his characters alive, but Bellow has developed a style of dialogue that accurately reflects the rhythms and sounds of living conversation. Sandor Himmelstein is a stereotype; but Sandor comes alive when he, Beatrice (his wife), and Herzog discuss the custody of Herzog's daughter as a consequence of the divorce from Madeleine (Valentine Gersbach is the man for whom Madeleine leaves Herzog):

> Beatrice tried to restrain Sandor, but he said, "Shut up." He then turned to Moses again, shaking his head so that it gradually sank toward his disfigured breast, and his shoulder blades jutted behind, caracoid through the white-on-white shirt. "What . . . does *he* know what it is to face facts. All he wants is everybody should love him. If not, he's going to scream and holler. . . . And what about his pal Valentine Gersbach? *There's* a man for you! That gimpy redhead knows what real suffering is. But he lives it up—three men with six legs couldn't get around like that effing peg-leg. It's okay, Bea—Moses can take it. Otherwise, he'd be just another Professor Jerk. . . .
> Herzog was incoherent with anger. "What do you mean? . . . what *about* the child?"
> "Now, don't stand there rubbing your hands like a goddam fool—Christ, I hate a fool," Sandor shouted. His green eyes were violently clear, his lips were continually tensing. He must have been convinced that he was cutting the dead weight of deception from Herzog's soul, and his long white fingers, thumbs and forefingers worked nervously.
> "What! Die? Hair? What the hell are you babbling! I only said they'd give the kid to a young mother."
> "Madeleine put you up to that. She planted this, too. To keep me from suing."
> "She *nothing*! I'm trying to tell you for your own good. This time, she calls the shots. She wins, and you lose. Maybe she wants somebody else."
> "Does she? Did she tell you that?"
> "She told me nothing. I said *maybe*. Now calm down. Pour him a drink, Bea. Out of his own bottle. He doesn't like Scotch."
> Beatrice went to fetch Herzog's own bottle of Guckenheimer's 86 proof.
>   (83–84)

The scene comes alive because Bellow casts the passage into a dramatic format. We catch the full visual and emotional impact of Sandor as Bellow interrupts the dialogue to describe Sandor's physical actions as well as his intellectual turmoil. These descriptions of Sandor's movements act as stage directions, as does Bellow's use of italics. Then, tones range dramatically from extreme agitation to the offhanded calmness of "Pour him a drink, Bea."

Bellow's use of Beatrice is one of the most interesting aspects of this drama. She says nothing, but her presence is essential as a piece of stage business. Sandor uses her to dramatize his arguments. Then, she provides for the rhythm of the scene: Sandor first talks to his wife about Herzog; then he swings his full attention to Herzog; finally, he brings the discussion back to his wife, and she walks off stage. The event is dramatically symmetrical. The point is—Bellow puts his characters on stage, we see them, and believe in their presence.

In this passage, Sandor, along with Herzog, is animated through the dynamics of language: the short, terse, explosive speech patterns, which are sprinkled with colloquialisms, ring true to his character and the occasion. Bellow punctuates dialogue in units of thought rather than in accordance with the mechanics of grammar, a style which adds to the verisimilitude.

In his development as a stylist, Bellow shows an increasing disregard for conventional patterns of space and time in his presentation of dialogue. He seems to be trying to break through the limits of such restraints in order to catch the full dramatic intensity of the moment; hence, he never hesitates to interrupt dialogue with descriptive narrative that conjures up the complete vitality of a particular character or point in time. In the above passage, we should notice the careful image of Sandor as a surgeon, which interrupts Sandor's lines directed at Herzog. Later Sandor shouts again at Herzog: " 'What's so great about your effing death?' . . . His figure straightened. He stood very close to Herzog, who was somewhat frightened by his shrillness and stared down, wide-eyed, at the face of his host. It was strong-cut and coarsely handsome. The small mustache bristled, a fierce green, milky poison rose to his eyes; his mouth twisted. 'I'm getting out of this case.' Himmelstein began to scream" (87). In this passage, Bellow is obviously not concerned about the unrealistic time lapse between Sandor's shouts of rage. He is more concerned that we see and feel the full, precise impact of Sandor's personality.

In his later work, Bellows exacting insistence upon the poetic truth of the instant results in fewer set speeches of any length and in relatively shorter stretches of dialogue. His thought units are shorter, and his punctuation grows more daringly flexible. He relies more and more on startling imagery. Also, in his later work, and especially in *Herzog*, Bellow shows a greater willingness to use the socially unacceptable word: but such words are seldom given to his protagonists—they think them, occasionally; they do not speak them, lest they sink to the desperate level of their antagonists.

In any case, owing to a wide variety of skills, Bellow's figures function successfully on two levels—as wide-ranging symbols and as characters in their own right. This achievement partially accounts for the broad spectrum of Bellow's appeal.

Distance and Point of View

In *Dangling Man* and *The Victim,* Bellow's use of distance and of point of view follows a rather simple pattern owing to the limited scope of the works themselves. In *Dangling Man,* Bellow effaces himself as author and allows his protagonist, Joseph, to recount his experiences through a diary. *The Victim* is somewhat more complicated in technique, for the events in the life of Asa Leventhal unfold through a semieffaced narrator who allows a substantial part of scene and event to filter through Asa's consciousness. Yet, with the peripheral exception of Schlossberg already noted, neither the protagonists nor the supporting characters are asked to represent more than what they seem to be— figures at strife in contemporary society; hence, distance and point of view remain relatively static and uncomplicated throughout the two books. Bellow's third novel presents another case: since Augie March functions as a character in his own right, and also acts as paradigm for American literature from realism to the present, Bellow uses a different distance for each role.

In order for his protagonist to come alive, Bellow diminishes the distance between Augie and the reader by having Augie tell his story in the first-person singular. Of even greater importance to this creation of proximity is the manner of Augie's telling: he describes his experiences in a frank, open fashion that catches our trust. Augie at the outset presents himself and describes his mother: "I am an American, Chicago born—Chicago, that somber city—and go at things as I have taught myself, free-style, and will make the record in my own way. . . . My own parents were not much to me, though I cared for my mother. She was simple-minded, and what I learned from her was not what she taught but on the order of object lessons. She didn't have much to teach, poor woman" (3). Moreover, we identify with Augie on a cultural and ideological basis: we agree with his values and goals; they are admirable in their familiarity.

However, Bellow's intention to include as theme the progress and state of American literature demands a measure of distance between Augie and the reader; for, even while we identify with Augie, we must be able to stand back of him and see him as the wandering spirit of that literature. Bellow achieves this distance, and allows another point of view, by imposing on his protagonist a detached, objective, philosophical style of nondramatic narration. Augie is candid, as stated above; and, because he is, we learn to see the world as he sees it. But these other narrative qualities in his voice are also present; and, because of them, we move away from him, as in his account of a watershed of his childhood:

The house was changed also for us; dinkier, darker, smaller; once shiny and venerated things losing their attraction and richness and importance. Tin showed cracks, black spots where enamel was hit off, threadbarer, design scuffed out of the center of the rug, all the glamour, lacquer, massiveness, florescence, wiped out. The old-paste odor of Winnie [their dog] in her last days apparently wasn't noticed by the house-dwelling women; it was by us, coming in fresh from outdoors. Winnie died in May of that year, and I laid her in a shoe box and buried her in the yard. (58)

This philosophical and emotional detachment extends even to his memories of what seem to have been moments of some stress. Such moments are always muted in nondramatic narration, as when Mrs. Renling, a mother figure with whom Augie lives for a time, accuses him of lustful intentions toward Thea, his future partner in an abortive romance. Augie reminisces: "I left the dining room without saying more. To walk around the shore road and get the shameful twists out of my guts and digest my trouble. It was awful, the feelings I was having, the disgrace and danger over Esther [sister to Thea] and the desire to conk Mrs. Renling over the head" (143). We cannot help feeling that Herzog would have had more to say about this episode. In any case, while we identify with Augie's vision, we do not identify with him as a person. He does not draw us into his feelings because he exhibits so little feeling.

Bellow continually passes up such opportunities to explore the heart and mind of Augie, for to do so would force our attention too directly on Augie as character in his own right; such an exploration would deter us from seeing through Augie and on into the significance of his experiences that hold Bellow's primary intentions. In his second role,

Augie acts only as an Emersonian "transparent eyeball" through which
Bellow's literary interpretations take shape and meaning. The effect is
to create distance between Augie and the reader, and to create a separate
point of view for the reader.

In *The Adventures of Augie March*, Bellow's use of distance and point of
view is highly effective for its purposes; but that use rests more on tone
and contextual attitudes than on the intricacies of prose style and
linguistic structure. The point becomes clear through comparison
between this story and Bellow's later novel, *Herzog*. These two novels
have a key similarity: on major levels, both describe historical arcs
through protagonists who function as media for those descriptions. In
the case of *Herzog*, Bellow means to offer a dramatic interpretation of
socioliterary events from the neoclassical age to the present; and encompassing that theme is the intention to depict the intellectual and
cultural development of Western man.

Owing to the similarities of purpose in these two works, Bellow
establishes at least two distances and two points of view for the same
reasons discussed earlier in connection with *Augie March*. But there is a
key difference: in *Herzog*, Bellow achieves his effects not only through
tone and psychological implications, but also through a remarkably
keen use of stylistic and structural techniques. With the opening line of
Herzog, "If I am out of my mind, it's all right with me," we are
projected immediately into the mind of Bellow's protagonist—indeed,
into his innermost thoughts. Moreover, throughout the story, we do
not for long retreat from that position; we often tend to become Herzog
(as we never could become Augie), to see and to feel the world through
him.

Bellow establishes this close relationship through a prose style that
dips deep into the twists and turns of Herzog's emotional and intellectual meanderings. The style at times resembles "stream of consciousness," but Bellow continually disallows such an immersion precisely for
the same reason he creates distance between Augie and the reader: while
Herzog is much more important as a character in his own right than is
Augie, he still must function as a medium for Bellow's ultimate
historical theme—and that theme demands a detachment between
reader and protagonist.

If we look once again at the first line of the book, we see that Bellow
establishes that detachment immediately. After we are projected into

Herzog's consciousness, we are sharply pulled back from that position by the proof of a narrator in the last three words—"thought Moses Herzog." Actually, Bellow straddles two distances and two points of view—all within the same sentence. Herzog *is* speaking—through his thoughts, to be sure—but the words are *his*. Yet Bellow casts these words into a narrative form, through a third-person point of view; and the results are a dual distance and a dual point of view that are almost simultaneously set in motion.

Further examples of like complexity can be drawn from almost any page in the book. A little later, Herzog reflects about his own character: "He went on taking stock, lying face down on the sofa. Was he a clever man or an idiot? Well, he could not at this time claim to be clever" (3). A close examination of this passage reveals that point of view and distance vary from almost one word to the next. In the first clause, we are outside of Herzog through the third-person usage; but we quickly enter his mind to learn that he is "taking stock," only to be pulled out of his mind as Bellow shows him lying on a sofa. In the second line, we are caught in a kind of no man's land: does the question belong to Herzog or to the narrator? It could belong to either: the tone and style are conversationally intimate, yet third-person narration is also present. Of course, the answer is that Bellow does not want a clear choice made; he wants us as readers to be in two places at once—inside the consciousness of his protagonist and outside it.

The fluidity of distance and of point of view that Bellow builds into his prose accounts for an artistic achievement of high order: it allows us to become both observer and participant; we watch Herzog and become Herzog. Aside from the technical excellence of such an achievement, the dual position we enjoy is highly appropriate to a theme that dramatizes a history of our own development.

Bellow as Humorist

Much of the comic spirit that pervades Bellow's novels is founded on a principle as old as comedy itself: human folly deserves our laughter. It is largely folly that drives Bellow's characters into one comedy of errors after another; it is folly that drives them to butt their heads against stone walls of misplaced values and impossible goals. They are frustrated beyond restraint; consequently, their behavior takes on comic dimensions of the absurd or the abnormal.

In *Seize the Day,* the protagonist Tommy Wilhelm is reduced to such irrational action as he searches desperately for some meaning in life. For help, he turns to his father, Dr. Adler (symbol for divinity), who asks with irritation just what his son expects of him: "'I expect *help!*' The words escaped him in a loud wild, frantic cry and startled the old man, and two or three breakfasters within hearing glanced their way" (53). And upon leaving the scene, Tommy reviles himself: "Ass! Idiot! Wild boar! Dumb mule! Lousy, wallowing hippopotamus! Wilhelm called himself as his bending legs carried him from the dining room. His pride! His inflamed feelings! His begging and feebleness. . . . Oh, how poor, contemptible, and ridiculous he was!" (55).

Bellow's novels are filled with such scenes, and they are invariably funny. We cannot help laughing at the discomfiture of these unfortunates, at their awkward and ungainly reactions to rejection and failure. Eugene Henderson, as his plan to clear the Arnewi water of frogs ends in catastrophe, exclaims, "Oh, God, what's happened. . . . This is ruination. I have made a disaster . . . kill me. All I've got to offer is my life. Go ahead, I'm waiting. . . . Stab me . . . don't ask me. Stab, I say. Use my knife if you haven't got your own. . . . Don't forgive me. I couldn't stand it. I'd rather be dead" (109).

However, Bellow's comedy is more than just funny; it is essential to the meaning of his work. In *Seize the Day,* Bellow means to label as folly Tommy's search for inner peace through divinity. Tommy experiences the same frustrations and exhibits much the same behavior when he turns for help to Dr. Tamkin, who symbolizes materialism and other contemporary panaceas. Bellow is saying that it is foolish, and fit material for comedy, to look for serenity in these outer forces. It should be noted that the comic spirit is not invoked in the last few pages of the novel when Tommy achieves that serenity; rather, the scene is set in lyrical tones of quiet triumph.

The same comic method is used in all of Bellow's novels; but *The Adventures of Augie March* presents a slightly different case in that we never laugh directly at the protagonist, nor do we laugh with him—as we do at Bellow's other protagonists. We can hardly laugh at or with a medium, which is Augie's function, as we discussed earlier. We can, however, react to the events that filter through Augie; hence, we are amused by the hypocritical contentions of Grandma Lausch and by the overwhelming pride and yen for power of Einhorn. In a way, Augie is like Huck Finn in that he stands aside from the comic implications of his own vision: he reports, and we interpret. Also, unlike the rest of Bellow's central characters, Augie never loses self-control. Occasionally, he reports an awkward or embarrassing moment; but his account of the event never describes an Augie given over to comic behavior.

Bellow's comedy often takes on ironic tones as it attacks inflated pretentions. Schlossberg of *The Victim* belongs in this category, as do Dr. Adler and Dr. Tamkin in *Seize the Day,* and a host of characters in *Herzog.* For example, Eugene Henderson in *Henderson the Rain King* explains to his guide, Romilayu, the "biggest problem of all":

> "which was to encounter death. We've just got to do something about it. It just isn't me. Millions of Americans have gone forth since the war to redeem the present and discover the future. I can swear to you, Romilayu, there are guys exactly like me in India and in China and South America and all over the place. . . . I am a high-spirited kind of guy. And it's the destiny of my generation of Americans to go out in the world and try to find the wisdom of life. It just is. Why the hell do you think I'm out here, anyway?
> "I don't know, sah."
> "I wouldn't agree to the death of my soul."
> "Me methodous, sah." (276–77)

Of course, Henderson is not aware of the implications here—that his profound and philosophical search for wisdom, truth, and immortality has been cut to the dimensions of the barely literate Romilayu's rough and unclear dedication to Methodism.

Moses Herzog is an interesting combination of several comic methods. Somewhat like Augie, he is often a medium in the sense that we laugh as his vision filters through to our mental and visual interpretation, as in the case of the announcement of Madeleine (his wife) that she wants a divorce, and Herzog's reaction:

> "It's painful to have to say I never loved you. I never will love you, either . . . so there's no point in going on."
> Herzog said, "I do love you, Madeleine."
> Step by step, Madeleine rose in distinction, in brilliance, in insight. Her color grew very rich, and her brows, and that nose of hers, rose, moved; her

blue eyes gained by the flush that kept deepening, rising from her chest and her throat. She was in an ecstasy of consciousness. It occurred to Herzog that she had beaten him so badly, her pride was so fully satisfied, that there was an overflow of strength into her intelligence. He realized that he was witnessing one of the very greatest moments of her life.
"You should hold on to that feeling . . . I believe it's true. You do love me. But I think you also understand what a humiliation it is to me to admit defeat in this marriage. I've put all I had into it. I'm crushed by this."
Crushed? She had never looked more glorious. (9)

Through Herzog's account, we are amused by the theatrics of Madeleine as she swells into caricature. But the comic effects do not stop there; for Herzog, unlike Augie, is deeply and personally involved. Like Augie, he is observer and reporter: but he is much more the participant; and we not only image Madeleine's posturings: we are also moved to laughter by the picture of the inept and innocent Herzog, as he gazes wide-eyed at a force beyond his control—Madeleine. Herzog is not amused, but we are; and we laugh directly at him for the same reason we laugh at Tommy Wilhelm: his impotence to deal with the world around him—always an appropriate subject for comedy so long as we "sport with human follies, not with crime."

Herzog is singular among Bellow's protagonists in that we sometimes laugh with him, for he is blessed with an awareness of the ironic that is unmatched by the others. On one occasion, he returns to his now-vacant and run-down house in the Berkshires: "Someone came in the night and left a used sanitary napkin in a covered dish on his desk, where he kept bundles of notes for his Romantic studies. That was his reception by the natives. A momentary light of self-humor passed over his face . . ." (48). Of course, we do laugh at Herzog here; but, for the most part, we are smiling with him since he knows what we know—reality always has the last word.

In its most subtle form, Bellow's comedy is based on irony. Often that irony is pointed and brief, as in the example above; at other times, it reflects a major theme of the entire novel, as in the case of *The Victim*—in which there is no victim.[1]

Something happens to the humor in Bellow's last two novels. In *Mr. Sammler's Planet,* there are indeed the usual driven comic figures—among others, Mr. Sammler's daughter, Shula; and his hyperactive nephew, Wallace. But for the first time we have a protagonist at whom we do not laugh. While Mr. Sammler, like Herzog, is quite aware of the ironies of life, they are not funny—to him or to us. Perhaps his advanced age along with his haunted past deny the luxury. In any case, we feel that his pain is set, not transient, not to be modified with laughter. Charlie Citrine is also a different kind of hero. Here is a younger man in the style of Herzog, surrounded too by figures in the comic mold, and going through agonies of the spirit reminiscent of those suffered by Herzog. As we laugh at Herzog, so we do at Charlie; for example, in his volatile relationship with the petty gangster Cantabile, or in his running frustrations with the sex-goddess Renata. But somehow we do not laugh with him. Somehow Charlie Citrine is not us, at least as much as Herzog is. We all know what Herzog is after, some heartfelt peace and quiet; with Charlie, we are a little puzzled.[2] One hesitates to make the judgment, but perhaps the cause lies in Bellow's thematic efforts in both *Mr. Sammler's Planet* and *Humboldt's Gift* wherein we seem to be returning to the messianic inclinations of his early writing. In the case of Charlie Citrine, perhaps his metaphysical impulses estrange us to the point where we disengage. In an age of scientific logic, such impulses make us uncomfortable.

Novelist of the City

Saul Bellow fills his novels with the sensuous details of the city—the peeling paint, the shimmering heat waves, the clanging streetcars, the all-night hamburger stands, children on skates, fire hydrants, brick rubble, cigarette butts, the ring of cash registers. These sights, sounds, and smells greet Bellow's protagonists every time they look out of their windows or walk in the street. Moreover, all of Bellow's people, in one way or another, are affected by their physical environment: Asa Leventhal of *The Victim* is confused and bewildered; Tommy Wilhelm of *Seize the Day* is heavily oppressed and frustrated; Herzog is forced to a painful assessment of how he fits into such a world.

The whole issue of urban man has come into focus through other writers—including Theodore Dreiser, John Dos Passos, James Farrell, Nelson Algren, Nathaniel West. Like Bellow, they see the city as oppressive and stultifying, as a force of alienation and distraction, and as a setting in which man is caught up in a confusing jungle of distorted aims and values. Their characters are lost in and become part of that environment, as are Bellow's creatures. But the distinction is that, while these writers see that environment as central to and definitive of man's ignominy, Bellow sees it as only a peripheral factor to man's fate. This is a key distinction: for Bellow's protagonists, through their experience, learn that they need not be defined by the grey ugliness of the city, by its stolid indifference and powerful drives toward corruption and greed. They manage to escape such a definition when they learn the meaning of self.

Unlike these other writers, Bellow sees nothing inherently evil about the city. Nor does he indulge in recrimination and diatribes against that environment. He sees it merely as another extension of man's will, and, as such, within the control of man—if he understands his power.

Thematic Patterns and Implications for the Future

Bellow is consistent in his affirmation of man's potentialities. In all of his novels, he shows his protagonists to be responsible for their particular conditions, their dilemmas and conflicts: but they are also regarded as capable of altering those conditions, whether or not they are aware of these responsibilities and powers. And, within this awareness, a pattern becomes evident. In *Dangling Man* and *The Victim,* Bellow depicts protagonists who fail to recognize their human possibilities. Both Joseph and Asa Leventhal remain mystified; unable to see themselves as decision makers, they mistakenly assume that they are in the grip of unknown and perhaps deterministic forces.

The Adventures of Augie March and *Seize the Day* project different states of consciousness, for Augie and Tommy Wilhelm become aware of the dignity of their human condition. Augie is a failure, but he senses that failure is not substantive to a definition of himself or of others as human beings. And Tommy Wilhelm sees through a glass darkly, through a bedimmed and tearful vision, that a definition of self depends on day by day living of that life. He nods in vague understanding that tomorrow brings irrevocable removal of his defining power. *Henderson the Rain King* and *Herzog* are success stories, for their heroes end in a clear self-awareness, an illumination of their human possibilities, at ease, or at least reconciled with their humanness in all its limitations.

After *Herzog,* however, there is a kind of launching out into space. With the publications of *Mr. Sammler's Planet* and *Humboldt's Gift,* it became a critical commonplace to observe that Bellow's work was growing increasingly philosophic, even metaphysical. In his earlier novels, Bellow's protagonists seem to find their earthbound condition sufficient unto the day: "The world has removed its wrath" from Henderson, and Herzog's last letter concludes, "I am pretty well satisfied to be." But with old Mr. Sammler and Charlie Citrine one is not so sure, since neither Sammler nor Citrine achieve such contentment within the terrestrial. I am reminded of Wallace Stevens's poem "Sunday Morning" in which, after the narrator explains to the woman the positive terms of her being human, she laments, "But in contentment I still feel the need of some imperishable bliss." Perhaps after *Herzog* Bellow felt his work to be incomplete, that man needed more than a simple satisfaction with his tenure on earth, perhaps a wider vision of what it means to be human. In any case, in his last two novels, Bellow grows more daring. Most unlike his earlier protagonists, Mr. Sammler is a quasi-religious figure; and at the end of *Humboldt's Gift*, Charlie Citrine lights out for a mystical territory that can be approached only through the imagination. In fact, these last two novels point to the change in Bellow's career that Bellow himself comments on in a late 1976 interview: "Whatever the reasons, I feel it is time to write about people who make a more spirited resistance to the forces of our time."[3] Surely Sammler and Citrine, but none of Bellow's earlier heroes, fit into this resistance movement; moreover, Bellow's further words in description of his own development are clear echoes of Charlie Citrine's progress: "I think that I have, till recently, held for the most part to modernist assumptions about history. It is only recently that it has begun to occur to me that in fact we did not live with these assumptions, and that we were deeply moved by others. Therefore, I have begun to think of shucking these old assumptions off."

Yet if by "the forces of our time" Bellow is referring to conditions more narrowly contemporary than those explored in his last two novels—and that is the view of this writer—we can expect Bellow to turn his attention to the problems he sees at his elbow. He says, "We're going through an interregnum at present, a terrible time of impatience. People are unquestionably more troubled, agonized, less certain of themselves. They are not only often without kindness but actively wickeder to one another. The cost of real virtue has gone up. Instead we have the false virtue of phony liberalism. In the midst of this one turns to the novelist and says: 'Well, Bud, what have you got to say about this?' " If Bellow's future bent is to address such ravages of the spirit, a direction clearly initiated in his last two novels and in his *To Jerusalem and Back,* no more will we see the likes of Henderson and Herzog, and perhaps, sadly enough, we will see less of the comic spirit that marked their trails. Rather, we will have the heirs of Mr. Sammler and Charlie Citrine, pilgrims who confront the world on a quest not only for self-justification or for self-realization, but offering themselves as point-men for our passage through the debilitating thicket of today's moral and spiritual malaise. It all smacks of a crusade—dangerous territory for the artist—but Bellow himself denies such presumptions. When he made the above pronouncement about its being "time to write about people who make a more spirited resistance to the forces of our time," he adds hastily, "I am not saying that as a novelist, I have become super-ambitious. Not at all. What I am saying is that I think that it is time for me to move on now." In spite of the demur, one can see Bellow moving into the arena of what he calls "great public matters." We have the hint in his own words: "In the book I recently did on Israel [*To Jerusalem and Back*] I discovered that it was as easy to write about great public matters as about private ones. All it required was more confidence and daring. Possibly the award of the Nobel Prize has, in an indirect way, bolstered that confidence further." So Bellow will move on. As for us, we fear the cost; we are always reluctant to leave familiar territory.

Notes and References

Chapter One

1. "Saul Bellow: Novelist of the Intellectuals," in *American Moderns: From Rebellion to Conformity* (New York, 1958), p. 210.
2. "A Discipline of Nobility: Saul Bellow's Fiction," in *After Alienation: American Novels in Mid-Century* (New York, 1964), p. 34.
3. "Distractions of a Fiction Writer," in *The Living Novel: A Symposium*, ed. Granville Hicks (New York, 1957), p. 15.
4. Ibid., p. 25.
5. "The Writer as Moralist," *Atlantic*, March 1963, p. 61.
6. "The Nobel Lecture," *American Scholar* 46 (Summer 1977): 316.
7. "Starting Out in the Thirties," *American Scholar* 44 (Winter 1974): 74–75.
8. Alfred Kazin, *New York Jew* (New York: Knopf, 1978), pp. 40–42; 47–48. Kazin's illuminating sketches describe his friend Bellow in New York at this time as a young intellectual, largely unestablished, energetic and eager to write.
9. *Library Journal*, 1 October 1965, p. 4030.
10. For a sympathetic and appreciative essay on *The Last Analysis*, yet one that notes its failings, see Irving Malin, "Bummy's Analysis," in *Saul Bellow: A Collection of Essays*, ed. Earl Rovit (Englewood Cliffs, N.J., 1975).
11. "Mr. Bellow's Planet," *New Republic*, 6 November 1976, pp. 6–7.
12. "The Nobel Lecture," p. 325.

Chapter Two

1. Ihab Hassan, *Radical Innocence: The Contemporary American Novel* (Princeton, 1961), p. 21. Hassan's definition of the antihero is useful here: "In fiction, the unnerving rubric 'anti-hero' refers to a ragged assembly of victims: the fool, the clown, the hipster, the criminal, the poor soul, the freak, the outsider, the scapegoat, the scrubby opportunist, the rebel without a cause, the 'hero' in the ashcan and 'hero' on the leash."
2. *Dangling Man* (New York, 1960), p. 2; hereafter cited in the text.
3. "Distractions of a Fiction Writer," p. 13.
4. "Saul Bellow: Man Alive, Sustained by Love," in *Fiction of the Forties* (Chicago, 1963), pp. 346–47.

5. *After Alienation,* pp. 35–36.

6. The name of "Allbee" obviously holds the symbolic intent of Every-man. On one level, he functions as an exposition of the relationship that exists between the individual (Asa) and his fellow man.

7. *The Victim* (New York, 1947), p. 26; hereafter cited in the text.

8. Jonothan Baumbach, "The Double Vision: *The Victim* by Saul Bel-low," in *The Landscape of Nightmare: Studies in the Contemporary Novel* (New York, 1965), p. 49.

9. "The Fool of Experience: Saul Bellow's Fiction," in *Contemporary American Novelists,* ed. Harry Moore (Carbondale, 1964), p. 88.

10. Hassan, p. 178. Hassan uses the Greek word *eiron* to define the "humble, self-deprecating man" as his partial definition of the contemporary literary hero (see p. 114).

11. Bellow often extends the scope of these images to include the world of art in general. In *Dangling Man,* John Pearl realizes no peace, no sense of value, when he uses his artistic skills as a means of escape.

12. Baumbach, pp. 35–54, thoroughly examines Allbee as alter ego.

13. Any interpretation of *The Victim* that does not see the relationship between Asa and Allbee as an intense and personal symbolic self-encounter is bound to end in confusion. Such is probably the case when Robert G. Davis states: "What remains unexplained is the meaning and use of Asa's summer of suffering" (Robert G. Davis, "Individualist Tradition: Bellow and Sty-ron," *The Creative Present: Notes on Contemporary Fiction,* ed. Nona Balakian and Charles Simmons [New York, 1963], p. 119).

14. *Writers at Work: Third Series* (New York: Viking, 1967), pp. 175–96.

Chapter Three

1. Robert Penn Warren originated the terminology in "The Man with no Commitments," *New Republic,* 2 November 1953, p. 22.

2. *The Adventures of Augie March* (New York, 1960), p. 28; hereafter cited in the text.

3. Malin, p. 97.

4. (New York, 1957), p. 22.

5. Warren, pp. 22–23.

6. Hoffman, p. 90.

7. Geismar, p. 218.

8. "The Thinking Man's Waste Land," *Saturday Review,* 3 April 1965, p. 20.

9. Augie is a great believer in what he calls his "axial lines"—the attainment of a life founded on "truth, love, peace, bounty, usefulness, harmony" (i.e., pp. 414, 454).

10. Einhorn's useless legs can be seen as symbolic of frustrated desires, much in the way that Hemingway uses physical disabilities to depict creative disabilities.

11. And Augie's words that "you could always get part of the truth from Einhorn" show Bellow's appreciation of the positive aspects of the literature of alienation.

12. "Distractions of a Fiction Writer," p. 20.

13. Hassan, p. 309.

14. "Distractions of a Fiction Writer," p. 13.

15. "The Absurd Man as Picaro: The Novels of Saul Bellow," *Texas Studies in Language and Literature,* (Summer 1964): 238.

16. "Distractions of a Fiction Writer," p. 14.

17. Grandma Lausch is a good example of how Bellow builds and supports the functions of his characters. Grandma Lausch represents authority, both in the March household and in the history of literature. Here, Bellow widens her role by showing her as a figure of middle-class standards, likening her authority to that which held realism to be immoral.

Chapter Four

1. *Seize the Day* (New York, 1961), p. 6; hereafter cited in the text.

2. The relationship between Tommy and Margaret acts as support for the two major conflicts. Tommy is estranged from Margaret, not divorced, as he finds it impossible to break the tie once and for all. He hopes that she will come to sympathize with him and help in his plight, all of which is close to the situation he faces with both Dr. Adler and Dr. Tamkin.

3. *The Portable Russian Reader,* ed. Bernard G. Guerney (New York, 1947), p. 147.

4. Ibid., p. 161.

5. For an interesting but overly winding psychological interpretation of *Seize the Day,* which makes much of father-son motifs, see Daniel Weiss, "A Psychoanalytic Study on the Novel *Seize the Day,* by Saul Bellow," *Psychoanalysis and American Fiction,* ed. Irving Malin (New York, 1965), pp. 279f.

6. Of technical importance is the way in which Bellow gives imagistic support to Tommy's struggle for life. The many times that Tommy experiences the mental isolation of a drowning man, he is also enveloped in all of the appropriate accompanying physical pain. While describing to his father the effect that his wife has on him, he "began to choke himself," complaining "she's strangling me." He "can't catch his breath." He will "be struck down by suffocation or apoplexy" (48). Tommy is ever feeling chest pains (49, 89, 91). He has trouble breathing (109, 113, 114). And Bellow uses the word

"congestion" at least seven times to describe Tommy's appearance or state of being (17, 30, 36, 43, 52, 53, 96).

Chapter Five

    1. *Henderson the Rain King* (New York, 1959), p. 3; hereafter cited in the text.
    2. "The Uses of Adversity," *Reporter* 25 (1 October 1959): 45.
    3. For example, see pp. 67, 76, 77, 78, 79, 212.

Chapter Six

    1. *Herzog* (New York, 1964), p. 1; hereafter cited in the text.
    2. Several references to *Hamlet* convey the image of Herzog's divided personality as well as show his reticence to action. Herzog discovers an advantage, a "certain wisdom" (23) in his alleged madness. Like Hamlet, madness would serve a purpose: Herzog must admit and accept certain "mad" elements dormant within himself and control them. The scene in which Herzog watches Gersbach giving little June a bath (257) is clearly reminiscent of Claudius at the altar, but Herzog senses a reversal of Claudius's ironic position. Herzog, like Hamlet, sees his adulterous archenemy as a kind human being busily engaged in a warm and moving gesture of love. It is enough to give Herzog second thoughts about his own amphibian nature. He exclaims, "The human soul is an amphibian and I have touched its sides" (257–58).
    3. See pages 16, 21, 61, 82, 194, 254.

Chapter Seven

    1. *Mr. Sammler's Planet* (New York, 1970), p. 3; hereafter cited in the text.
    2. Alfred North Whitehead, *Science and the Modern World,* (New York, 1960), p. 260.
    3. Ibid., p. 270. For a revealing study of Bellow's turn from an ethical perspective to a religious faith see James N. Harris, "One Critical Approach to *Mr. Sammler's Planet,*" *Twentieth Century Literature* 18 (1972): 235–50.
    4. In "Mr. Bellow's Perigee; or The Lowered Horizons of *Mr. Sammler's Planet,*" Max Schulz finds Bellow has indeed given us "an impoverished view of man," and disapproves of Bellow's vision (in *Contemporary American-Jewish Literature,* ed. Irving Malin. [Bloomington: Indiana University Press, 1973], p. 131).

Chapter Eight

1. This chapter was originally set down in a paper, excerpts of which the author of this book presented to a Modern Language Association meeting at Chicago (1977), in a special session entitled "Saul Bellow—Since *Herzog.*"
2. Whitehead, *Science and the Modern World,* p. 260.
3. Ibid., p. 270.
4. *Humboldt's Gift* (New York, 1975), p. 17; hereafter cited in the text.
5. Whitehead, *Adventures of Ideas* (New York, 1961), pp. 309–81.
6. Ibid., p. 328.
7. Ibid., p. 331.
8. Ibid., p. 371.
9. Ibid., p. 372.
10. Ibid., p. 367.
11. Ibid., p. 371–72.
12. Ibid., p. 368.
13. Ibid., p. 367.
14. The novel is also the story of Saul Bellow. A philosophic exercise, it is Bellow's mind thinking about Bellow's mind. Through Charlie, Bellow is discovering his own history and nature, and hence, the history and nature of mankind. The philosopher Hegel, reference to whom appears again and again in this novel, puts it this way: "It may be said that world history is the exhibition of spirit striving to attain knowledge of its own nature. As the germ bears within itself the whole nature of the tree, the shape and taste of its fruit, so also the first traces of spirit virtually contain the whole of history." (George Wilhelm Friedrich Hegel, "The Philosophy of History," *The Philosophy of Right: The Philosophy of History,* trans. J. Sibree, Great Books of the Western World Series [Chicago: University of Chicago Press, 1952], p. 161.) It comes to mind that Bellow worked on the Great Books Series. One wonders if he was involved in the section on Hegel. Back to the point: Alfred Kazin is right, of course, when he says that Bellow "has invented and re-invented himself in book after book" (*New Republic,* 6 November 1976, p. 7). Each book offers a different perspective.
15. Whitehead, *Adventures of Ideas,* p. 378.
16. Ibid., p. 354.
17. Ibid., p. 375.
18. Perhaps somewhat more than "figure." In response to an interviewer's question concerning Bellow's use of Steiner, Bellow said," I think people were confused by seeing Rudolph Steiner's work pop up in a novel a good part of which was comic in intent. I do admit to being intrigued with Steiner. I do not know enough to call myself a Steinerian. . . . I think it

enough now to say that Rudolph Steiner had a great vision and was a
powerful poet as well as philosopher and scientist" (*New York Times Book
Review*, 5 December 1976, p. 93).
    19. Whitehead, *Adventures of Ideas*, p. 368.
    20. Ibid., p. 364.
    21. Ibid., p. 369.
    22. Ibid., p. 354.
    23. Ibid., p. 364.
    24. Ibid.

Chapter Nine

    1. *Mosby's Memoirs and Other Stories* (New York, 1968), p. 22; hereafter
cited in the text. "Looking for Mr. Green" originally appeared in *Commentary*, (1951); "The Gonzaga Manuscripts" in *Discovery No. 4* (1954); "Leaving the Yellow House" in *Esquire* (1957); "A Father-to-be" (1955) and
"Mosby's Memoirs" (1968) in the *New Yorker*; "The Old System" in *Playboy*
(1967).
    2. *To Jerusalem and Back: A Personal Account* (New York, 1976), p. 9;
hereafter cited in the text. A substantial part of this book originally appeared
in the *New Yorker*, 12 July and 19 July 1976 under the title "Reflections—
The Middle East I and II." For reviews of this book the reader is referred to
the *New York Times Book Review*, 17 October 1976; *Harpers*, December 1976,
pp. 82–85; *Commentary*, November 1976, pp. 80–84.
    3. It was inevitable that there would be some political reaction to
Bellow's book, although there was not the amount one might expect. Most
reviewers read the work as something other than a political statement. John
J. Clayton is one of the exceptions. In his *Saul Bellow: In Defense of Man*, 2d
ed. (Bloomington, 1979), he accuses Bellow of betraying his own principles,
claiming Bellow takes "a stand in favor of the old regime. Yet it isn't clear
that capitalist societies make accessible much spiritual space to the majority
of people. . . . It is easy for the class in power to appear neutral, to make the
class *out* of power look like ideologues. Easy and misleading. Bellow is a
'dangerous thinker' when he puts sensibility at the service of those in power
and permits us to retreat in spiritual comfort from the pain of other people"
(p. 261). Clayton's attack is best read in the light of the preface to his second
edition wherein he points to his own growth in political awareness since the
publication of his earlier work in 1967.

Chapter Ten

    1. Sarah Cohen's *The Enigmatic Laughter of Saul Bellow* (Urbana, 1974)
builds on the thesis that Bellow's comedy is a counter to despair. She is right,

of course; but I think it goes further than that. Bellow uses comedy to put despair into a perspective that shows the folly of despair. That is, Bellow's comedy not only offsets despair; in a sense, it defeats it. Cohen's book is quite interesting and very often thought-provoking; yet I want to believe that Bellow's humor is less complex than the number of pages she gives to it. Perhaps not. I do like Bellow's response to an enquiry concerning his comic element. On President Nixon's televised explanation regarding his behavior: "Sometimes you think, what else can you do but laugh at these things" (*Salmagundi*, Summer 1975, p. 15).

2. Among the reviews—highly favorable, with minor reservations—that reflect this confusion are John W. Aldridge, "Saul Bellow at 60: A Turn to the Mystical," *Saturday Review*, 6 September 1975, p. 25; Richard Gilman, *"Humboldt's Gift,"* *New York Times Book Review*, 17 August 1975, p. 2; Roger Sale, "The Realms of Gold," *Hudson Review*, Winter 1975–76, pp. 623–25.

3. Joseph Epstein, "A Talk with Saul Bellow," *New York Times Book Review* 5 December 1976, pp. 92–3. The other comments by Bellow are drawn from this article.

Selected Bibliography

PRIMARY SOURCES

1. Fiction

The Adventures of Augie March. New York: Viking Press, 1953.
Dangling Man, New York: Vanguard Press, 1944; New York: World, 1960.
Henderson the Rain King. New York: Viking Press, 1959.
Herzog. New York: Viking Press, 1964.
Humboldt's Gift. New York: Viking Press, 1975.
Mosby's Memoirs and Other Stories. New York: Viking Press, 1968. Includes "Leaving the Yellow House," "The Old System," "Looking for Mr. Green," "The Gonzaga Manuscripts," "A Father-to-be," and "Mosby's Memoirs."
Mr. Sammler's Planet. New York: Viking Press, 1970.
Seize the Day. New York: Viking Press, 1956.
The Victim. New York: Vanguard Press, 1947.

2. Uncollected Short Stories

"Address by Gooley MacDowell to the Hasbeens Club of Chicago." *Hudson Review* 4 (Summer 1951): 222–27. Reprinted in *Nelson Algren's Book of Lonesome Monsters,* edited by Nelson Algren. New York: Lancer Books, 1962.
"By the Rock Wall." *Harper's Bazaar,* April, 1951, 135; 205–08; 214–16.
"Dora." *Harper's Bazaar,* November, 1949, 118; 188–90; 198–99.
"The Mexican General." *Partisan Review* 9 (May–June 1942): 178–94. Reprinted in *More Stories in the Modern Manner* (New York: Avon, 1954).
"Sermon by Doctor Pep." *Partisan Review* 16 (May–June 1949): 455–62. Reprinted: *Best American Short Stories, 1950,* edited by Martha Foley (Boston: Houghton Mifflin, 1950); *The New Partisan Reader, 1945–1953* (New York: Harcourt, Brace, 1953); *Fiction of the Fifties,* edited by Herbert Gold (New York: Doubleday, 1959).
"A Silver Dish." *New Yorker,* 25 September 1978, pp. 40–62. Reprinted in *The Best American Short Stories: 1979,* edited by Joyce Carol Oates (Boston: Houghton Mifflin, 1979).

"Trip to Galena." *Partisan Review* (November–December 1950): 779–94.
"Two Morning Monologues." *Partisan Review* 8 (May–June 1941): 230–36. Reprinted in *Partisan Reader* (New York: Dial Press, 1946).

3. Plays
"A Wen." *Esquire,* January 1965, pp. 72–74, 111.
The Last Analysis. New York: Viking Press, 1965.
"Orange Soufflé." *Esquire,* October 1965, pp. 130–31, 134, 136.
"The Wrecker." *New World Writing* 6 (1954): 271–87. Reprinted in *Seize the Day.*

4. Nonfiction
To Jerusalem and Back: A Personal Account. New York: Viking Press, 1976.

5. Articles and Essays
"Deep Readers of the World, Beware!" *New York Times Book Review.* 15 February 1959, pp. 1, 34.
"Dreiser and the Triumph of Art." *Commentary* 11 (May 1951): 502–3.
"Distractions of a Fiction Writer." In *The Living Novel: A Symposium,* edited by Granville Hicks, pp. 1–20. New York: MacMillan, 1957.
"How I Wrote Augie March's Story." *New York Times Book Review,* 31 January 1954, p. 3.
"Isaac Rosenfield." *Partisan Review* 23 (Fall 1956): 565–67.
"Some Notes on Recent American Fiction." *Encounter* 21 (November 1963): 22–29.
"Starting Out in Chicago." *American Scholar* 44, (Winter 1974–75): 71–77.
"The Thinking Man's Wasteland." *Saturday Review,* 3 April 1965, p. 20.
"The Uses of Adversity." *Reporter,* 1 October 1959, pp. 42, 44–45.
"Where Do We Go From Here: The Future of Fiction." *Michigan Quarterly Review* 1 (Winter 1962): 27–33. Reprinted in *Saul Bellow and the Critics,* edited by Irving Malin (New York: New York University Press, 1967).
"The Writer and the Audience." *Perspectives U.S.A.,* 9 (Autumn 1954): 99–102.
"The Writer as Moralist." *Atlantic Monthly,* (March 1963), pp. 58–62.

6. Lecture
"The Nobel Lecture." *American Scholar* 46 (Summer 1977): 316–25.

SECONDARY SOURCES

Since the publication of the first edition of this book, criticizing Saul
Bellow's writing has become an industry: books, essays, reviews, interviews,
dissertations—it has reached the point at which no student can attend them
all. For this revised edition, I have held the listing of these sources to some of
my earlier entries and some later work that I found of direct or peripheral
interest. I am sure that there are others of equal value.

1. Bibliography
Nault, Marianne. *Saul Bellow: His Works and His Critics: An Annotated
    International Bibliography.* New York: Garland Publishers, 1977. This
    book is a comprehensive reference guide to work about Bellow the man
    and about his writing. There is a generous sprinkling of references to
    critical voices from abroad.
Noreen, Robert G. *Saul Bellow: A Reference Guide.* Boston: G. K. Hall,
    1978. An annotated bibliography of writings about Bellow from 1944
    to 1976. Annotations are careful to echo both praises and complaints.
    Some foreign criticism is cited. The work is quite comprehensive.

2. Books
Clayton, John J. *Saul Bellow: In Defense of Man.* Bloomington: Indiana
    University Press, 1967. Bellow is examined as a psychological novelist,
    with studies on *The Victim, Henderson the Rain King,* and *Herzog.*
    Included are brief discussions of the short stories and plays. The book
    sets forth interesting interpretations as well as exploring unity and
    development. Clayton's second edition (1979) is now available, wherein
    we find some measure of rethinking, especially when Clayton casts
    some shadows of his newly acquired political inclinations on Bellow's
    work.
Cohen, Sarah Blacher. *The Enigmatic Laughter of Saul Bellow.* Urbana: Univer-
    sity of Illinois Press, 1974. Through an examination of Bellow's novels,
    Cohen proposes to show that Bellow inevitably uses comedy as a counter
    to despair. She looks at this equation as one of the factors in Bellow's
    work that "sharpen the mystery of life." The book is thoughtful and
    interesting, but heavily detailed.
Opdahl, Keith M. *The Novels of Saul Bellow.* University Park: Pennsylvania
    State University Press, 1967. Explores the first six novels as well as
    some of the shorter fiction. A revised dissertation, this book traces the

ideological themes in the novels, relating the reactions of the heroes to their environment. Includes a lucid, intelligent introductory survey of Bellow's writing.

Porter, M. Gilbert. *Whence the Power? The Artistry and Humanity of Saul Bellow.* Columbia: University of Missouri Press, 1974. Porter centers his work on psychological interpretations of the behavior of Bellow's heroes. Some interesting conclusions, but by nature of the work, often highly speculative.

3. Collections of Essays

Critical Essays on Saul Bellow. Edited by Stanley Trachtenberg, Boston: G. K. Hall, 1979. A collection of twelve reviews on Bellow in general or on individual novels. Also, ten critical essays on Bellow's fiction. Trachtenberg writes a lengthy and thoughtful introductory essay on Bellow.

Critique: Studies in Modern Fiction 7 (Spring–Summer 1965). Five studies of Bellow's writings: "Bellow's View of the Heart" by James Dean Young; "Theme in *Augie March*" by Robert D. Crozier, S.J.; "Bellow's Henderson" by Allen Guttman; "The Theme of *Seize the Day*" by James C. Mathis; and "Clown and Saint: The Hero in Current American Fiction" by David D. Galloway.

Critique: Studies in Modern Fiction 9, no. 3 (1967). Three studies of Bellow's writings: "Saul Bellow's *Luftmenschen*: The Compromise with Reality" by Stanley Trachtenberg; "Water Imagery in *Seize the Day*" by Clinton W. Trowbridge; and "Bellow and Milton: Professor Herzog in His Garden" by Franklin R. Baruch.

Modern Fiction Studies 25 (Spring 1979). This is a special Saul Bellow issue with eleven essays on his writing, most of them centering on a particular novel, with others more general. An excellent introductory essay on Bellow by Field, and a comprehensive bibliography of criticism on Bellow.

Salmagundi 30 (Summer 1975). Included are five essays on various aspects of Bellow and his fiction, along with Robert T. Boyers's "Literature and Culture: An Interview with Saul Bellow."

Saul Bellow: A Collection of Critical Essays. Edited by Earl Rovit. Twentieth Century Views. Englewood Cliffs: Prentice-Hall, 1975. Twelve essays, nine of which are original with this collection. Not usually included in these critical collections, an essay on *The Last Analysis*. Also present is Gordon Lloyd Harper's 1967 interview with Saul Bellow.

Saul Bellow and the Critics. Edited by Irving Malin. New York: New York
   University Press, 1967. Another collection of critical essays, and a good
   source for a comprehensive view of Bellow's techniques and themes.
   Bellow's "Where Do We Go From Here: The Future of Fiction" is
   included. Among others are essays by Leslie Fiedler, Maxwell Geismar,
   Irving Malin, and Marcus Klein.

4. Parts of Books

Baumbach, Jonothan. "The Double Vision: *The Victim* by Saul Bellow." In
   The Landscape of Nightmare: Studies in the Contemporary Novel. New York:
   New York University Press, 1965, pp. 35–54. *The Victim* is examined
   as one of the important novels of our times with an insight into man's
   confrontation with his distorted image and a recognition of guilt. The
   emphasis is placed on the confrontation with a double in the Dostoevski
   tradition. Baumbach also discusses other Bellow novels up to *Henderson
   the Rain King.*
Davis, Robert G. "Individualist Tradition: Bellow and Styron." In *The
   Creative Present: Notes on Contemporary Fiction,* edited by Nona Balakian
   and Charles Simmons. New York: Doubleday, 1963, pp. 111–41. The
   novels of Bellow and William Styron are compared as to their focus on
   the sense of alienation prevalent in man. Although Davis asserts the
   positive nature of Bellow's themes, he fails to recognize the affirmations
   of self undergone by the protagonists in Bellow's novels.
Eisinger, Chester E. "Saul Bellow: Man Alive, Sustained by Love." *Fiction of
   the Forties,* Chicago: University of Chicago Press, 1963, pp. 341–62.
   Bellow's first three novels provide a basis for an examination of the
   relationship of man to his society, the individual against the inhuman
   world. Includes an illuminating study of *Augie March.*
Galloway, David G. "The Absurd Man as Picaro: The Novels of Saul
   Bellow." In *The Absurd Hero in American Fiction: Updike, Styron, Bellow,
   Salinger.* Austin: University of Texas Press, 1966, pp. 82–139. The
   protagonists in the first five novels are discussed as "absurd heroes,"
   rebels from the pressures of the world. Galloway perceives the achievement of Bellow's heroes in their attempts at self-realization. A comprehensive and engrossing essay. The book also contains a comprehensive list of the writings of Bellow, as well as critical essays and reviews of
   Bellow's works.
Geismar, Maxwell. "Saul Bellow: Novelist of the Intellectuals." In *American
   Moderns: From Rebellion to Conformity.* New York: Hill and Wang, 1958,
   pp. 210–24. Bellow is described as a novelist appealing only to intellectuals, as one who is attempting to break out of these attitudinal confines

in his first four novels. The Jewish sensibility of sorrow and compassion is emphasized. *Augie March* is dismissed as being "everything but authentic," but other of Geismar's observations have validity.

Hassan, Ihab. *Radical Innocence: The Contemporary American Novel.* Princeton: Princeton University Press, 1961, pp. 290–324. Discusses the affirmative capability of man, leading to an awareness of the "common soul of humankind," in the first five novels. An illuminating study in which Hassan perceives the basic thematic patterns functioning in Bellow's writing.

Hoffman, Frederick. "The Fool of Experience: Saul Bellow's Fiction." In *Contemporary American Novelists,* edited by Harry T. Moore. Carbondale: Southern Illinois University Press, 1964, pp. 80–94. The protagonists in the first five novels are examined as examples of the middle-class "schlemiel" struggling against the loss of identity, trying to survive in the modern world.

Klein, Marcus. "A Discipline of Nobility: Saul Bellow's Fiction." In *After Alienation: American Novels in Mid-Century.* New York: World, 1964, pp. 33–70. Examines the progress of man in his movement away from "alienation" toward "accommodation" in the first five novels. Includes a perceptive analysis of the facets of all Bellow's writing: the effect of the city and the personality and qualities of the characters.

Malin, Irving. *Jews and Americans.* Carbondale: Southern Illinois University Press, 1965, pp. 73–75, 97–98. Examines Bellow's writings as expressions of Jewish literature and traditions. His heroes are "Jewish ironists," caught between dream and fact. A source for the examination of the Jewish conscience in Bellow's writing.

McConnell, Frank D. "Saul Bellow and the Terms of our Contract." In *Four Post-War American Novelists: Bellow, Mailer, Barth, and Pynchon.* Chicago: University of Chicago Press, 1977, pp. 1–57. Treats all of Bellow's novels—often comparing Bellow's vision to those of Mailer, Barth, and Pynchon. Interested in the prophetic perspectives evinced by these writers. Reads Bellow as grittily optimistic in his vision.

Weinberg, Helen. *The New Novel in America: The Kafkan Mode in Contemporary Fiction.* Ithaca, N. Y.: Cornell University Press, 1970, pp. 29–107. Proposes that Bellow's protagonists move progressively through his novels as different kinds of heroes: the victim hero, the rebel hero, the activist hero, and the hero as fool (Herzog). Weinberg's thesis is that all of the heroes are searching for the same truth in spite of individual differences.

Index